THE U.S. AND WORLD DEVELOPMENT
AGENDA FOR ACTION
1976

THE U.S. AND WORLD DEVELOPMENT

AGENDA FOR ACTION
1976

Roger D. Hansen
and the Staff of the Overseas Development Council

PUBLISHED FOR THE OVERSEAS DEVELOPMENT COUNCIL
PRAEGER PUBLISHERS
NEW YORK/ LONDON

Library of Congress Cataloging in Publication Data

Hansen, Roger D
  The U.S. and world development.

  (Praeger special studies in international economics
and development)
    1. Economic assistance, American—Addresses,
essays, lectures.   2. Food supply—Addresses, essays,
lectures.   3. Energy policy—Addresses, essays, lectures.
I. Overseas Development Council.   II. Title.
HC60.H313   309.2'233'73   76-4936
ISBN 0-275-56510-6
ISBN 0-275-85670-4 student ed.

PRAEGER PUBLISHERS
200 Park Avenue, New York, N.Y. 10017, U.S.A.

Published in the United States of America in 1976
by Praeger Publishers, Inc.

789 008 98765432

Printed in the United States of America

Introduction

Theodore M. Hesburgh and James P. Grant

This year, the fourth in which the Overseas Development Council has published an *Agenda for Action*, may mark the beginning of major changes in this country's policies, both national and international. It is a year in which we will be choosing national leadership to guide us into the last quarter century of this millenium. It is also the 200th anniversary of the establishment of this nation as a bold new social experiment based on the view that "all men are created equal." Finally, this year marks the beginning of what may be the most extensive period of international negotiations, involving more nations and more economic and social issues affecting more people than any that have taken place at any time since World War II, and perhaps before. The nations of the world are beginning the long process of creating a new set of international economic—and political—relationships for the decades ahead. We therefore have an opportunity to advance significantly the extent and quality of cooperation between the rich nations of the Northern hemisphere and the poorer nations of the South.

The coming negotiations, which are analyzed in detail in this volume, involve issues which the poor nations of the world have been pressing for more than a decade. These issues have gained more prominence recently as the rich countries have come to realize that the demands of the poor countries have not only considerable merit but also bargaining power behind them. Thus we are paying attention to the expressed needs of the developing countries both because it is right to do so, on grounds of justice and equity, and because it is perceived to be in our own self-interest.

The negotiations ahead hold the promise of allowing all sides to gain from a new series of "global bargains" on economic issues. Perhaps the clearest example of the gains that can be made is to be found in the approach to the world food situation. At the 1974 World Food Conference, most of the nations of the world agreed upon a comprehensive series of recommendations which should, if implemented, help to increase food production and improve the quality of life in the developing countries. In addition, they should greatly reduce the wide fluctuations in grain prices of the recent past, and thus benefit consumers in both developed and developing countries. Similar global bargains should be possible in other fields, notably energy —for which this *Agenda* proposes a global approach that is badly needed.

In a more general sense, rich and poor countries alike stand to benefit from the more open international economy that could result from the negotiations ahead. The United States would gain from access to larger markets for its capital-intensive goods and from assured access to the raw materials it increasingly needs. The developing countries would benefit from access to markets in the rich countries for their primary products and labor-intensive manufactures and from access to the capital and relevant technology necessary for their own development.

Moreover, a successful outcome of these negotiations should increase the willingness and capacity of the developing countries to take part in future cooperative efforts to address the problems common to both rich and poor countries. For even if one does not fully accept the prognostications of the "doomsday" school, it is clear that our globe does have certain finite limits beyond which we cannot go without endangering the well-being and perhaps the very lives of all.

A further promise of these major negotiations is that they provide all nations, rich and poor, with a great opportunity to begin the difficult task of creating a more just and equitable world. A world that is increasingly divided between the very rich and the very poor will be subject to severe social and political strains, threatening the viability of the present international system. Yet is is within our capacity both to avoid such a disaster and to advance human well-being. That is the promise and opportunity before us as we enter the last quarter of this century.

Two dilemmas are inherent in the negotiations that are now being launched on a global scale. The first is that in these high-level technical negotiations between *governments*, we run the risk of losing sight of the fact that development essentially concerns *people*. For it is people, not governments, who ultimately count. Development, after all, is but a shorthand phrase for the measures that will allow people to improve their own lives and control their own destiny. The language of economists and officials and the technical aspects of these difficult issues tend to obscure the very fundamental problems facing individuals whose lives are a deadening combination of poverty and lack of opportunity.

The need to concentrate on programs that help people, especially poor people, to help themselves is obscured by many in this country who now maintain that America's role in the world should be to champion human rights and political liberty—that we should not be afraid to call to task those countries which violate the accepted standards of political freedom. However, the proponents of this view miss the central point. It is not that we should be less concerned with political freedom throughout the world. Indeed, we must be more effective in promoting it. But our efforts will be convincing only when we also demonstrate our concern for the essentials of human well-being and especially for the very right to survival of the hundreds of millions of people who are acutely hungry and malnourished. Official expressions of concern can sound very hollow indeed when our government uses long-term development aid to win support in international forums; such action debases rather than enhances all that is best in this country. And while flashy oratory in international organizations may attract widespread attention and an approving echo of public opinion, it ignores the basic problem: How is this country to respond to governments and people—abroad *and* at home—who are struggling to achieve self-reliant development and some modicum of economic security?

A second dilemma related to the negotiations now just under way is that Americans and others in the developed world may have to *give* now in order to *gain* in the longer run. Both rich and poor nations will ultimately benefit from a more equitable and efficient international economic system. Our domestic experience since the 1930s and our international experience since 1945 clearly demonstrate the gains that can be made *by all sides* when policies and institutions are designed for that purpose. The postwar system of development cooperation, for instance, resulted in unparalleled economic growth by both developed and developing countries during the 1950s and 1960s. But just as there were short-run costs then for some Americans in making the adjustments in our own economy that were necessary to meet the needs of that new era, so there will be costs for some in meeting the needs of the era ahead. To pretend otherwise is both intellectually dishonest and politically naive. The central question therefore is: Who must bear the costs, and how can the burden be spread fairly so that all can benefit from the ultimate gains? In this regard, lessons can be learned from the Trade Act of 1974, under which workers whose jobs are threatened because of the broader national interest in a liberal world trading system can claim compensation for their losses in income and receive assistance in finding new jobs.

Awareness of the opportunities and the dilemmas confronting us at the present moment brings us to the central issue of the place of *values* in the shaping of U.S. policy—international as well as domestic. It is fitting, in the year when the United States is celebrating its 200th anniversary as an independent nation, that we look ahead to the kind of country and world we want two and a half decades hence. There is a growing mood in this country to return to our founding principles and to look once again at the values inherent in that event of 200 years ago. The signers of the Declaration of Independence took that momentous step out of "a decent respect to the opinions of mankind" and espoused the radical doctrine that "all men are created equal, that they are endowed by their Creator with certain inalienable rights, that among these are life, liberty, and the pursuit of happiness." In the years ahead, we must decide whether we genuinely believe that these truths apply to all, or only to a small, largely white minority that comprises only about 6 per cent of the world's population.

Many Americans seem infected with a growing mood of pessimism about the future. We are plagued with a series of revelations about corruption in high places and in the institutions that many consider to be the basic support of our society. To some, these developments seem reason enough to withdraw from international affairs, taking refuge in our own liberties and economic well-being; to others, they seem to justify outright resignation to the seeming inevitability of ecological disaster.

There are also those who now propose to apply the battlefield medical principle of "triage" to the world—designating some poor countries as beyond saving. Still others reach the same conclusion, envisioning us in a precarious "lifeboat" surrounded by many more survivors than can be taken aboard. These "prophets of doom" conclude that assistance and cooperation should be denied to the many millions whom they consider to be either beyond hope or not "worthy" of our help.

Other Americans, however, have reached exactly the opposite conclusion. One of the heartening developments of the past twenty-four months has been the reestablishment of the "constituency of conscience," including not only many religious as well as secular groups but also many individuals in the Congress. It was partly the pressure generated by these groups and individuals that led the Administration to take a global approach to the world food problem and to increase its food aid last year in the face of considerable resistance within the federal bureaucracy. Similarly, it was the perceived desire of many Americans to designate aid for those who need help the most that led some members of Congress to finally separate the legislation governing economic and humanitarian assistance from our programs of military aid and to focus the assistance on the poorest people rather than on political "allies." Broad public support of this legislation influenced its passage in Congress by an unprecedented margin. The changing mood in America also has been reflected in recent opinion polls, which show that many are willing to reduce their consumption of meat and nonessential uses of fertilizer to help hungry people overseas. There are also growing doubts about the ultimate value of our materialistic style of life.

Although some observers both here and abroad maintain that Americans should feel "guilty" about causing the conditions that led to the plight of the poor countries, we must not let the endless argument about the causes of underdevelopment obscure the more essential conclusion that, regardless of the past, we have a *responsibility* for helping to create conditions that will henceforth contribute to a better life for all people. Even where there is no guilt, all of us have a responsibility, rooted in justice, to promote the development of the world's poor majority.

Nevertheless we should not ignore the fact that many of the issues involved in reshaping the international economy are controversial. The question of who loses and who gains, and how the costs and benefits are to be distributed both nationally and internationally, will be paramount.

Certainly no new systems in which only a few gain and the many pay will find broad support or have serious durability. In the long run, it should be possible for all of us to benefit, as is demonstrated in the *Agenda* in both the food and energy areas. The need is to devise strategies with enough ingenuity and commitment to ensure that outcome. This viewpoint is not yet shared by all Americans. But because our system works best when all of us participate in political and economic decisions, it is important that alternative solutions to these issues be examined, and that their domestic costs and benefits, as well as their claims to justice, become the subject of extensive public consultation and discussion.

What are the central development objectives for 1976 and beyond? As spelled out in this *Agenda for Action*, the first is to make sure that the U.S. government pursues the general lines laid out by the Secretary of State at the Seventh Special Session of the U.N. General Assembly last fall. His speech marked a constructive U.S. response to the growing demands of the developing countries for major changes in the world's economic structure and was warmly welcomed by developed and developing countries alike. The commitment to negotiate seriously implicit in that speech needs to be followed up with public support and pressure for continued progress in the negotiations.

Second, we need to find additional ways of addressing the pressing needs of the poorest countries and the poorest people. The response of Americans in meeting emergency needs in the past has been admirable. We now need to go further, however, to address the root causes of hunger and poverty. Hunger and malnutrition are after all just symptoms; the real disease to be corrected is the underlying situation of poverty and lack of opportunity. Unfortunately no serious proposals for attempting to meet the essential needs of the world's poorest people within a reasonable time period are currently under consideration by governments. There clearly is a need for a renewed commitment on the part of both developing and developed countries. The leaders of the developing countries must seek new ways to address the most essential needs of their poor majorities—for food, health, education, and some real control over their own destiny—through programs that can be put on a self-sustaining basis within a reasonable period of time. The rich countries (both market-economy and centrally planned) must commit themselves to a much higher level of assistance, moving more rapidly toward the 0.7 per cent of GNP target agreed to in 1970 by most members of the United Nations—but not the United States. Increased assistance should be linked specifically to programs aimed at the most essential needs of the world's poorest billion people. A renewed commitment to this more focused objective by both developing and developed countries would be mutually reinforcing. Past experience indicates that the public in the rich countries will support programs aimed at the poorest people; but neither Americans nor Western Europeans are likely to support increased appropriations until they are persuaded that developing-country leaders are themselves committed to attacking the problems of poverty in their own countries. And if leaders in the poor countries are to launch the necessary reforms, they will need assurance of long-range financial support from the developed world. The initiation of a "compact" between rich and poor countries focusing on meeting the most essential human needs would be a major advance toward providing the world's poorest billion people access to the prerequisites for "life, liberty, and the pursuit of happiness," and initiation of serious discussion of such an effort would be a more appropriate celebration of our Bicentennial than many of the activities that will be taking place in this country during the coming year.

Finally, we need to begin a major new process of renewal among ourselves. We cannot lose sight either of the need for changes in our own system to allow more equitable participation by *all* Americans, or of the need for extensive discussion and debate about the values—international as well as domestic—that we consider important in the decades ahead. For it is not enough to be concerned about the poor majority in the developing countries. We must be equally committed to supporting programs aimed at the poor and powerless in our own country. And unless Americans can regain, in their own eyes and those of others, a position of moral leadership in providing both liberty and equality of opportunity at home, they will not be able, whatever their military and economic power, to exercise such leadership internationally.

The world currently is experiencing one more major chapter in the long struggle to ensure that ever more people share in the control of their own well-being and destiny. This effort traces its origins at least to the Magna Carta. Its most recent manifestations include the explosive ending of the colonial era after World War II and the struggle of workers and minorities to achieve full participation in the American political system. In the past, these conflicts have led to extremist responses, with both sides feeling that right and justice resided solely with them; all too often, the result has been violence and chaos. In the final analysis, progress comes to the poor and disadvantaged only when they undertake to improve their own lot. This effort is now taking place on an unprecedented world scale. Whether it leads to hostile confrontation or to renewed cooperation will depend at least partly on how we choose to respond to the aspirations of the world's poorest countries and people. Do we merely want to win points in a debate about the inequities of the world—playing for applause in the galleries, particularly in the press and Congress? Or do we now have the vision to respond constructively to the current challenges posed by the poor countries—by seeking new modes of mutually beneficial cooperation? We are on the threshold of a great opportunity to reshape relations among nations and to provide hope and justice for all humanity. It is one of the most exciting prospects of any period in history. We do possess the means to succeed in this venture. The question is whether or not we have the will and the vision to cross the threshold and begin the task.

THE U.S. AND WORLD DEVELOPMENT

Acknowledgments

Roger D. Hansen, *Project Director*
Valeriana Kallab, *Executive Editor*
Nancy J. Krekeler, *Assistant Editor*
Rosemarie Philips, *Assistant Editor*

The Overseas Development Council wishes to express its appreciation for the generous counsel given to those preparing this Agenda for Action *by many distinguished authorities in the World Bank, the International Monetary Fund, the United Nations, and the U.S. government. Advice was also gratefully received from several members of the Council's Board of Directors, especially from the Chairman of its Executive Committee, Davidson Sommers, and from Lincoln Gordon and Anthony Lake. The preparation and publication of this* Agenda for Action *has been partially supported by a grant from the Edna McConnell Clark Foundation.*

 The Project Director is indebted to the many members of the Council's Staff who participated in the preparation of this volume.

 Individual chapters in this Agenda for Action *represent the views of their authors and not necessarily those of the Overseas Development Council or of the Project Director.*

Table of Contents

OVERVIEW
ESSAY

The U.S. and World Development: A Year of Opportunity

In past years the Overseas Development Council's *Agenda for Action* has had two essential purposes: to identify developmental issues which the Council felt *should* be included on governmental and other agendas; and to propose policies to deal effectively with those issues.

In 1976 the task facing us is in many ways very different. In the first place, there is no need to propose an agenda of issues to be considered during the year; thanks to events of the past year, that international agenda is already before the world's developed and developing countries. In the second place, the number of forums in which discussions and negotiations will be taking place is so extensive that an identification of them and of their major tasks becomes necessary. Finally, the number of issues being considered by these various negotiating forums is so large, and the individual proposals so divergent, that it is impossible in a single short volume to do justice to the complexities of the issues. For all these reasons, this volume of the *Agenda for Action* and particularly this "overview" chapter focus on the overall dimensions of the major issues to be examined in "North-South"[1] forums throughout the world this year.

The year ahead presents a unique opportunity to advance the search for mutually accommodative resolutions to problems which presently strain relations between developed and developing countries and which hinder individual and mutual efforts to accelerate the pace of economic and social development with the world's developing countries. This chance to bring

---

[1]Throughout this overview essay, the term "North" is used as a shorthand description of the world's "developed" or "industrialized" countries; the term "South"—unless otherwise indicated in context—encompasses the "less developed" countries, ranging from the newly rich but nonindustrialized members of OPEC to the poorest and "least developed" countries of Africa, Asia, and Latin America.

about change exists not only because of the array of meetings to be held and the legion of issues to be discussed, but also because of the perceptions, both Northern and Southern, that continued tactics of confrontation are not in the best interests of either party. These perceptions are accurate, but they may not be lasting. They could change with a major and rapid swing in the business cycle, with an outbreak of war in the Middle East leading to further OECD-OPEC tensions, or any one of a hundred other events peripheral to the real issues at stake but crucial to the *perceptions* of those issues. And that, above all, is why 1976 may present the world with an opportunity which will not reappear for some time to come. To sacrifice this occasion could prove to be a very costly folly for all parties involved. A brief review of the past year helps us to understand both how the opportunity arose and how fleeting it may be.

From Confrontation to Negotiation

The past year opened with the U.S. government still preoccupied by the energy crisis to the exclusion of many other North-South issues and still discussing publicly those conditions under which it might be deemed necessary to apply military power in the Middle East to assure access to oil supplies. Furthermore, the U.S. government refused to open serious discussions with the Organization of Petroleum Exporting Countries (OPEC), and chose instead to continue with the development of the International Energy Agency—composed of members of the Organisation for Economic Co-operation and Development (OECD)—and domestic programs in an attempt to gradually decrease the dependence of the United States and other industrialized countries on OPEC-controlled energy supplies. Finally, when developed and developing countries did gather in April 1975 to prepare for a September energy conference, the meeting reached a deadlock and dissolved in failure when the United States and other developed countries refused to accommodate developing-country demands to add discussion of other development questions to the agenda of the proposed September "consumer-producer" conference.

Despite this uninspiring beginning, the dialogue between developed and developing countries slowly led to thoughts of compromise. By September, changing attitudes bore their first fruit in the form of a comprehensive consensus resolution unanimously endorsed by the Seventh Special Session of the U.N. General Assembly on Development and International Economic Cooperation.[2] Shortly thereafter, another planning session was convened to organize the consumer-producer conference (now officially entitled the Conference on International Economic Cooperation), which held its first ministerial session in Paris in December. A somewhat parallel set of formal and informal developed-country discussions—which

---

[2]See U.N. General Assembly, Seventh Special Session, Resolution 3362 (S-VII), September 16, 1975.

culminated in the meeting of six of the most important of those countries at Rambouillet, France, in November 1975—helped to overcome many differences among the developed countries and to prepare for negotiations on several of the major issues facing the developed countries in the coming year.

What caused this movement from confrontation through compromise to the opening of the broad range of negotiations that face us in 1976? Most probably it was a calculation on the part of the large majority of parties concerned that the potential benefits of compromise and negotiation would considerably outweigh their costs, and that the costs of continuing confrontation were fast becoming disproportionate to any further benefits which such a strategy might produce.

This is not to say that confrontation policies are always, or even generally, inappropriate to the achievement of moderate—even mutually beneficial—ends. Former Assistant Secretary of State Thomas O. Enders stated that the turning point for U.S. policy occurred in April 1975, "when it became clear that the conservative members of OPEC were going to join the radical ones in bidding for the political leadership of the Third World."[3] His remark suggests that the "united front" confrontation tactics resorted to by OPEC and the developing countries last April in Paris were an essential ingredient in the gradual evolution of a U.S. policy response that eventually accepted the developing-country proposal to broaden the Paris agenda to include all major development issues.

The failure of the Paris discussions in April finally demonstrated to the United States the capability of the OPEC countries to act as a fairly cohesive unit, at least for a period of several years. This led the United States to recognize the potential costs of continued "stonewalling," which, in these circumstances, seemed guaranteed to forestall any OECD-OPEC talks on energy issues, and to increase the OPEC country-developing country "bloc" tactics on a wide range of international issues that were a constant source of U.S. governmental complaints. Additionally, this scenario lent some further credence to the possibility that the OPEC countries might devote increasingly large sums of their oil proceeds to the financing of other developing-country producer cartels, a possibility discussed in some detail at Third World caucuses in Dakar and Algiers early in 1975.

Beyond these short-term considerations, many senior government officials began to speculate more seriously about the changing role of both the United States and the developing countries in the global economy. They considered a host of trends, all of which suggested that an attempt at compromise was an eminently sensible course of action. Among those trends were the rapidly rising share of U.S. exports and imports as a percentage of U.S. gross national product; a growing reliance of the United States on raw materials located overseas, often in developing countries; the increased bargaining strength of developing countries vis-a-vis U.S. and other devel-

---

[3]Richard S. Frank, "Economic Report/U.S. Takes Steps to Meet Demands of Third World Nations," *National Journal*, Vol. 7, No. 43 (October 25, 1975), p. 1480.

oped-country multinational firms; and the not insubstantial role of developing countries as markets for U.S. exports and as locations for foreign direct investment.

Among the officials concerned with rapidly deteriorating U.S.-Third World economic relations were others whose major worries were often more political than economic in nature. This latter group included representatives from all of the major segments of the U.S. government who had been involved in one of the many global forums convened in recent years. These officials were increasingly becoming aware that the world is moving into an era which will be noted for its need to manage *global* problems, quite often through the process of *multilateral* diplomacy. For example, the Third Law of the Sea Conference is viewed by many as embodying a large number of the problems to be faced in a variety of negotiating forums in the near future. At the Law of the Sea Conference, two issues are particularly salient. First, how will nations come together to establish new regimes to manage issues which, like those encompassed by the seas, are global in nature? The current Law of the Sea Conference evokes different problems for different audiences: 1) managing a global commons, 2) setting and policing environmental standards, 3) establishing efficient regimes for the management of fisheries and other resources, and 4) many additional problems ranging from national security to scientific investigation. Second, how can the United States best develop major support for its own proposals in the various multilateral arenas that attempt to apply such global approaches?

To the extent that the agenda of major issues facing the U.S. government in its third century is laden with such global issues—be it oceans and other "commons" problems, the environment, nuclear proliferation, the international ramifications of domestic economic programs throughout the world, and many others—the United States will find that it cannot resolve its "own" problems without recourse to multilateral diplomacy. And it obviously cannot *succeed* in its multilateral diplomatic efforts unless it can achieve majority support for its proposals.

The recognition of this broader issue, together with the more immediate concern with the short-term economic implications of further North-South confrontation in 1975 and 1976, provided much of the impetus needed to reconsider U.S. policies toward the OPEC countries in particular and the Third World in general in the late spring and early summer of 1975. The resulting shift in U.S. positions was enough to produce a consensus resolution on development and international economic cooperation at the Seventh Special Session of the U.N. General Assembly in September of 1975 and to resuscitate plans for the Conference on International Economic Cooperation, now fully launched in Paris. Will the U.S. shift prove to have been permanent or temporary? Will it develop support throughout the Executive Branch or remain an outlook of but a few senior officials in the State Department? And even if it gains full Executive Branch support, will it be sustained by the U.S. Congress? If these questions were answerable with any degree of certitude, the course of the 1976 negotiations would be considerably easier to predict.

The willingness of the United States to include the developing world on its 1975-76 diplomatic agenda was all that was needed to elicit a constructive response from the world's developing countries. As noted in Chapter I, the "Group of 77" developing countries accepted the Kissinger speech at the United Nations (delivered by Ambassador Daniel P. Moynihan) as signaling a willingness to negotiate, worked hard to produce a compromise resolution throughout the Special Session, and ultimately supported a final draft which considerably diluted their earlier demands. Like the United States, the developing countries, too, had come to the recognition that rhetorical victories over a "new international economic order" empty of substance were no longer worth the price that such a strategy imposed upon most of them.[4] They needed actions of a positive nature to overcome the deepening economic difficulties that the energy, food, and fertilizer price rises[5] and the global recession were posing for them; and most of these actions required a great deal of developed-country cooperation. If the United States and other developed countries were finally prepared to discuss specifically a broad range of short-term and longer-term developmental problems, the developing countries were anxious to begin such discussions immediately.

OPEC countries aside, the short-term problems of the developing countries in the aggregate were of major proportions. The rapid rises in energy, food, and fertilizer costs, the depressed state of the economies of the OECD countries, and continued worldwide inflation have all contributed to the serious cyclical—and, in some cases, secular—difficulties now being faced by the developing world. The current-account deficit for the non-oil-exporting developing countries in 1975 will probably equal or slightly exceed $35 billion, a fourfold increase from the 1973 figure of $9 billion. Much of this increase reflects not only a stagnation of (and in some cases an absolute decline in) export earnings due to depressed global economic conditions, but also a rather rapid deterioration in aggregate developing-country terms of trade. In 1974, developing-country export prices rose by 27 per cent while their import prices increased by 40 per cent; in 1975, their export prices remained almost constant while the prices of their imports rose by approximately 6 per cent. Excluding oil, the purchasing power of primary commodities, accounting for approximately two thirds of developing-country export earnings, is estimated to have fallen by about 13 per cent during 1975.

While the consequences of these trends vary considerably from country to country, the aggregates are very discouraging. Growth rates have deteriorated rapidly. Addressing himself to the situation in the poorest countries

---

[4]As later events in the U.N. Thirtieth General Assembly suggested, the developing countries were not prepared to adopt this more conciliatory approach on many other unrelated issues.

[5]See Tables B-5, p. 156, B-6, p. 157, and B-8, p. 159.

(i.e., those with per capita incomes below $200), World Bank President Robert McNamara noted that:

> In 1974, per capita incomes of the one billion people living in these nations *declined* an average .5%. For the hundreds of millions of them already severely deprived, it meant hunger, illness, and an erosion of hope.
>
> This year [1975] the outlook is for a further weakening of these economies, and the per capita incomes of the one billion people are likely to fall again.[6]

By late 1975, the number of countries designated by the United Nations as "most seriously affected" by the adverse global economic conditions had reached 42—an increase of 9 countries over the 1974 figure of 33.[7] The situations of individual countries in the "most-seriously-affected" category have changed in various ways over the period since the group was initially identified in August of 1974. Those whose difficulty was attributable in significant measure to the need to import high-priced food and fertilizers have found their problems eased considerably by better-than-average weather, some decline in world food prices, and, in late 1975, a sharp drop in fertilizer prices. For the majority of these countries, however, the problems of external financing worsened even more during 1975 than they did for the non-oil-exporting developing countries as a whole.[8] Serious concern has been expressed that the incurring of further indebtedness could seriously strain their debt-servicing capacity and thus add substantially to their longer-range development problems.[9]

Most developing countries at higher levels of income and industrialization fared better during 1974 than their poorer counterparts, most notably because they were in a position to draw on substantial foreign exchange reserves (which continued to accumulate, but at a slowing pace), to borrow in international markets, and to augment the financing of imports through suppliers' credits. By these and other means, their per capita growth rates were bolstered during 1974, showing an aggregate average increase of almost 4 per cent.

For 1975, however, a negative per capita growth rate of approximately 1 per cent is projected, despite the drawing down of reserves and an increase in borrowing which, in the cases of some countries, already appears to be straining their creditworthiness. The increased reliance on short-term for-

---

[6]Robert S. McNamara, "Address to the Board of Governors," September 1, 1975 (Washington, D.C.: World Bank, 1975), pp. 3–4.

[7]See the list of countries provided as a note to Table E–4, p. 200.

[8]See Table E–2, p. 194, which includes the most-seriously-affected countries.

[9]For a discussion of the "least developed" countries, see Helen C. Low and James W. Howe, "Focus on the Fourth World," in James W. Howe and the staff of the Overseas Development Council, *The U.S. and World Development: Agenda for Action, 1975* (New York: Praeger Publishers, Inc., 1975), pp. 35–54.

eign borrowings, which has been an integral part of the picture for most of these countries, may well raise questions of future debt-servicing capability, although at this point in time the dimensions of the problem are not clear.

How much more developing countries can cut their imports and how they can finance their growing current-account deficits are crucial problems to be faced during 1976. As will be noted below, these problems and policies to ameliorate them will be considered in many of the old and new negotiating arenas throughout the year. Perhaps no other single issue on the agenda for 1976 is of greater *short-term* urgency; and one can also at least hope that short-term policies in this area contain the potential for evolution into *longer-term* policies of resource transfers to enhance jointly supported North-South efforts to accelerate the development process. Both aspects are important, since the new problems faced by many of the developing countries are structural as well as cyclical. The increase in energy costs alone suggests the medium- to long-term nature of some of the problems that must be overcome before many developing countries recover completely from the adverse impact of events of the past two years.

In retrospect, it seems clear that it was a careful reassessment of self-interest that led the United States and other developed countries on the one hand and the developing countries on the other to substitute an attempt at negotiation for a policy of continued confrontation. Throughout this year, at a variety of meetings, the wisdom of such a strategy and its potential for mutual accommodation will be tested. It is to be hoped that by this time next year the wisdom of the strategy will, at the very least, have begun to become apparent to all major actors and elements represented in the negotiating process, and that the *potential* for mutual accommodation creating new opportunities for economic and social development will have begun to be realized.

Nevertheless, the difficulties in achieving significant progress should not be underestimated. Indeed, to underestimate them is probably to guarantee failure. As a prescient observer of the fissures within present-day American society recently wrote: "Freedom, the underlying principle of a democratic society, requires a commitment to *restraint*, a willingness not to do anything to undermine the basic set of conventions which enable men of different values and interests to live together."[10] The international system, however, never has been a "democratic society," nor does it yet possess "the basic set of conventions" that will permit states representing differing values and interests to live together in assured patterns of peace and mutual accommodation. It is above all for these reasons that international analogies drawn from domestic societies are often quite misleading.

Without the existence of anything approaching a democratic international society or the conventions to support it, the commitment to *restraint* in search of mutual accommodations will be sorely tested before the year is

---

[10]Seymour Martin Lipset, "The Paradox of American Politics," *The Public Interest*, No. 41 (Fall 1975), p. 165. Emphasis added.

out. But only this recognition—and a weighing of the potential costs of failure—can bolster that crucial commitment.

Forums New and Old

The Conference on International Economic Cooperation. The newest of the forums in which negotiations on international economic reforms will be taking place is the Conference on International Economic Cooperation, which held its inaugural session in Paris in December of 1975 and is expected to meet throughout 1976, if not longer. The major substantive work of the Conference will be addressed by four different subgroups or commissions focusing on energy, raw materials, the general problems of development, and the problems of financing as related to each of the problem areas examined in the other three groupings.

There are several reasons for hoping that this new forum will lead to some significant progress in negotiations over the coming year. First, the necessary actors are present, as is a representative balance among contending forces and aspirations. Representing the OPEC countries are Algeria, Indonesia, Iran, Iraq, Nigeria, Saudi Arabia, and Venezuela; representing other developing countries are Argentina, Brazil, Cameroon, Egypt, India, Jamaica, Mexico, Pakistan, Peru, Yugoslavia, Zaire, and Zambia; and the European Community, Japan, the United States, Canada, Australia, Spain, Sweden, and Switzerland represent the world's developed countries. Since the European Commission will be representing its nine member countries, however, the tilt in the membership toward the developing countries is not as great as initial appearances suggest. Nevertheless, the interests of developed, developing, and oil-producing states will all find a voice in the Conference itself and in the work of its subgroups.

Second, the group seems small enough to avoid the pitfalls of the forums of multilateral diplomacy in which very large numbers of states are engaged (e.g., the U.N. General Assembly and the Law of the Sea Conference). If it can avoid the endless speeches and public posturing that typically characterize (and often paralyze) larger international convocations, the Conference may be able to combine the attributes of representativeness and feasible size necessary to undertake serious negotiations with better-than-even probabilities of achieving some significant progress.[11]

Of course, any tangible progress will remain contingent upon the motives of the major actors, including above all their desire to seek mutually accommodative results across the broad range of issues to be discussed. And here, perhaps, lies the third and major reason for some optimism. The agenda of issues to be considered by the Conference is large enough to

---

[11]On the need for smaller, more informal, and less "public" negotiating processes, see the Report of the Group of Experts on the Structure of the United Nations System, *A New United Nations Structure for Global Economic Co-operation,* U.N. Pub. Sales No. E/AC. 62/9 (New York: United Nations, 1975).

encourage the search for a balanced package of proposals which could, in the *aggregate*, produce benefits for all, even if some gained more than others.

There is much discussion and analysis these days about the pros and cons of "linkage politics"—that is, the growing propensity of countries to link the settlement of some problems on which their bargaining position is relatively weak to others on which they hold a much stronger hand. Regardless of the opposing views on the potential for such linkage strategies to produce positive negotiating outcomes, it seems accurate to say that the issues at stake within the four subgroups of the Conference *already* have been linked by many of the active participants. Given this starting point, the breadth of the agenda may well serve more as an opportunity to produce mutually balanced concessions—e.g., Northern access to needed raw materials in exchange for a larger developing-country role in the control of raw material sources, their processing, and their assured access to Northern markets—than as an obstacle to progress in the negotiations.

UNCTAD IV. The year also will witness the convening of the fourth session of the U.N. Conference on Trade and Development. Opening in Nairobi in May, UNCTAD IV will try again to make progress on many of the issues that have characterized its work since it was established in 1964. The agenda will focus on commodities; manufactures and semi-manufactures; money, finance, and the transfer of real resources for development; the transfer of technology; and the problems of the least developed countries.

For three reasons, however, it is difficult to be very optimistic about the prospects for significant progress in North-South negotiations in the UNCTAD forum unless major negotiating progress on the UNCTAD commodity proposals is somehow made prior to the May meeting in Nairobi. First, UNCTAD suffers from many of the debilitating effects of large-scale multilateral diplomacy noted above. With over 140 nations in attendance, with endless plenary speeches and rhetorical flourishes from all sides, and with all the publicity attending an international conference of this size and scope, the chances for serious negotiations are often undermined by the session's very structure.

Second, UNCTAD suffers from a history of confrontational politics. Of all of the existing international organizations, it is perhaps the one most widely perceived within the governing circles of the United States and other developed countries as unsuited for serious negotiations on issues of major importance in the trade and development fields. Whether valid or not, this perception presents a serious stumbling block to attempts at mutual accommodation.

Finally, the major issue on the UNCTAD IV agenda promises to be one of the most controversial of all those to be dealt with during 1976—the UNCTAD Secretariat's proposal for an "integrated commodity program." As presently envisaged, the program calls for:

(a) A series of buffer-stock arrangements for ten "core" commodities;

(b) A common fund for the financing of these buffer stocks;

(c) Multilateral commitments among producers and consumers to undertake systematic appraisals of future supply and demand conditions and, in some cases, to undertake sales and purchases over specified time periods within mutually agreed price ranges;

(d) A greatly expanded and revised system of compensatory financing to provide loans at concessional rates of interest to those countries experiencing significant deterioration in their export earnings due to falling prices of their raw material and other commodity exports; and

(e) An expansion of commodity-processing facilities in developing countries to serve as part of an export diversification program in raw material-exporting developing countries.

It is doubtful that the program as presently envisaged by the UNCTAD Secretariat and many of the developing countries can make much headway against the opposition to it from many quarters. The United States strongly opposes the scheme, as do a significant number of other major developed countries, and many of the net raw material importers among the developing countries also have reservations. The reasons for objections run the gamut from the highly ideological (e.g., too much interference with the "free market") to the highly pragmatic (e.g., whether such a scheme would strengthen or weaken a particular country's balance-of-payments position).

Present views on the subject may change. Within the United States, a number of respected economists are suggesting that the potential benefits that might be derived from an "integrated commodity program"—assured access to supplies, more limited price fluctuations, and an international political atmosphere more conducive to the search for and development of new sources of raw materials—are likely to outweigh the potential costs, which include the initial purchasing costs of buffer stocks, the propensity of such an approach to gradually increase the prices of raw materials included in the program, and others of a more hypothetical nature. And if a way can be found to manage the scheme so that it transfers income to resource-poor developing countries which would otherwise suffer net losses on their trade account as a result of its operation, some developing-country doubts also may be dispelled.

On balance, however, the slow development of convincing analytical support for the scheme, together with the strong opposition of some major actors, does not suggest that much short-term progress can be expected. Therefore, the perceived "success" or "failure" of UNCTAD IV is likely to hinge on the Conference's ability to make some significant negotiating progress on other issues of its agenda, or to reach agreement on some specific segments of the commodities program, e.g., the areas of compensatory financing or accelerated commodity processing within developing countries. In these other areas, the probability of some success is higher, since the developing countries are perceived to have more bargaining strength on these issues than they had at the first three sessions of the Conference.

The "Tokyo Round" of Trade Negotiations. In another Geneva forum, the multilateral trade negotiations being conducted under the General Agreement on Tariffs and Trade (GATT) are moving very slowly. The pace of the negotiations in 1975 reflected disagreements on both technical and substantive issues between the major industrialized participants—the United States and the European Community. The interests of other developed and developing countries that are participating in the negotiations have been sidelined temporarily while the two major participants attempt to reconcile their differences. Only after such a reconciliation will the trade negotiations, which are of great potential importance to the developing countries, begin to move forward with any speed. It is to be hoped that the discussions of the six OECD nations at Rambouillet in November of 1975 have helped in that process of reconciliation.

The International Monetary Fund. In the International Monetary Fund (IMF), negotiations continue on such international monetary reform issues as the phasing out of gold as a major international reserve; the shape of a new exchange-rate regime; and the changing role of Special Drawing Rights. In addition to these general international monetary reform issues, all of which have distinct ramifications for the North-South dialogue, the Interim Committee of the IMF will be considering some very special issues much more directly linked to development problems and the present foreign exchange scarcities of some of the *poorest* of the developing countries. Two such issues are proposals for changes in the Fund's present compensatory financing facility, and proposals to establish a Special Trust Fund to lend money on highly concessional terms to developing countries experiencing serious balance-of-payments difficulties. If the process of economic recovery in the industrialized countries should continue to be slow in coming, the short-term and medium-term needs for emergency-type lending and/or outright grants to some of the lower-income countries—and some other special-case countries as well—will become increasingly important. Therefore the work of the IMF and its Interim Committee (twenty finance ministers chosen to represent all IMF member countries) in the area of enhancing the capacity of that body to respond more effectively to short-term payments problems assumes major importance during 1976.[12]

The World Bank. In the World Bank, negotiations with governments are now beginning on the scale of the fifth replenishment of the International Development Association (IDA), the institution established to provide 50-year loans at a service charge of 0.75 per cent to the lower-income countries. Its fourth replenishment of $4.5 billion, of which the U.S. share is $1.5 billion, will be fully committed by the end of fiscal year 1977. The fifth

---

[12]Substantial progress on most of the issues noted in this paragraph was made at the January 1976 meeting of the Interim Committee in Jamaica. For a summary report, see *IMF Survey,* January 19, 1976.

replenishment will need to be nearly double the current figure if the sharp inflation of recent years is to be offset and some increase in purchasing power is to be provided along the lines of all earlier replenishments. The issue of a capital increase to enable the World Bank to maintain a high volume of development lending (presently at a level of $5.5 billion per year) also will be considered in 1976. In addition, the Bank has added a "Third Window" to its channels for providing longer-term funds to developing countries. Lending through this facility will be available chiefly to countries with per capita incomes below $375, with an interest rate subsidy of 4 per cent. It now appears that the level of donations to this new fund will set a limit of approximately $600 million for its development loans—unless contributions are forthcoming from such major developed countries as the United States, the Federal Republic of Germany, and Japan, which thus far have been critical of yet another special fund.

Finally, the Joint World Bank-IMF Committee on the Transfer of Real Resources will continue throughout the year to attempt to shape agreements among developed and developing countries to ease some emergency problems and to institute some longer-term reforms to accelerate the process of economic development. Issues on the agenda of this "Development Committee" range from short-term considerations of how to increase financial support for the Third Window to examination of such longer-term problems as increasing developing-country access to Northern capital markets (national and international) and stabilizing raw material prices.

Action on the World Food Problem. At least four major tasks in the food area—all identified by the 1974 World Food Conference—await serious attention in 1976: a global system of food reserves, to be discussed by the World Food Council; a global system of food aid; a major effort (financial, technological, and socio-political), led by the Consultative Group on Food Production and Investment in Developing Countries, to accelerate food production and improve nutrition within the developing countries, particularly among their small farmers; and the problem of how to treat such major sources of instability in the world food system as the Soviet Union's sporadic and unpredictable purchasing forays into the international market.[13]

The Law of the Sea Conference. Yet another major forum of debate deserving of mention in this context is the March 1976 session of the Third U.N. Law of the Sea Conference. At the previous session of the Conference, held in Geneva last year, the 141 attending nations succeeded, with some bureaucratic sleight of hand, in producing a "single negotiating text" that will constitute the basic agenda when the Conference reconvenes in New York in March. Whether the Conference can produce a consensus document that will form the basis of a new global oceans regime before the end of the year is in considerable doubt. The greatest North-South "split" at the

---

[13]See Chapter II.

Conference continues to center on the issue of a "deep seabed regime." What will be the role of such a regime? What will be the role of private enterprise in exploring for minerals and extracting them from the deep seabed?

Developing countries desire to limit and control the activity of private enterprise in this arena because only Western companies thus far have the technology needed to mine the deep seabed. Conversely, most of the developed countries, led by the United States, seek wide degrees of freedom for private enterprise to search for and recover minerals from the seabed. Of all the unresolved issues facing the Conference, this is the most difficult; it is likely to become more so if and as unilateral actions, adding to the complexities already involved, are taken prior to a negotiated agreement. Compromise positions are being developed so that there still is some hope that a successful resolution of this issue can be achieved this year—a resolution which would, by reserving perhaps 50 per cent of the major mineral finds to an international deep seabed regime, provide a source of funds that could be used exclusively for developmental purposes within the less developed countries.

Even if such an agreement is reached, however, it is certain to mock the original idea that the oceans are "the common heritage of mankind," and that that entire heritage should be nurtured and used for support of the development process. The Conference seems very likely to approve 200-mile "economic zones" for all coastal states, thus gutting the remaining "common heritage" of the overwhelming portion of its potential wealth. This outcome is the result of pressures from coastal states, developing and developed alike. Perhaps the most that can be hoped for in the short run—and this in itself would be a significant step forward—is that as a result of the Conference, the oceans will not be overfished and overpolluted. For the longer run, one can hope that the minimal proceeds for developmental purposes provided by a treaty—if a treaty is produced by the Conference—become the first of a series of more "automatic" sources of funds for the process of economic and social development within the South.

Reform of the U.N. System. Within the United Nations, considerable effort will be devoted over the next year to studying various proposals to reform the structure and functioning of the U.N. system as it affects issues of economic and social development. The resolution adopted by the Seventh Special Session of the General Assembly established an Ad Hoc Committee on the Restructuring of the Economic and Social Sectors of the U.N. System to begin its work immediately and to submit a final report to the 1976 regular session of the General Assembly. This Committee was instructed to take into account the report submitted by a group of experts early in 1975, entitled *A New United Nations Structure for Global Economic Co-operation.*[14] The degree of progress in this particular setting is likely to be significantly affected by the progress—or lack of it—in many of the other

---

[14]Report of the Group of Experts, *A New United Nations Structure*, op. cit.

negotiating forums throughout the year. Progress in other arenas should enhance the prospects for proposals seeking to strengthen the U.N. system's capacity to bargain and to accommodate; lack of progress may support present tendencies to use the system to confront and to exacerbate.

The Major Issues for Negotiation

Seven somewhat distinct but often overlapping issues seem to be the most prominent among those on the 1976 agendas of the various organizations and conferences described in the preceding section:

(1) Export earnings of the developing countries;
(2) International trade reforms;
(3) Global food programs;
(4) Resource transfers;
(5) Other programs to accelerate the growth and development process;
(6) Organizational restructuring and institutional reforms to aid development; and
(7) The problems of the poorest countries and "absolute" poverty.

Most of these problems have confronted international organizations and conferences and individual governments for years; some of them (e.g., the food problem) are novel at least in their urgency and the insistence with which their solutions are being sought by one or another major group participating in the debate (e.g., as in the case of institutional reform).

If there is any reason for some optimism about the way in which the 1976 agenda may be dealt with, it lies in the kind of calculation that both developed and developing countries appear to have made during the past twelve months. As noted at the outset, there is some reason to believe that the potential costs and benefits of an outright failure in the attempt at negotiations over these issues have been rather carefully considered, and that cooler heads in both developed and developing countries have—at least temporarily—prevailed. Secretary of State Kissinger's speech delivered at the Seventh Special Session of the General Assembly noted that "we profoundly believe that neither the poor nor the rich nations can achieve their purposes in isolation. . . . The reality is that ample incentives exist for cooperation on the basis of mutual respect."

About one week before that speech was to be delivered, a special task force of the Third World Forum expressed a similar view at its meeting in Mexico City:

We believe that it is possible to evolve proposals which balance the longer-term interests of the developed countries and the Third World and which, as such, are acceptable to the entire international community. For instance, security of earnings of the [raw material] producing countries can be counter-balanced by security of supplies to the consuming countries. Greater share in benefits to the host countries from the exploitation of their natural resources can be matched by longer-term assurances to the [transnational corporations] for the protection of their investments. The democratization of the international financial institutions can be carried out in such a way as to increase the voice of the Third World without losing the interest of the rich nations in the continuation and growth of these institutions.[15]

If the thought processes and the analysis leading to such viewpoints prevail during the course of this year's negotiations, then a) this changing perspective on the part of major actors and blocs of actors, b) the range of forums available, and c) the wide spectrum of issues represented on the various international agendas all offer considerable opportunity for the successful start of serious and mutually accommodative negotiations on global economic issues of importance to both developed and developing countries.

Pessimists may view 1976 as a year in which the discussion of too many issues in too many forums by too many governments with divergent interests guarantees failure. Optimists will judge the range of issues, forums, and interests as a major opportunity to develop a broad series of balanced bargains. When all is said and done, the crucial ingredient most probably will be that of changing governmental *perceptions* of the need to search out mutually accommodative bargains where the "gains" are divided among the parties to the negotiation. If perceptions of such a need are not gaining ground in both developed and developing countries, then the year may end with leading elements of the former group rallying around the increasingly inadequate banner of "free markets," with leading elements of the latter group hopelessly demanding "reparations" for colonial injustices, and with all efforts at constructive negotiation stalled and failing. Given the range of opportunities presented this year and the uncertainty that they will recur in the near future, one must wonder whether the world can easily accommodate the potential costs—economic, political, and ethical—of such a failure.

1. *Developing-Country Export Earnings.* In recent years, exports have accounted for approximately 80 per cent of the developing countries' total inflows of foreign exchange. Furthermore, it is recognized that the instability of export earnings for the developing countries—generally reflecting the larger cyclical swings in raw material prices and export volumes—is considerably greater than it is for developed countries. Finally, it is argued that this instability in foreign exchange earnings often complicates the planning and implementation of development programs. The net result is that programs to stabilize developing-country export earnings have been on international agendas for years and once again occupy a very prominent place in 1976.

---

[15]*Proposals for a New International Economic Order,* prepared by a special task force of the Third World Forum, Mexico City, August 21–24, 1975, p. 14. (Available from the Third World Forum, Provisional Secretariat, Casilla 179-D, Santiago, Chile.) The Third World Forum, formed in 1973, is an association of prominent social scientists from Asia, Africa, and Latin America.

U.S. recognition of the problem and apparent willingness to take some action to resolve it claimed first place in Secretary Kissinger's listing of action programs and proposals at the General Assembly's Seventh Special Session. In a section of his speech entitled "Ensuring Economic Security," the Secretary stated that "the international community must undertake a new approach to reduce drastic fluctuations in the export earnings of the developing countries." The United States rejected the general UNCTAD *price*-stabilization approach, arguing that for many commodities such stabilization would be difficult to achieve "without severe restrictions on production or exports, extremely expensive buffer stocks, or price levels which could stimulate substitutes and thereby work to the long run disadvantage of producers." Instead, the United States proposed the creation within the IMF of what it called a "development security facility" to stabilize overall export *earnings* of developing countries.

To a large degree, the U.S. proposal amounts to an expansion of the compensatory financing scheme which has existed within the Fund for over a decade. But the proposed changes are significant: access to such loans is considerably eased; the volume of funds available for lending is significantly expanded; and provision is made for the poorest countries to convert their loans into grants under prescribed conditions. Furthermore, unlike commodity-price stabilization schemes, the U.S. proposal, geared to export *earnings,* would cover shortfalls in the export earnings of manufactured products as well as raw materials. But it would *not* in any way guarantee the *purchasing power* of those earnings vis-a-vis manufactured and capital-goods imports.

The U.S. proposal in this field thus is, at first glance, far different from the proposals of most developing countries that still support the UNCTAD commodity-price support scheme discussed above. The crucial question facing negotiators over the coming year is whether or not the two approaches can be reconciled as part of a package of mutually accommodative agreements. Such an outcome certainly is not out of the question. In the first place, the United States has not ruled out examination and negotiation of specific commodity agreements. Indeed, the Kissinger speech recommended that "a consumer-producer forum be established for every key commodity to discuss how to promote the efficiency, growth and stability of its market." It also announced that the United States intended to sign a new international tin agreement, to participate in the cocoa and sugar negotiations, and to continue negotiations on an international coffee arrangement. In the second place, many developing countries appear to be having further thoughts about the wisdom of UNCTAD's integrated commodity approach. As noted above, many of them, in examining the approach in detail, recognize the distinct possibility that it might consitute a net drain on their foreign exchange position. Obviously, this is particularly likely for the resource-poor developing countries, many of which are among the poorest of the developing countries.

The fact that a special task force of the Third World Forum proposed support for a more limited "integrated" commodity scheme—one to stabilize the prices of coffee, rubber, tin, copper, and tea—suggests that careful examination of individual commodity problems in particular and export earnings in general might well produce a package of proposals on which most if not all developed and developing countries could agree. It would probably combine elements of many proposals now being discussed—increased access to larger volumes of compensatory financing, some individual commodity agreements designed to fit the requirements of a particular product, and some schemes covering more than one commodity in instances where such a group or groupings proved to be the most cost-effective way to achieve shared goals.

A serious examination of the raw material and commodity controversy suggests that there are many obstacles to be cleared in this area of negotiations, not the least of which concerns the ideological arguments which still color most attempts to analyze the subject. Perhaps the most fundamental issue is one that often remains hidden: Should compensatory financing arrangements and international commodity agreements serve the single function of stabilizing earnings and price fluctuations around underlying trends, as argued by most developed-country governments and most economists, or should they also attempt to serve as mechanisms to transfer income from developed to developing countries, as generally proposed by the latter group? If this were the only issue being negotiated this year, the probabilities for a successful outcome would be very small; a compelling economic case for income transfers through artificially elevated commodity prices simply has not yet been made, if indeed it can be made convincingly. However, since many other problems under discussion offer the opportunity for accelerated economic development through a combination of increased economic opportunities and/or increased resource transfers—direct or indirect—the pessimism raised by this one major clash of views easily can be overdrawn.

2. *International Trade Reforms.* Another issue linked to limiting price and earnings fluctuations of raw materials and other exports from developing countries involves a set of trade reforms to increase developing-country capacity to earn scarce foreign exchange and accelerate economic growth.[16]

In this area, an apparent willingness of the United States to discuss a broad set of trade reform issues is directly responsive to long-standing developing-country complaints about major aspects of the present international trade regime. The United States has proposed a fivefold approach in the present "Tokyo round" of the GATT negotiations to achieve greater developing-country access to developed-country markets for its products:

(a) *Special treatment for products of the least developed countries,*

---

[16]See Table C–5, p. 181.

extended through a variety of means "such as preferences, favorable concessions and exceptions which reflect their economic status."

(b) *The implementation of generalized tariff preferences* for almost all developing countries; this will be of particular benefit to the manufacturing sectors of the more advanced developing countries. The U.S. generalized system of preferences (GSP) became effective on January 1, 1976.

(c) *The adaptation of general rules regarding trade policies to reflect the special needs of the development process.* For example, the present negotiations in the non-tariff-barrier field are to take into account —and therefore make exceptions favoring—the special situations of the developing countries. The United States has promised that in at least two specific areas—government procurement practices and the use of export subsidies, which generally trigger the U.S. countervailing duty statute—the United States "will negotiate special considerations for the developing countries."

(d) *The dismantling of much of the present developed-country tariff system of protection,* which favors the import of developing-country raw materials over the latter's processed goods and manufactured products. Such an effort, if successful, would lower the high tariff rates now levied against developing-country processed and manufactured goods, thus increasing the capacity of those countries to accelerate the export of a much broader range of semi-finished and finished products and diminishing their present high degree of dependence on the export of unprocessed raw materials and other commodities.

(e) *Early agreement on tariff cuts for tropical products,* which are of particular importance to many developing countries.

There is a clear parallel between the present U.S. position on the trade issues summarized here and its position adopted on the issues of commodity trade noted above. Once again, U.S. proposals fall well short of present developing-country desires; but once again they may still serve as the basis for a successful negotiation.

The developing countries will not find any willingness on the part of the United States to accept the concept of "indexing," whereby the prices of the typical developing-country export basket of products would be automatically stabilized vis-a-vis the costs of their typical import basket. They will be discouraged, moreover, that the generalized tariff preferences extended to them by the United States and other developed countries whose GSP programs have been in effect for some years continue to be severely limited both in terms of product coverage and product-by-product volume coverage. Mainly because of pressures for protection within all of the larger industrial societies, many of the products that the developing countries are most able to export are not eligible for preferences; in the cases of many of their other products, volume limitations established by legislative or administrative actions appear to offer little incentive to develop an export capacity that would achieve optimal scales of production. Finally, the developing countries will be disappointed with the very slow pace of negotiations now proceeding in Geneva and will question whether or not the General Agreement on Tariffs and Trade (GATT) is the proper forum in which to focus on the special trade problems of the developing countries. A special task force of the Third World Forum already has recommended that this range of issues "be taken up in a much broader perspective than the usual discussion in terms of tariffs and quotas on individual commodities. The U.N. General Assembly should set up a special commission for this purpose, with a balanced representation from the international community."[17]

Thus these issues seem destined to be discussed in Geneva (GATT), Nairobi (UNCTAD IV), Paris (the Conference on International Economic Cooperation), and perhaps in New York (the United Nations) as well. Again the crucial question is whether the United States and other developed countries have offered enough by way of an initial negotiating position to engage the developing countries in a serious debate on trade reforms that will increase market access for developing-country products—particularly processed and manufactured products—in the North. A second crucial question concerns the ability of developed-country government executive branches to make the results of negotiations in this area acceptable to their national parliaments or legislative bodies where that process—as in the United States—is in certain areas a necessity. Some parts of a package on trade reforms (e.g., certain levels of tariff reductions) would not require additional legislative approval. Other parts (e.g., codes on non-tariff barriers) will require U.S. congressional approval. Therefore many trade reform issues of major importance to the developing countries will require the simultaneous conduct of *international* and *domestic* negotiations to ensure progress.[18]

Once again, however, a difficult task may be made somewhat easier by the very breadth of the issues under consideration. One example should suffice to make the point. In passing the Trade Act of 1974, the U.S. Congress, concerned with achieving access to supplies of raw materials (often located in developing countries), authorized "reciprocal concessions or comparable trade obligations, or both, by the United States" in order to achieve such access.[19] This type of linkage again suggests the possibility of

---

[17]*Proposals for a New International Economic Order*, Third World Forum, op. cit., p. 8.

[18]Because so many of the issues raised in the 1976 negotiations have immediate *domestic* as well as international ramifications, they raise a fundamental question alluded to in this paragraph that requires much more thorough analysis than it has yet received: the organization of domestic political systems to make foreign policy decisions in the *national* interest when so many sectoral as well as private interest groups are attempting to influence these "foreign" policy outcomes. This issue will be examined in future ODC publications.

[19]See Harald B. Malmgren's illuminating discussion of this point in his monograph, *The Raw Material and Commodity Controversy,* International Economic Studies Institute, Contemporary Issues No. 1, October 1975.

negotiations that can shape results reflecting an international *convergence* of interests; it also allows room for some optimism that these results will be acceptable domestically if any significant effort is undertaken to explain, defend, and press for their approval with publics at large and legislatures in particular.

3. *Global Food Programs.* In the area of global food programs, the proposals set forth by the United States and other developed countries are closer to the requests of the developing countries than in any other area of the coming year's North-South discussions. All parties to the negotiations seem to have attained a high degree of agreement on the following propositions:

(a) The solution to world food problems lies primarily in rapidly increasing food production in the developing countries.

(b) Developed and developing countries in a position to do so should substantially increase the volume of assistance to developing countries for agriculture and food production.

(c) The Consultative Group on Food Production and Investment in Developing Countries should quickly identify developing countries with potential for the most rapid and efficient increase in food production and help to mobilize the resources needed to capitalize on that potential.

(d) Developed and developing countries in a position to do so should pledge and appropriate at least $1 billion for the International Fund for Agricultural Development so that it may begin the process of investing in projects to increase agricultural production within developing countries.

(e) A minimum international food-aid target for 1975-76 should be 10 million tons of food grains.

(f) Assistance in the food area should be granted on the most concessional terms possible to those countries most seriously affected by the economic difficulties of the past two years.

(g) A global system of food-grain reserves—held nationally or, in some instances, regionally—should be established promptly. The total reserves of food grains should reach at least 30 million tons (25 million of wheat and 5 million of rice).

Other specific issues exhibiting convergent interests have been articulated by both sides, but the seven noted above cover the major points of agreement. The problems of moving from verbal agreement to program development and implementation are another matter, however, and as Chapter II indicates, many of these problems remain far short of resolution. Thus, for example, there is as yet no agreement on the rationale or operation of a global food-reserve program. This delay has resulted mainly from differences among developed countries, and the obstacles yet to be surmounted are substantial.

Nor has the International Fund for Agricultural Development (IFAD) yet received enough financial backing to begin its crucial contribution to increasing food production within developing countries. The U.S. Congress has authorized a contribution of $200 million, but the money has not yet been appropriated. Furthermore, the Executive Branch has made the full U.S. contribution contingent upon total global commitments of $1 billion.

The problem of the availability of fertilizer—the major input needed to accelerate the production of food in developing countries—likewise has not been directly addressed by the developed countries. The problem has been indirectly addressed in U.S. proposals and congressionally approved programs which would (or already do) channel the overwhelming percentage of U.S. concessional lending (and food aid) to the poorest countries; these are the countries whose present balance-of-payments deficits have made it difficult to import needed amounts of fertilizers at the high price levels of 1974 and most of 1975.

Also unresolved is the "free rider" issue—which the United States itself probably has exacerbated rather than eased. The Soviet Union has shown almost no willingness to partake in the gradual development of a set of institutions that will improve the world's capacity to manage global food problems. Yet the United States signed a long-term grain agreement with the U.S.S.R. in 1975 that exchanges a U.S. guarantee of Soviet access to U.S. grain supplies for a Soviet guarantee of a certain level of purchases each year. It can, of course, be argued that this agreement to some extent regularizes Soviet intervention in grain markets and therefore somewhat limits price fluctuations as well as (for some of the poorer developing countries) the inability to purchase food on the international market that sometimes results from those fluctuations. Nevertheless, a long-term guarantee to a major buyer that refuses to partake in the work of the institutions now being constituted to create a greater degree of stability in international grain markets and to increase developing-country production capacity may well prove counterproductive to the major efforts agreed upon in principle at the 1974 World Food Conference in Rome.

Finally, the developed and developing countries remain far apart on the issue of increased access to the former's markets for the latter's exports of temperate-zone food products. Agricultural protectionism remains very high in many developed countries and highest of all within the European Common Market. It is difficult to be optimistic that the present round of negotiations—in Geneva, London, or elsewhere—will accomplish much in this area. In fact, the agricultural sector is one that poses serious obstacles to effective negotiations between *developed* countries.

In sum, however, the agricultural arena would appear to be one in which some major and mutually accommodative bargains could be struck. It is an area in which producers and consumers in both developed and developing countries stand to gain from well-conceived reforms, as does the state of political and economic relations between developed and developing countries. An added incentive to progress in the agricultural field is the prospect for OECD-OPEC cooperation in the International Fund for Agricultural Development and the potential for the spread of such cooperation into other development arenas. The creation of the Fund is contingent upon matching commitments of $500 million each from the OPEC and OECD countries. The United States and the European Community have each indicated a willingness to provide $200 million, and the remaining $100 million is expected from Japan, Canada, and other OECD members. The OPEC countries, which were the primary proponents of the Fund at the World Food Conference, were still lagging at the end of 1975 in organizing for their contribution. Voting rights within the projected Fund are to be divided equally by assigning nine votes each to the developed, OPEC, and developing countries. The enhanced status implicit in equal voting power with the developed countries is greatly desired by the OPEC countries; OPEC willingness to join in a major developmental effort on a "fifty-fifty" cash basis should be greatly desired by the developed countries; and provision for both an equal vote and a substantial financial resource transfer for their agricultural sectors should please the developing countries. If successful, the Fund might well serve as a model for such tripartite cooperation in other areas, e.g., global energy research and development programs.

It will undoubtedly prove difficult to convince many producers that policies and institutions that potentially place limits on short-term profit maximization can also serve their longer-term interests, but the task should not prove insurmountable. Furthermore, policy makers have a natural counterweight in domestic consumer interests, diffuse as such interests have tended to be in the past. Once again, while North-South accommodation cannot be guaranteed to emerge from negotiations over the course of the year, the environment for positive progress is not inauspicious.

4. *Resource Transfers.* During 1976, a great deal of discussion undoubtedly will focus upon the subject of North-South resource transfers. At least at first glance, the requests of the developing countries and the responses (thus far) of the developed countries appear to leave a major gap between expectations and potential results.

Nevertheless, the gap can begin to be narrowed once a distinction is made between reforms to redistribute existing wealth between North and South on the one hand and reforms to move more rapidly toward a global equality of economic opportunity on the other. It was, after all, a special task force of the Third World Forum that made this vital distinction—one that is too easily overlooked by many analysts of the current state of developed-developing country relations. The task force put the issue in the following manner: "We wish to make it clear that the Third World is not demanding a massive redistribution of wealth of the rich nations. Nor is it seeking equality of income. It is asking for equality of opportunity."[20]

---

[20]*Proposals for a New International Economic Order,* Third World Forum, op. cit., p. 3.

There are, of course, several developing-country requests that would, if implemented, take the form of increased income transfers. One of the most prominent is the continued request that the developed countries meet the commitment which most of them (excluding the United States) accepted in 1970—as part of the International Strategy for the Second U.N. Development Decade—to transfer 0.7 per cent of their GNP annually in the form of official development assistance to developing countries. As Table E-7, p. 203 illustrates, the OECD countries as a group are not fulfilling even half of that target, and the United States renewed its opposition to any such target figure at the 1975 Special Session of the General Assembly. Another request which would amount to an income transfer involves the call for a conference to consider various forms of debt relief in the near future. As noted much earlier in this essay, the international reserve position and the import capacity of many developing countries have been strained by the recent global recession; for many, the present burden of debt repayment has increased considerably. Debt reschedulings of significant proportions would obviously assist in the short-term management problems faced by many developing countries as well as relieve the longer-term drain on future resources reflected in heavy debt schedules; hence the call for a conference on the issue within the next twelve months.

The prospects for such a conference are highly uncertain. In 1972 at the third session of UNCTAD, developed and developing countries were unable to generate a mutually acceptable approach to the debt problem. The developing countries proposed that debt relief be granted with some degree of automaticity based on statistical indicators; the creditor countries argued that debtor countries did not devote enough attention to the role of proper domestic financial policies, and feared that increasing the availability of debt relief would be likely to invite rather than to prevent further debt crises. They also voiced concern that increasing use of debt relief would adversely affect the capacity of developing countries to borrow in private capital markets. Despite the lack of change in general attitudes regarding debt relief since the 1972 UNCTAD session, a new examination of the subject might not prove fruitless *if* global economic conditions place increasingly heavy burdens on the foreign exchange positions of many developing countries during 1976.

Most developing-country proposals in the resource-transfer field would introduce *new* and *automatic* sources of income. Among those receiving the most attention are: the linking of the creation of international reserves to development needs; royalties from the commercial exploitation of international commons like the oceans and space; and new forms of international taxation, e.g., a tax on consumption of nonrenewable resources, with the proceeds going to the developing countries.

A new source of funds that is closer to realization is the proposed Special Trust Fund of the IMF. The Interim Committee of the IMF is presently attempting to agree on the establishment of such a Fund, initially to be financed through the proceeds from IMF gold sales and contributions from IMF members.[21] The IMF has been considering various aspects of U.S. and other proposals for such a Trust Fund for the past year, and the figure of approximately $2-$3 billion is most often mentioned as the Fund's initial goal. The money would be loaned at concessional interest rates to the least developed countries facing serious balance-of-payments difficulties. While the United States and other developed countries often refer to the Fund as a "one-time" affair, the developing countries continue to suggest that it should be envisioned as a permanent part of the IMF funded by replenishments somewhat on the order of the triennial International Development Association replenishment scheme.

Beyond the proposed Special Trust Fund, there is little reason to be sanguine about the responsiveness of the United States and many other developed countries to developing-country requests in the general area of resource transfers. For short-term cyclical reasons the developed countries find themselves facing low or negative growth rates, historically high rates of unemployment, and, in some instances, very large governmental deficits. *Analytically*, not all of these developed-country problems suggest limiting old or new forms of resource transfers to developing countries; indeed, the second-order effects of such transfers could ease the unemployment and growth-rate problems for the North in the aggregate as developing-country imports expand. *Politically*, however, these problems pose major road-blocks; this is particularly true of aid transfers per se. But surely there is maneuvering room for some debt rescheduling and for the early establishment of the Special Trust Fund, since neither is likely to raise serious legislative problems in the United States or elsewhere if handled carefully.

As for longer-term responses, the figures on official development assistance (ODA) suggest the difficulty of counting on any swift and significant improvement in the aggregate levels of aid transfers. Table E-7, p. 203 illustrates the unwillingness of political leadership (or the inability of political systems) within most developed countries to reach the 0.7 per cent target for ODA. However, a close look at the figures confirms that it is for the most part the poor record of the United States that is responsible for the aggregate ODA figure of 0.33 per cent in 1974 and the even lower figure for 1973. In those two years, the U.S. contribution was 0.25 per cent and 0.23 per cent respectively. However, it is worth noting that, despite worsening economic conditions in all of the major donor countries in 1974, Sweden became the first member country to reach the 0.7 per cent goal, and six other countries exceeded 0.5 per cent.

At the same time that the U.S. Executive Branch was requesting $3.4 billion in multilateral and bilateral development assistance for the poor countries for FY 1976, it was requesting $3.2 billion for military and security supporting assistance (the latter mainly for the Middle East).

---

[21]Agreement on the constitution of the Special Trust Fund was finally reached at the January 1976 meeting of the Interim Committee. For details see *IMF Survey*, January 19, 1976.

Such figures obviously suggest that the issue is one of priorities. And while the Administration has been making its own priorities clear, so has the U.S. Congress. In the International Development and Food Assistance Act of 1975, the Congress for the first time separated military and supporting assistance from economic development assistance and authorized expenditures for the latter as a category of its own. This was but the latest congressional indication that there remains a constituency for economic development assistance which is strong enough to pass legislation on Capitol Hill even without Executive Branch leadership. It seems clear, therefore, that a higher priority for foreign economic assistance within the White House could very possibly produce a more generous U.S. foreign assistance program.

All this suggests that mutual accommodation over the short term in the resource-transfer area—if it can be achieved at all—may have to be found in some of the newer suggestions advanced by the developing countries. There is, of course, no little irony in the fact that the first U.S. proposal on a seabed regime would have provided a rather significant new source of funds to be allocated to the developing countries. But it was blocked by the developing countries, all of whom were suspicious of U.S. motives and many of whom preferred to claim 200-mile "economic zones" for themselves. Gradually the U.S. position has also moved in the same direction. And the end result, which may be endorsed by the Law of the Sea Conference during 1976, leaves so little of the "common heritage of mankind" to the poorest countries and people of the world that it should stand as a constant reminder of the fate which awaits most "egalitarian" ideas not strategically and tactically planned and grounded in the realities of international politics.

Even if accommodation between developed and developing countries in the traditional resource-transfer sphere is limited to the establishment of the Special Trust Fund and some limited development funds resulting from the revenues and profits engendered by the operations of an "international seabed regime," both initiatives contain a degree of novelty which could lead to more significant developments at later stages. The Trust Fund *could* become a permanent mechanism for assisting the least developed countries with their balance-of-payment difficulties; together with an enhanced compensatory financing scheme containing a potential grant element for the least developed countries, the Trust Fund could turn out to be far more beneficial than the more narrow readings of certain proposals suggest. And however small the proceeds from a new seabed regime, its very institution would help to establish a precedent for other forms of "automatic" resource flows whose proceeds were to be earmarked for economic and social development.

Finally, the role of OPEC in resource transfers to the developing countries should be noted. The total net flow of development resources from OPEC countries rose from less than $1 billion in 1973 to an estimated $4.5 billion in 1974 and is projected to exceed $6 billion in 1975. Further forecasts depend heavily on assumptions concerning changes in OPEC current-account surpluses. Of the 1974 total volume, $2.7 billion was transferred on concessional terms, with a grant element of about 65 per cent. Of the nonconcessional amount, $1.4 billion consisted of purchases of World Bank bonds, largely by Saudi Arabia and Venezuela.[22]

Almost three fourths of Arab OPEC bilateral aid in 1974 was committed to Arab countries, mostly to Syria and Egypt; nine tenths of the total was directed to Arab and Moslem countries.[23] With the tapering off of aid flows from Iran and Venezuela in 1975, overall OPEC disbursements are likely to become even more highly concentrated in these groups of countries unless more special efforts, such as that envisioned with IFAD, are made to involve the OPEC countries in a broad range of international economic development efforts. One encouraging sign is that while only Kuwait has contributed to IDA heretofore, several OPEC countries are participating in the current discussions concerning the fifth IDA replenishment.

In November 1975, the OPEC countries made a provisional decision to establish a new fund for developing countries, to be financed by means of a levy of ten cents on each barrel of OPEC oil exported. Such a fund would provide $1 billion in development assistance per year at present levels of oil production. While the manner in which this money would be distributed was left for later discussion, it was expected that some of it would take the form of interest-free loans to replenish depleted monetary reserves and some would be transmitted as interest-free, long-term loans for specific development projects. No final provisions for the implementation of this scheme had been made as of the end of 1975.

Given the concentration of OPEC aid in the Moslem world in general and the Middle East in particular, it is clear that OPEC development-assistance funds are as yet of marginal assistance to most developing countries, and in many of them do not begin to cover the foreign exchange losses created by the oil-price increases. The coming year's efforts to find mutually accommodative solutions to major global economic problems will test the nature of OPEC statesmanship as well as that of all other parties to the negotiations.

5. *Other Programs to Accelerate Development.* Three other major categories of programs are being suggested to speed growth rates and industrial expansion in developing countries and will be addressed in one guise or another in various forums throughout 1976.

The first of these involves an *upgrading of scientific and technological skills* available to the developing countries. The developing countries would like to establish an international code covering the transfer of technology "corresponding in particular to the special needs of the developing countries."[24] They would also like to revise existing international conventions on

---

[22]See Table E-18, p. 214.

[23]See Table E-17, p. 213.

[24]U.N. General Assembly, Seventh Special Session, Resolution 3362 (S-VII), September 16, 1975, section III, para. 3.

patents and trademarks. The objective in both instances would be to make Northern technologies available to developing countries at lower costs.

Since most Northern technologies are in private rather than public hands, progress in these areas is likely to be minimal. However, several other U.S. suggestions at the Seventh Special Session of the General Assembly may provide room for joint efforts of a mutually beneficial nature. The United States proposed the creation of an International Energy Institute to work in the field of new energy development. As Chapter III of this volume suggests, the potential payoff to developing countries of a joint effort in this field—whether located within or outside such an institute—may be very sizable. Little, if any, present thinking about the world's energy needs is being done on a global basis. Generally, studies focus on national needs; occasionally the target is a region (the European Community or the OECD countries as a whole). A major consequence of the limited scope of these approaches is that little consideration is being given to developing-country energy needs, to their energy production potential, and to the implications of both for development strategies in many areas of the Third World. Chapter III suggests that few topics on the 1976 agenda for negotiation are likely to have the pervasive long-term importance that should be accorded to this one and calls for intensive preliminary research in this area to be followed by a World Energy Conference. This proposal would serve the needs of developed as well as developing countries.

At the Seventh Special Session, the United States also supported a developing-country proposal for a clearinghouse for the sharing of information and research relevant to all forms of development and called for the creation of an International Center for the Exchange of Technological Information to perform this task. Finally, the United States proposed the creation of an International Industrialization Institute to sponsor and conduct research on industrial technology with the governments, industries, and research facilities of developing countries. Prospects for progress in these areas appear good; it remains far more difficult to determine whether or not the *impact* of such progress will be more than marginal.

The second category of efforts to accelerate development concerns *greater developing-country access to international and Northern national capital markets to borrow for developmental purposes.* The United Nations, the Joint World Bank-IMF Development Committee, and the United States are independently exploring such possibilities. Here, too, major problems —including wide differences of viewpoint regarding the role of private direct investment—must be overcome if mutual accommodation is to be reached. It is not much of an oversimplification to say that the developing countries seek more *public* capital (via the IBRD and regional development banks) and loans to government agencies while the United States and other Northern governments favor more *private* borrowing and lending directly to private-sector activities within developing countries. Thus the major U.S. proposals at the General Assembly's Special Session were to pledge support for a significant expansion of the IBRD's International Finance

Corporation (IFC) and to propose the creation of an International Investment Trust, under the IFC's management, to mobilize portfolio capital for investment in private-sector enterprises within developing countries. A major effort will have to be made in many of the forums during upcoming negotiations if these U.S. proposals are to gain support, financial and political, from other developed countries, the OPEC countries, and the potential borrowers from such institutions. If such programs are proposed as part of a larger program containing a variety of opportunities for developing-country access to Northern capital markets rather than as an *alternative* to public-sector borrowing, they may make more than a marginal contribution to the potential resolution of outstanding North-South issues.

The third category concerns *the role of the multinational corporations (MNCs) in development*. Most developing countries continue to want MNCs to locate facilities within their borders; at the same time, many of them are altering the terms of the bargains they strike with such companies in order to increase MNC contributions to developing-country economic growth. Most companies and developed countries, on the other hand, are looking for greater stability in the "rules of the game" and less altering of the terms of investment once these have been accepted. The nature of this problem is such that one cannot look for much short-term progress; but there is probably less and less reason to be concerned about the lack of *formal* progress captured in a globally agreed "code," "convention," or treaty. The slowly increasing bargaining strengths of developing countries and their growing knowledge concerning the operations of multinational corporations suggest that there is no *short-term* need on their part for a formal multinational agreement in this field; thus there is little likelihood that developed countries can achieve their goals very quickly. In the longer term, agreement undoubtedly will be needed if a potentially chaotic and inefficient de facto state of affairs is to be avoided.[25]

6. *Organizational Restructuring.* The range of issues in this area may have been raised initially with developmental questions in mind but has been broadened rapidly over the past two years to encompass questions of power, status, and hierarchy in the international system and its leading institutions. What many developing countries are now demanding is a more "equal" place at all the world's bargaining tables.

A good deal of progress toward the realization of this goal was made during 1975. OPEC's voting power within the IMF was doubled to approximately 10 per cent of the total; the other developing countries maintained their proportional share of IMF votes; and the developed countries absorbed the losses. Developing-country representation in the IMF's Interim Committee and the Joint World Bank-IMF Development Committee exceeds 40 per cent. The Conference on International Economic Cooperation

---

[25]C. Fred Bergsten, "Coming Investment Wars?" *Foreign Affairs,* Vol. 53, No. 1 (October 1974).

was established with seven representatives from OPEC, twelve representatives from other developing countries, and eight seats for the developed countries. And an ad hoc committee of the entire U.N. membership began its study of institutional reform to achieve the major goals of increasing the importance of developmental issues in the U.N. structure, enhancing the capacity of the United Nations to act effectively in these areas, and increasing the role of developing-country representation throughout the U.N. system.

Under these new and evolving circumstances, the issues will probably not demand any less attention during 1976. The year may serve more as a test period for some changes that already have been introduced. Particularly at the Paris meetings, bargaining in an arena where developing-country *representation* is more than equal to that of the developed countries will be watched to see whether a new form of global "concurrent majority" machinery is emerging.

This observation is not meant to suggest that other efforts to examine the issues and propose modifications in the present system be postponed. It is simply offered to suggest that 1976 may not be the year to spend a great deal of negotiating effort on the issue of institutional reform. Such efforts would seem to be more profitably undertaken after one can observe and place in some perspective the successes and failures of all the efforts in the various institutions dealing with the major substantive 1976 agenda. It is probable that no single organizational formula will be appropriate to all issue areas on the international economic agenda, and that any attempt by the North or the South to impose one would undermine rather than enhance efforts at mutual accommodation.

7. *The Poorest Countries and the Poorest People: A Crosscutting Problem.* One final major issue remains on the 1976 agenda for discussion and negotiation. It concerns the treatment of the world's poorest *countries* and, at least in some forums, of the world's poorest *people*—whether or not they happen to reside in one of those countries. Thus the issue clearly involves, but increasingly appears to go beyond, traditional interstate relations.

At the traditional interstate level, all major parties to the present negotiations have declared themselves in favor of special forms of assistance to the least developed countries. All documents of the Group of 77 developing countries reflect this position. The final resolution of the Seventh Special Session called for many special measures for these countries across all functional fields—trade, industrialization, agricultural development, aid, etc. The developed countries repeated the pledge, and several U.S. proposals were geared specifically to an implementation of that pledge. For example, the proposed development security facility would be permitted to convert loans into grants for the poorest countries under prescribed conditions; and the Special Trust Fund would be established to give balance-of-payments support to these countries at highly concessional rates. Additionally, the

September 1975 Kissinger speech noted that the poorest countries should receive—and are receiving—preferential access to concessional financial aid in U.S. bilateral aid programs.

In this latter area, the Kissinger speech simply reflected the will of Congress, which for the last three years has been insisting that U.S. programs to accelerate development allocate an increasing portion of their funds and attention to the problems of the poorest nations and the world's poorest people—those suffering from what has come to be denominated as "absolute poverty." The U.S. aid authorization bill for fiscal year 1976 (the International Development and Food Assistance Act of 1975) is the most recent example of this trend. It requires the President increasingly to concentrate the bulk of U.S. aid in those poor countries that make the greatest efforts in four fields: land reform, increased agricultural self-sufficiency, reduced infant mortality, and the control of population growth. Thus as congressional disenchantment with foreign aid as a general proposition wanes, and as military aid—at least in the congressional authorization process—is finally separated from economic aid and scrutinized even more closely at congressional insistence, the one general exception to the trend increasingly appears to be support for aid to the poorest nations and to other developing nations whose *domestic* policies are specifically directed to raising the living standards of the poorest people in their societies.

Are these congressional concerns of the past several years a temporary phenomenon, or do they represent a steadily growing commitment to targeting most, if not all, U.S. economic assistance on those developing countries which appear to be attempting to deal directly with the poverty problem within their own societies? While the question cannot be answered with certainty, it is fair to note that it is applicable not only to the U.S. Congress but also to other developed-country governments, legislatures, and nongovernmental groups that are interested in accelerating the development process (e.g., the United Kingdom, the Netherlands, and Sweden at the governmental level).[26]

Thus a dilemma of potentially major proportions is posed at this point in North-South relations. Increasing levels of global interdependence, population, and economic production are likely to necessitate the expansion of multilateral diplomacy to cope with such issues as the oceans, environmental degradation, nuclear proliferation, and many others. To be able to strike mutually accommodative bargains in such areas, the United States and other industrial nations will need the cooperation of developing-country governments at the United Nations, the Law of the Sea Conference, and in other multilateral forums that will have to address these issues in the future. Thus success in negotiating on many of the "global agenda" items for

---

[26]Cf. the recent British White Paper, *Overseas Development: The Changing Emphasis in British Aid Policies—More Help for the Poorest,* Presented to Parliament by the Minister of Overseas Development, Cmnd. 6270 (London: Her Majesty's Stationery Office, 1975).

the near- to medium-term future is likely to be contingent upon interstate accommodation, as are many of the gains to be derived from the present year of negotiation on international economic reforms.

But the dilemma is posed by the cost of such cooperative efforts and the distribution of such costs. If the United States, with its eye on the "global agenda" problems, decides that intergovernmental amity is more important for policy makers than economic and social development that is targeted upon the poorest countries and peoples in the world, what are the longer-run implications for the so-called "forgotten 40 per cent" of humanity? Those persons who are primarily concerned with "global agenda" issues and those who are leery of the oft-revealed interventionist and technocratic positivist tendencies within American society will oppose any attempt to key U.S. policies relating to economic development on performance criteria which attempt to gauge and promote increased economic opportunity within developing countries.

On the other hand, those persons more concerned with absolute poverty and related issues will oppose the primacy of "global agenda" reasoning on three grounds. First, they will tend to agree with the view expressed by a special task force of the Third World Forum when it stated that "reforms in the international order will be *meaningless* . . . without corresponding reforms in national orders" and pointed out that it does not advocate that developing countries "find a convenient alibi in the international order for every lack of progress on the domestic front."[27] In short, these critics will argue that without domestic reforms within developing countries, none of the goals established under the banner of the new international economic order will be achieved.

Second, and closely related, they will argue that the older "trickle-down" strategy of economic development within developing countries cannot alone produce the kinds of results which will aid the poorest people in *most* countries within the South. Without major reforms, job opportunities cannot be expected to keep pace with population growth, and the poverty problem will steadily worsen.

Third, they will argue that Northern public support for economic and social development cannot be sustained if the developing countries themselves do not directly address the basic poverty problems experienced by most of their citizens. Recent U.S. congressional directives are the most dramatic evidence in support of the proposition.

Obviously an optimal solution to this problem would be a guiding mechanism for the entire complex of negotiations during 1976 and beyond that kept *both* the *interstate equity* and the *intrastate equity issues in mind*—a mechanism which, in balancing the needs for interstate cooperation on the one hand and the problems of the poorest people within societies on the other, remained responsive to the legitimate nature of each call for

---

[27]*Proposals for a New International Economic Order,* Third World Forum, op. cit., p. 3. Emphasis added.

redress. Once this obvious point is made, however, one must recognize that international negotiations are conducted *among* governments *by* government officials. The forgotten 40 per cent may be excused for wondering, therefore, if the fox hasn't been asked to guard the henhouse.

Again, however, there may be somewhat more room for optimism than the preceding paragraph suggests. It is natural to expect intergovernmental relations to emphasize one set of issues—those raised by slowly growing developing-country bargaining strength (obviously not slow in the case of the OPEC states) and those global issues which will increasingly require the attention and the cooperation of the great majority of states—over the intra-state issues of equity and increasing equality of opportunity.

But there remain ways for those who would give a higher priority to the latter set of issues to influence the course of events. First, they can and do work within and outside of the governmental arena for the rather formal quid pro quos of the type which may eventually evolve as a result of the 1974 World Food Conference and from the present negotiations over the Special Trust Fund of the IMF. In both cases, the major beneficiaries will be the poorest countries; and in the agricultural field, most of the beneficiaries should be among the least advantaged within their own societies. Second, they can work to influence the legislative bodies that have a major role in determining the flow of bilateral and multilateral development assistance. The "new directions" program which the U.S. Congress has adopted in attempting to reorient U.S. aid flows over the past three years to concentrate directly on the problems of the poor again suggests that progress can be made in the area of intrastate equity with a minimum of overt "intervention" if aid programs are designed so as to reach only targeted recipients.[28] While the governments on the receiving end of such flows can obviously minimize the intended impact of such aid programs by tilting other domestic policies in favor of more advantaged groups, this problem too may be capable of minimization if properly monitored by the donor state.

Finally, those people and institutions more concerned with the individual "justice" and "equity" aspects of North-South bargaining can continue to work in the marketplace of ideas. Indeed, the first two avenues of influence

---

[28]In the Foreign Assitance Act of 1973, Congress took a commendable initiative in establishing the Development Coordination Committee (DCC), chaired by the Administrator of the Agency for International Development (AID). The first report of the DCC, which superbly anticipated many of the issues of the new international economic order, reflected a basic dilemma: Was the DCC designed to let the interested agencies of the U.S. government review and comment on the work of AID or was it for AID, as the one agency exclusively working with developing countries, to comment on how the many nonaid actions taken by the U.S. government—domestic and international—impact on those countries? Given the already overelaborate machinery for reviewing AID's work, another committee is not needed for that purpose. However, the DCC could perform a useful role in advocating U.S. government actions that would impact beneficially on developing countries and in commenting critically on harmful policies. To permit this evolution, one important change is needed in the law. Instead of asking the DCC to make an annual report on development, the Foreign Assistance Act should require the Chairman of the DCC to make the report. As a report of the Chairman, it can be more independent and critical of current U.S. government policy than if it must clear the entire committee.

noted above clearly imply that these ideas are already achieving results, however marginal they still may be. This suggests the need for a continued examination and discussion of the issue, and the development of proposals that balance the scales of interstate and intrastate equality of opportunity. For instance, a cooperative attack on absolute poverty that a) could be supported through official development assistance (raised to the U.N. target of 0.7 per cent of GNP) and that b) held the prospect of significantly raising average life expectancies, sharply decreasing birth rates, and assuring literacy for virtually all in the younger generation *before the end of this century* should be vastly more popular with Americans and Western Europeans than existing foreign aid programs. The developing-country contribution to this "cooperative attack"—much needed political, economic, and social reforms guaranteeing that the fruits of Northern assistance result in sustained improvement in the standards of living for the world's poorest billion—would not only increase economic opportunities for those whose interests are most likely to be overlooked by the forthcoming international economic negotiations, but also would be likely to enhance greatly the basis of Northern financial support and political cooperation in developmental reforms.

Perhaps this section is best ended with the question: global reforms, economic and otherwise—for *what*, and for *whom*? The question should not be avoided, in 1976 or thereafter, simply because the answer is difficult to generate.[29]

Some Priority Goals for the United States in 1976

In assessing the problems and the prospects confronting the United States in the field of global economic and social development, it may be helpful to think of three different types of policy goals that might be achieved.

1. The *first* concerns those goals directly linked to the substantive negotiations to be held throughout the year. Since the issues of negotiation and the forums in which they will be taking place have been reviewed in some detail, little more need be said about them here. At issue is the search for accommodative reforms of present international economic systems in which both North and South gain. While the view taken here is that a major share of these gains should be used to create new economic opportunities for developing countries and accelerate their rates of growth, it is essential to search out and construct trade-offs which intially assure *mutual* accommodation. It will be far easier to argue the case for shifting the majority of the gains to the world's poorer countries as it is demonstrated that "positive-sum" solutions can be found to many of today's international economic problems. In and across the seven categories of issues analyzed earlier in this overview, such solutions are possible and should be sought. This implies the following minimum targets for U.S. policy during the 1976 negotiations:

---

[29]For a lengthier discussion of these themes, see Chapter I.

(1) Support of substantial changes in global compensatory financing mechanisms to increase the stability of developing-country export earnings;

(2) Support of major trade-liberalization efforts to further lower import barriers to developing-country agricultural goods, processed raw materials, and manufactured goods;

(3) Support for the major resolutions of the 1974 World Food Conference, including financial support for the International Fund for Agricultural Development, a global food-reserve program, and increased food aid;

(4) Support for some new and more automatic resource-transfer mechanisms, e.g., funds from an international seabed regime and from the creation of the Special Trust Fund within the IMF; and support for some old forms of resource transfers, e.g., the fifth replenishment of IDA and increased capital for the World Bank and the International Finance Corporation;

(5) Support for special new endeavors in the fields of finance and technology (such as the proposals on energy in Chapter III);

(6) A willingness to try new negotiating forums in which developing-country representation is considerably increased, and in some of which OPEC countries share an equal voice and equal financial commitments with the developed countries; and

(7) A continued search for methods and programs to reach the poor majority within developing countries.

Programs to ease the domestic distributional impact of certain elements of such reforms also must be evolved. The area of trade presents the classic example of socially optimal economic policies being rejected because the gains to society in the aggregate are not distributed in a manner that helps the short-term losers to adjust to new conditions. To put this more simply, U.S. trade liberalization should improve the economic welfare of all Americans *in the aggregate;* but unless some government money is spent to retrain, relocate, and otherwise help reemploy workers who lose their jobs because of the increased flow of cheaper imports, a small but important portion of American society will be forced to pay a very high price for the gains which the rest of us will share.

Lest the seven targets listed above seem to be loaded in favor of the developing countries, however, we should remind ourselves of the potential benefits to the United States that are most likely to flow from their achievement: uninterrupted access to low-cost raw materials and other exports, lower rates of global inflation, greater cooperation on global economic issues, and a generally more benign atmosphere for international negotiations in general.

2. The *second* type of goal the United States should seek is to prevent important but not centrally related issues—which will undoubtedly flare up—from being used to undermine the atmosphere for a successful set of

negotiations. One example of such an issue is provided by the recent U.N. votes on different aspects of the Middle East situation, particularly the November 1975 General Assembly vote on Zionism. What the United States needs to do in such instances is to *de-link* the economic negotiations to the greatest extent possible from such important but peripheral events. This policy need in no way silence U.S. objections to votes (or actions) of which it disapproves. But it should stop well short of linking the success of the 1976 international economic negotiations to issues *which are not integral to those negotiations themselves.* In this regard, the recent reports that U.S. aid is to be linked to how recipient nations vote in the United Nations and other international bodies is a step in precisely the wrong direction. Other examples of such issues that could be used in an attempt to derail serious international economic negotiations are the intervention by several major powers in Angola and the continuing conflict between the United States and Panama over a new Panama Canal treaty. U.S. involvement in Angola is a clear example of a case in which U.S. actions, while described as related to one major set of U.S. policy concerns—U.S. relations with the Soviet Union—have had an immediate impact on U.S. relations with African countries. Continued U.S. involvement could have further serious repercussions on U.S. relations with developing countries generally, thus affecting the achievement of U.S. policy goals in the various forums of international economic negotiation in the course of 1976. The Canal Zone issue is one that has many layers of meaning for Latin America and other developing countries. It embodies many of the political and psychological symbols—including that of colonialism—which have led to the growing North-South clash of the past two years; and it must not be forgotten that the political and psychological factors weigh *at least* as heavily in the origins of today's unsettled North-South relationships as do the economic issues now being negotiated. The negotiations themselves reflect this fact in their consideration of many institutional and organizational reforms that would increase the role and status of the developing countries. In these circumstances, a very delicate hand may need to be played to avoid a negative spillover from the one set of negotiations to the other.

3. The *third* type of goal the United States should aim at during the coming year is to avoid foreclosing future options. The debate and negotiating process between developed and developing countries will continue for as long as we can, with any validity, project into the future. There will be no "answers" discovered in 1976, but with luck, good will, and determination, the developed and developing countries may begin to find some new *processes*—institutional and informal—intra-Northern, intra-Southern, and North-South, which can together deal with the problems of international reform and economic development in a more cooperative, comprehensive, and productive manner.

A major additional reason for keeping options open concerns the eventual roles of the Soviet Union and the People's Republic of China in nascent international frameworks. It is as yet too early to predict the nature of those roles, as evidenced by the apparently very limited Soviet and Chinese interest and involvement in the events of the U.N. General Assembly's Seventh Special Session in 1975 and by their absence from almost all of the major negotiating tables in 1976. While it seems unlikely that two countries with such *potential* impact on international economic relations can remain on the sidelines much longer—as the dramatic Soviet entry into global grain trade and the less dramatic but substantial Chinese entry into the global trade and technology regimes over the past several years suggest—neither country yet appears ready or willing to commit itself in any substantial way to discussion of the major issues on the 1976 agenda or to the related organizations now being created or reformed.

These issues and organizational reforms cannot await the further thoughts of the Soviet Union and China. But the ramifications of the absence of these two countries should be noted as negotiations proceed and new structures, e.g., a global food regime, are constructed. In which areas are agreements least affected by their absence, thus minimizing problems for the future? In which areas is their absence most likely to limit the effectiveness of agreements? In these areas, is it possible to engage the two countries in dialogue in the near future? If not, can rules be established which minimize the potential impact of nonparticipants on agreements?

These are but a few of the major procedural and substantive questions which the absence of China and the Soviet Union poses for the negotiations. They do not address the issue of the relationship of these two countries to strategies of global development. This issue merits far more consideration than it has been given by any parties to the present negotiations and those which will inevitably follow. Moreover, it is probably worth far more consideration by the two absent states themselves. The negotiations inevitably will impinge upon some of their interests; their responses will affect the interests of others. All might be better served by a representation of those interests sooner rather than later.

In concluding this examination of the major development issues to be debated in the various negotiating forums this year, attention should be drawn once again to the tension between the opportunities for progress presented in 1976 and the *potential* obstacles to significant progress. The potential obstacles can be divided into three categories. The first concerns *governmental intentions.* The crowded 1976 negotiating calendar is the result of a willingness on the part of the governments of almost all countries, developed and developing, to discuss a host of controversies that have plagued North-South relations for years. But a crucial question remains to be answered: Are most of these governments—particularly the most influential within the developed, OPEC, and developing countries—prepared to negotiate seriously in a search for quid pro quos that might produce significant progress for all rather than in just another "winners-losers" competition? Or is their commitment to "discuss" issues simply part of the same old delaying tactic in which mutually accommodative solutions to problems on the agenda are not a primary goal?

The second category of obstacles concerns *groups (and governments)* *within each "bloc" that remain opposed to the search for compromise.* Chapter I analyzes some of the ideas prevalent in the United States that underlie opposition to compromise within this country. But ideas and adherents opposing compromise can be found in the South and in the OPEC countries as well as in the United States and other developed countries. Will their voices grow stronger or weaker? If the former is the case in either the North or the South, the prospects for progress will undoubtedly diminish.

Finally, the third potential obstacle concerns the linking of "non-related" issues and events to the economic and organizational negotiations. Of course, if the events are *perceived* by major groups of governments as related—e.g., the vote on Zionism or unpredictable events in the Canal Zone or in Southern Africa—then it is somewhat misleading to call these issues "unrelated." They may be unrelated in any functional sense, but highly related where the perceptions of major groups of countries in the negotiations lead them to make such linkages. For this reason, a commitment on the part of all parties to considering how their actions in other areas may play back into these negotiations and acting in those other areas in ways which will *minimize* such linkage potential will be of utmost importance. If such a commitment is missing, it will simply strengthen the hands of those governments and groups which would prefer that the negotiations fail.

The negotiations will be difficult enough under the best of circumstances. They will most likely fail if the international environment in which they are undertaken is plagued by conflicts—rhetorical or otherwise—that further heighten the domestic constraints on international compromise which face negotiators. Thus the delicate nature of this "year of opportunity." The opportunity is real, but so are the obstacles. To underestimate the obstacles will most likely waste the opportunity. While most countries could survive this waste, the same cannot be said for hundreds of thousands of human beings. One hopes that this distinction will be kept in mind.

SELECTED
POLICY ISSUES

CHAPTER I

The "Crisis of Interdependence": Where Do We Go from Here?

Roger D. Hansen

When the editor of the highly respected academic journal, *International Organization*, wrote of "the crisis of interdependence" late in the spring of 1975, nobody accused him of hyperbole.[1] Many other observers described the international economic and political events of 1974 and 1975—particularly the North-South aspects of international relations—in far more apocalyptic terms.

Geoffrey Barraclough, for one, proclaimed in August 1975 that what we are witnessing is "the opening stage of a struggle for a new world order, a search for positions of strength in a global realignment, in which the weapons (backed, naturally, by the ultimate sanction of force) are food and fuel. . . . The essential point to grasp is that the situation in the 1970s is as fluid and unpredictable as the situation in the 1930s, and as fraught with danger."[2] Addressing the issue of interdependence directly, Barraclough challenged the widely held but superficial notion that the "fact" of growing global interdependence guarantees a dilution of state sovereignty and the appearance of the more benign contributions to world order that often are posited as the inevitable results of such a process. "Today," he noted, "the slogan is interdependence. The question is whether interdependence will

---

[1]Robert O. Keohane, *"International Organization* and the Crisis of Interdependence," *International Organization*, Vol. 29, No. 2 (Spring 1975), pp. 357 ff. In this chapter, interdependence can be said to exist to the extent that "events occurring in any given part or within any given component unit of the world system affect (either physically or perceptually) events taking place in each of the other parts or component units of the system." Oran Young, "Interdependencies in World Politics," *International Journal*, Vol. 24, No. 4 (Autumn 1969), p. 226.

[2]Geoffrey Barraclough, "Wealth and Power: The Politics of Food and Oil," *The New York Review of Books,* August 7, 1975, p. 23.

prove more effective as a rallying cry in the 1970s than collective security was in the 1930s. . . . Too often, the call for 'constructive relations of global interdependence' reflects little more than a pious hope with no discernible structural underpinning."[3] And noting (rightly or wrongly) that all governments accept the concept of interdependence provided they can secure it on their own terms, Barraclough concluded that as "the old international political and economic structures begin to topple and disintegrate, the struggle for wealth and power is developing into a struggle of all against all."[4]

Also writing in the summer of 1975, Irving Kristol indicated his concurrence with the spreading public perception that the North-South conflict, as it developed between April 1974 and September 1975—the period between the Sixth and Seventh Special Sessions of the U.N. General Assembly—represented "the world's new cold war." Kristol analyzed the conflict as taking place essentially between the "mainly affluent" liberal capitalist societies and "those societies—whether communist, socialist, or neo-fascist (this latter category prevailing especially in Africa)—which, whether poor or less affluent, are opposed to liberal capitalism in principle."[5] His analysis of the "North-South" conflict led him to the following provocative conclusion echoing much of the message contained in Daniel Moynihan's article in the March 1975 issue of *Commentary*:

> There is always a good case, in both principle and prudence, for the more affluent being charitable toward the poor—even to those whose poverty is largely their own fault. Nor is there any reason to expect, much less insist on, gratitude: Such benevolence is supposed to be its own reward. But when the poor start "mau-mauing" their actual or potential benefactors, when they begin vilifying them, insulting them, demanding as of right what it is not their right to demand—then one's sense of self-respect may properly take precedence over one's self-imposed humanitarian obligations. If the United States is to gain the respect of world opinion, it first has to demonstrate that it respects itself —its own institutions, its own way of life, the political and social philosophy that is the basis of its institutions and its way of life. Such a sense of self-respect and self-affirmation seems to be a missing element in our foreign policy. It is no wonder, therefore, that we are making such a mess of the "new cold war."[6]

Keohane, Barraclough, and Kristol have been joined throughout the past year by many others who view global interdependence either as the

---

[3]Ibid., p. 24.
[4]Ibid.
[5]Irving Kristol, *Wall Street Journal*, July 17, 1975.
[6]Ibid.

essential *cause* of a crisis (e.g., Robert W. Tucker) or as a phenomenon that is itself *in* a state of crisis (e.g., the views emerging from the project entitled "Reviewing the International Order," launched at the suggestion of the Club of Rome and directed by Jan Tinbergen, as well as from The Hague Symposium on a New International Economic Order, sponsored by the Netherlands government).[7] As a result of both the *events* and *analyses* of the past two years, the complexity of the relationship between "global interdependence"[8] on the one hand and a more pacific and more "equitable" international system on the other has become increasingly apparent. Those who have assumed a generally positive correlation between the two are being forced to reexamine their initial assumptions. Those who have always doubted the benign potential attributed to the growth of interdependence appear to feel vindicated by the heightened degree of confrontation (rhetorical and actual) in North-South relations that characterized 1974 and the first nine months of 1975.

Whatever the merits of individual views, an understanding of 1) *what* has happened to the course of North-South relations during the past year, 2) *why* these trends have emerged, and 3) *how we are best to interpret them* is indispensable to the process of considering various U.S. policy options concerning the developing world and of proposing specific courses of action. While no brief analysis of trends still unfolding can hope to capture more than a fragment of reality, this essay offers a first approximation of the present state of North-South relations and the implications for the designing of U.S. policy affecting the world's developing countries.

The Context of the "Interdependence" Debate: April 1974–September 1975

Prior to the unfolding of the Seventh Special Session of the U.N. General Assembly (September 1-16, 1975), the term "crisis of interdependence" seemed an appropriate characterization of both governmental action (or inaction) and of the unofficial analyses of "interdependence" issues (offered by both individuals and organizations) that achieved a remarkably high degree of prominence.

---

[7]Robert W. Tucker, "Egalitarianism and International Politics," *Commentary*, September 1975, pp. 27–40, and Tucker, "A New International Order?" *Commentary*, February 1975, pp. 38–50; "Reviewing the International Order" Project (Project RIO), *Reviewing the International Order (RIO): Interim Report* (document RIO 25), prepared during the project's second general meeting, held June 17–20, 1975, in Rotterdam, the Netherlands (Rotterdam: Project RIO, c/o Bouwcentrum International Education, Postbus 299, 1975); and *Report of the Symposium on a New International Economic Order*, held at The Hague, the Netherlands, May 22–24, 1975.

[8]For a recent review of the economic content of this term, see Richard Rosecrance and Arthur Stein, "Interdependence: Myth or Reality?" *World Politics*, Vol. 26, No. 1 (October 1973), pp. 1-27. For a broader theoretical and empirical treatment of some major aspects of the interdependence concept in the world of the 1970s and beyond, see the thought-provoking essays by John Gerard Ruggie and Ernst B. Haas in *International Organization*, Vol. 29, No. 3 (Summer 1975).

While all serious observers of the phenomenon of international "interdependence" have from the outset recognized its Janus-like quality, until 1974-75, most public discussion had focused upon its pacific face with a general disregard for its less benign aspect. Organizations and individuals, often guided by different sets of values and norms, all sought in "interdependence" answers to their normative goals as well as to their policy problems. Some saw interdependence as a necessary condition to universalize their norms regarding such controversial issues as "limits to growth," the management of the world's resources, and the problems of population and pollution. Others saw it as a desired end product of the internationalization of the world economy and the business firm. Still others saw in it the necessary environment for the emergence of a "global humanism," heretofore artificially held in check by the salient role of the nation-state with its more "parochial" loyalties. A brief examination and analysis of events of the past two years is necessary to understand the growth of concern over the less benign potential of interdependence with particular reference to North-South issues.[9]

Southern and Northern Governmental Activity: Changing Perceptions and Goals. In most developing countries, the *perceptions* of global bargaining power changed radically with the success of the Organization of Petroleum Exporting Countries (OPEC) in quadrupling the price of oil in a single year. This altered perception was perhaps most clearly revealed at the Sixth Special Session of the U.N. General Assembly in April-May of 1974. At that Session, the Declaration of the Establishment of a New International Economic Order was pushed through the Assembly despite the clearly stated opposition of the United States and several other developed countries. The Declaration contained more than a decade of Southern proposals for international economic reforms. Eight months later, the General Assembly overwhelmingly endorsed the Charter of Economic Rights and Duties of States which, at the request of the developing countries, had been under consideration within the U.N. system for several years. Only six countries, all members of the Organisation for Economic Co-operation and Development (OECD) and led by the United States, voted against the Charter's adoption.

The pattern set by the U.N. meetings of 1974 was followed in a series of developing-country gatherings held in 1975. In Dakar in February, in Algiers shortly thereafter, and finally in Lima in August of 1975, the nonaligned bloc (now including some 110 Third World countries) met to reach a consensus on concrete proposals to reform the rules and norms of the present international economic system. They also pushed through

---

[9]In this chapter the term "North" is used as a shorthand description of the world's "developed" or "industrialized" countries; the term "South" encompasses the "less developed" countries, ranging from the newly rich but nonindustrialized members of OPEC to the poorest and "least developed" or "Fourth World" countries of Africa, Asia, and Latin America.

another set of proposals at the Second General Conference of the U.N. Industrial Development Organization (UNIDO) in March of 1975; these proposals drew a lone negative vote from the United States.

Prior to the U.N. Seventh Special Session, then, the South had won a series of "victories" through the United Nations and its constituent bodies —victories that were largely rhetorical in the sense that the General Assembly can only recommend, and results clearly are contingent upon the willingness of all states to implement those recommendations. And prior to the Seventh Special Session, there were few if any signs that the United States (and most other OECD members) had any intention of implementing recommendations that had been promulgated by the Southern bloc despite Northern disapproval.

Cumulatively, the Southern demands contained in these recommendations called for a much higher level of resource transfers—direct and indirect—from North to South.[10]

1. In the *trade* field, the demands were for a) various forms of international commodity agreements that would raise and stabilize the price of raw materials; b) nonreciprocal reductions in developed-country barriers to developing-country exports; c) expanded generalized trade preferences for the developing countries to better enable them to compete with industrial-country production in the markets of the North; and d) better-financed domestic adjustment-assistance programs in the North which, by easing the transitional pains accompanying the restructuring of Northern economies, would facilitate increased imports of Southern manufactured (and in some cases agricultural) goods. In sum, the South sought increased relative *prices* for its exports to the North as well as increases in the *volume* of such exports.

2. In the field of *aid*, the South's demands included the following: a) that the developed countries meet the aid targets most of them had agreed to in the International Development Strategy for the Second U.N. Development Decade (a minimum of 0.7 per cent of GNP in the form of official development assistance and 1.0 per cent of GNP including private capital flows to the South); b) that the North increase its financial commitments to those emergency funds created during the last eighteen months in response to the food and fuel crises of 1973-1975; and c) that the North be prepared to renegotiate the terms of debt for those Southern countries experiencing serious balance-of-payments problems aggravated by debt-repayment obligations.

3. In the area of *foreign investment*, there were again several distinct Southern goals: a) greater access to international capital markets; b) the elimination of the traditional international legal restraints on the expropria-

---

[10]Certainly not all demands fit this characterization. Particularly in the trade field, many demands are for systemic reforms that would increase the efficiency of global resource allocation and, in so doing, increase Southern growth opportunities.

tion of foreign direct investment, including the putative requirement of "full, prompt, and effective" compensation; and c) the engagement of Northern assistance in policing the activities of multinational corporations for the general purpose of increasing the level of economic benefits to the host countries. Such increased benefits might take various forms, e.g., greater North-South capital and technology flows, lower charges on technology transfer, more job creation in developing countries, and increased developing-country exports to the North.

4. In the field of *technology transfer*, Southern objectives included a) Northern financing earmarked for the creation, expansion, and modernization of Southern scientific and technological institutes; b) Northern support in "persuading" multinational corporations to adapt their technology to host-country development needs; and c) international support for changes in patent laws and other measures that would lower the costs of technology transfers to the South.

5. With regard to the *international monetary system*, the developing countries continued to demand a) a greater voice in the reform and management of that system, and b) an international reserve-creation process (in which Special Drawing Rights would gradually replace gold and national currencies as international reserves) that would enhance Southern access to global production by distributing a significantly greater magnitude of the growth in international liquidity to Southern countries than they receive under present International Monetary Fund arrangements.

6. To these rather traditional objectives the South added some *new demands*—new both in the range of ambition and the forcefulness of tone. Most prominent among these novel goals were the following: a) *a much greater role for the Southern countries in the process of international economic decision making* (within the International Monetary Fund, the World Bank, the General Agreement on Tariffs and Trade, and elsewhere) —a role that would, for example, ensure a greater *automaticity* in many types of North-South transfers; b) a consciously programmed *relocation of international economic production* (with an initial emphasis on the processing of developing-country raw materials), which would swiftly increase the relative share of global industrial output originating in developing countries; c) support for *a far greater degree of cooperation among developing countries* (or "collective self-reliance" in the South's own terminology) designed to strengthen both the Southern economic base and its bargaining position vis-a-vis industrialized countries (including international support for all developing-world raw material producer groups, preferential trade arrangements among developing countries, intra-South payments unions to increase trade among developing countries, and many others); d) explicit statements to the effect that, since "colonial injustice" and "neo-imperialism" are in great part responsible for the present inequities in the global distribution of income (a ratio favoring the North by perhaps as much as 20:1 in real per capita terms at the present time), the North must provide *increased net re-*

source transfers to the South in all the areas noted above in order to narrow the present income gap.[11]

Throughout 1975, the South's manifestos proliferated as rapidly as its specific demands. Support of the general developing-country position by the Organization of Petroleum Exporting Countries—best signified by OPEC's refusal to negotiate on energy issues with the OECD countries at the April 1975 Paris meeting until the agenda had been broadened to include all major development issues—led to a crescendo of rhetoric at the meeting of foreign ministers of the nonaligned countries in Lima in late August 1975.[12] The following paragraph from the Lima Programme for Mutual Assistance and Solidarity produced by that meeting reflects the radical tone of those countries which seemed to have captured the leadership of the Southern bloc during the eighteen-month period prior to the September 1975 Seventh Special Session of the U.N. General Assembly:

> Understanding that the struggle to establish The New International Economic Order is arduous, complex and long, a struggle for a second liberation, because of the fierce opposition of the imperialists and their obstinate defense of their privileged position which they do not abandon willingly; conscious therefore, that international aid in its present conception contributes in many cases to reinforce the structure of international domination, the Ministers of Foreign Affairs reaffirmed the urgent need for concerted efforts by the Non-Aligned Countries to mobilise their forces to consolidate their cohesion and their unity, to cooperate with and assist one another in the economic and social fields to strengthen their common front in the struggle against imperialism in order to assure the total independence of their peoples.[13]

One of the few public hints that the more "moderate" developing countries still were able to exercise significant influence within the nonaligned bloc when they chose to do so became apparent—initially at the July meeting of the Organization of African Unity and later at the Lima meeting of the nonaligned countries—when first the Africans and then the Asians and

---

[11]Income distribution figures for single countries are difficult enough to estimate; intercountry comparisons are even more uncertain. The RIO *Interim Report* cited in footnote 7 above suggests that the oft-quoted 20:1 ratio considerably *overstates* existing North-South average income inequalities. See Roger D. Hansen, "The Emerging Challenge: Global Distribution of Income and Economic Opportunity," in James W. Howe and the staff of the Overseas Development Council, *The U.S. and World Development: Agenda for Action, 1975* (New York: Praeger Publishers, Inc., 1975), pp. 157–88.

[12]The OPEC alignment with Brazil, India, and Zaire at the April 1975 Paris talks withstood all the pressures applied by the OECD countries in attendance.

[13]Conference of Ministers for Foreign Affairs of Non-Aligned Countries, "Lima Programme for Mutual Assistance and Solidarity," Lima, August 25-30, 1975, issued by the Conference as Doc. NAC/FM/CONF.5/15, and circulated by the U.N. General Assembly as U.N. Doc. No. A/10217, p. 38.

Latin Americans as well refused to give majority support to the hard-line Arab approach to the question of ousting Israel from the U.N. General Assembly.

If Southern actions (embargoes, producer cartels, "tyranny of the majority" voting tactics in U.N. bodies, etc.) appeared to raise fundamental questions about the potentially benign nature of interdependence, so, too, did many actions of Northern governments. During the winter of 1974-75, President Ford, Secretary of State Kissinger, and other top U.S. Administration officials openly discussed scenarios that might lead to U.S. military intervention in the Middle East. In addition, the United States gave clear priority to developing the International Energy Agency among the OECD countries rather than to negotiating with the OPEC countries. This course of action, combined with statements by highly placed U.S. government officials—mostly in the Treasury Department—appeared to confirm the view that the fundamental goal of U.S. foreign economic policy in late 1974 and early 1975 was to break the OPEC oil price and to develop requisite domestic (and OECD) political support for self-sufficiency attempts such as the U.S. Project Independence (and its OECD variant). Finally, the unwillingness of the OECD countries represented at the April Paris energy talks to expand the agenda to include other major issues of concern to developing countries again appeared to verify the unwillingness of the United States and other developed countries to enter into anything resembling serious negotiations with the South over the question of reforming the present international economic system.

While the U.S. government began to change the tone of its position on North-South issues in late spring 1975, throughout the summer it refused to divulge its plans for the Seventh Special Session of the General Assembly—a meeting that had been called specifically to discuss development and international economic cooperation. In fact the United States then had no position to reveal; the entire summer was characterized by bitter Administration infighting over the nature of *any* U.S. initiatives to be taken at the Special Session. Outwardly, however, there was little evidence to suggest a "forthcoming" U.S. response. Two events characterized the ambivalence of official U.S. thinking during the period. The first was Secretary Kissinger's newly announced willingness to reconsider—"on a case by case basis"—traditional U.S. opposition to commodity agreements. This apparent concession was in fact a convoluted restatement of more than a quarter century of U.S. policy regarding international commodity arrangements. The second event was the announcement in late May that the United States would support the International Fund for Agricultural Development[14]; three months after this pronouncement, however, the United States still had made no financial commitment to the Fund.

---

[14]For a discussion of the International Fund for Agricultural Development, see Chapter II.

Two "Schools" of Nongovernmental Analysis and Prescription. The past year's analyses and prescriptions for North-South relations produced by groups and individuals outside governments also attest to the accuracy of the term "crisis of interdependence." One major school of thought portrayed the "crisis" as inevitable and used it as an opportunity to advance a set of "egalitarian" principles. This school saw the crisis as inevitable for two basic reasons. First, the latter half of the twentieth century was envisioned by this group as a period in which the drive for "equality" on the part of the less developed states would be one of the powerful motive forces of international relations. And second, the successful actions of OPEC suggested to many members of this school that new avenues could and would be found to the reform of international economic and political systems, including an enhanced effort at Southern "self-help," funded where necessary by OPEC earnings.

Basically, the analysts of this general persuasion were inclined, like the spokesmen of many developing countries, to place the so-called "demands" of the developing countries in a historical and political perspective which freed the analysis of the issues at stake from the economist's efficiency criteria. They reconsidered the impact of the West on Asia, Africa, and Latin America; they analyzed the psychological, cultural, and the political as well as economic costs of colonialism to the developing countries; and they were willing to accept the pronounced escalation in developing-country demands for international economic and political changes as a natural consequence of the past two centuries of history. Many of them undoubtedly would have sympathized with French President Giscard d'Estaing's 1974 reference to the world's "revenge on Europe for the nineteenth century" and would have seen the demands of the developing countries as one expression of that revenge.

This school also emphasized that the dramatic events of 1973 and 1974 created a novel opportunity to conceptualize—if not to immediately implement—new measures for "closing the gap" between the world's rich and poor countries. The seizure of that opportunity is evidenced by such varied efforts as those of the new Third World Forum of eminent developing-country scholars,[15] as well as the previously mentioned May 1975 Symposium held in The Hague and the project being conducted by Jan Tinbergen and associated international economists.

The major goal of the organizers and many of the participants in these and similar efforts was to come to grips with what the Tinbergen group viewed as the world's three major problems over the years ahead: "peace, justice, and environmental integrity." Those analyzing the issue of *peace and international conflict* most often linked the problem of conflict to the Westphalian system of state sovereignty; the other barrier to peace to which

---

[15]See, for example, *Proposals for a New International Economic Order,* prepared by a special task force of the Third World Forum, Mexico City, August 21–24, 1975. (Available from the Third World Forum, Provisional Secretariat, Casilla 179-D, Santiago, Chile.)

they devoted a good deal of attention was the degree of developed-country versus developing-country conflict inherent in "capitalist and socialist imperialism."[16] Their prescriptions reached out in two directions, recommending the evolution of power from the nation-state a) "upward," to regional and international general-purpose agencies (e.g., the U.N. system) and special functional agencies (e.g., a World Central Bank); and b) "downward," to increasingly autonomous and more self-sufficient units within nation-states.

Those analyzing *justice* appeared to divide into two groups. The first focused on the issue of *absolute poverty* and presented proposals to "put a floor under poverty." The standard ingredients of such proposals were minimum levels of food, nutrition, housing, clothing, and education.[17] The second group focused most, if not all, of its attention on *states* rather than *individuals*. It was concerned far less with absolute poverty than with the "gap" between average standards of living in the rich and the poor countries. This second group raised all the old normative arguments against the gap (variously calculated at somewhere between 13:1 and 20:1 and still growing) and presented a host of proposals to narrow it considerably before the end of the century.[18] Far less was said about social injustice of a noneconomic nature; only a few references to ethnic and individual rights can be found within this strand of thought in the various symposia and reports.

A good deal of attention was paid to the third problem, *environmental integrity*. On the narrower issue of "limits to growth," both resource optimists and resource pessimists had their say. Perhaps the most balanced view on this subject was presented by Nurul Islam at The Hague Symposium:

> In the longer run the possibility of scarcity may emerge if the present rates of overall population growth and the income and consumption growth rates in the developed countries continue. Any such forecast, however, is subject to considerable uncertainty. This uncertainty necessitates a continuous analysis, assessment and forecasting of demand and supply, especially of non-renewable minerals, materials and food and of the problems and prospects of technological progress.[19]

---

[16]For the most sophisticated presentation of this proposition, see Johan Galtung's "Appraisal" in The Hague *Symposium Report,* op. cit., pp. 44–53. Galtung's theory "sees the two major forms of imperialism today (capitalist and socialist), not as a series of deliberate actions by dominance-oriented people, but as a structure, as a pattern of billions of acts, almost all of them routine, spun around the four themes of exploitation, penetration, fragmentation and marginalization" (p. 44).

[17]See, for example, James P. Grant and Mahbub ul Haq, "Income Redistribution and Financing of Development," Project RIO, "Reviewing the International Order" (draft document RIO-24), Part II, Chapter 8; and G. Adler-Karlsson, "New Way of Life in Developed Countries," discussion paper for The Hague *Symposium Report,* op. cit., pp. 67–70.

[18]See, for example, Project RIO, "Reviewing the International Order" (draft document RIO-19), Part I, Section 3.

[19]Nurul Islam, "Chairman's Report," The Hague *Symposium Report,* op. cit., p. 24.

It should be noted that the output of this first school—the school which viewed the "crisis of interdependence" as an opportunity to put forward new ideas and move toward a more "egalitarian" international economic and political system—is characterized by a major ambivalence about the distribution of income and economic opportunity, both globally and within nation-states.

Some groups and commentators within this school spoke insistently of "gap closing" at the global level and of various means of implementing such a suggestion. Included in such prescriptive exercises were calls for major North-South resource transfers, a deliberate slowing of growth within the North, a shifting of a great deal of the world's industrial production to the South, and a broad menu of additional programs of both a global and a Southern regional orientation to speed growth within the South. Such analyses and prescriptions showed an almost exclusive concern with the distribution of income and opportunity *between developed and developing countries.* They virtually ignored the distribution questions that are *internal to states,* both Northern and Southern.[20] Other groups within this school, while also limiting their attention to interstate distribution issues, distinguished clearly between *income redistribution issues* over the short and medium term and distribution issues which focused upon increasing global *economic opportunity* over the longer term. For example, the Third World Forum explicitly stated that "the Third World is not demanding a massive redistribution of wealth of the rich nations. Nor is it seeking equality of income. It is asking for equality of opportunity."[21]

Other members of this school did, however, directly or indirectly raise the domestic distributional issue.[22] As noted above, the issue of intrasocietal distribution of income and economic opportunity often was expressed in the form of a concern about building *minimum-needs* criteria that would be applicable globally. At least one prominent participant in the debate, Professor G. Adler-Karlsson of Denmark, also suggested the need for a *maximum income,* above which marginal tax rates would be set at 100 per cent. However, this idea appears to have received rather limited support. As the chairman of the working group to which Professor Adler-Karlsson proposed the notion at The Hague Symposium put it, "the idea of a maximum income suggested by Professor Adler-Karlsson did not find general acceptance."[23]

If the first group analyzed above for the most part welcomed increasing "interdependence" and was in the aggregate cautiously optimistic about the possibilities of using the present "crisis" to increase Southern bargaining

---

20See, for example, Project RIO, "Reviewing the International Order" (draft document RIO-19), Part I.

21*Proposals for a New International Economic Order,* Third World Forum, op. cit., p. 3.

22See, for example, "What Now: Another Development," *Development Dialogue,* No. 1/2, 1975 (The 1975 Dag Hammarskjold Report, prepared on the occasion of the Seventh Special Session of the United Nations General Assembly).

23The Hague, *Symposium Report,* op. cit., p. 73.

power and to enhance the cause of international egalitarianism (at the collective or the individual level), a second significant school of thought paid much more attention to the malevolent potential inherent in North-South interdependence. Its members saw in the crisis of North-South relations little cause for hope that a greater degree of global cooperation in matters of "peace, justice, and environmental integrity" would be forthcoming. In some cases, the far different conclusions reached were a result of different norms and values on the part of commentators; in others, the sharply divergent conclusions appeared to follow more directly from an analysis of the empirical problems involved irrespective of the norms and values of investigators. A brief examination of the recent writings of several leading commentators will suffice to portray the range of opinions representative of this school—views that are important to the shaping of foreign policy concerning U.S. relations with the world's developing countries.

According to Geoffrey Barraclough,

> In the wider perspective of history, it may well turn out that the long-term significance of the "oil crisis" is the way it has served as a catalyst for the wider and more fundamental confrontation between the poor nations and the rich, which threatens to engulf the world. The issue today is not oil . . . but whether the existing economic system, upon which Western preponderance is based, can withstand the challenge from the Third World.[24]

This challenge arose, according to Barraclough, as a direct response to the eighteen months (1974 to mid-1975) which the United States spent in trying to break up the OPEC cartel and lower the price of oil:

> The alliance between OPEC and the other developing countries, which emerged into broad daylight at the April [1975] meeting in Paris, was in a very real sense a response to Kissinger's intransigence. It has added a new dimension to the conflict. What might still, a year ago [summer 1974], have been handled as a purely practical negotiation about oil payments and debt transfers has turned into a question of principle and ideology.

> The question we are faced with today is no longer oil, or the price of oil, but a conflict between two *irreconcilable* conceptions of a just world order. That, in the end, is why the attempts of American liberals to patch over the differences are to all appearances doomed to failure.[25]

Viewing the "South" as a solid bloc of the Fourth World, Third World, and OPEC countries—all seen as committed to a principle of world order

---

[24]Barraclough, "Wealth and Power," op. cit., p. 29.
[25]Ibid. Emphasis added.

which is "irreconcilable" with any U.S. conception of the same set of phenomena—Barraclough quite logically concluded that "tests of strength" (not excluding the ultimate test of force itself) encompass the most probable future of North-South relations. His portrait left no room for compromise, none for the hope that the present "crisis of interdependence" can be resolved (at the least, contained) through the process of negotiation.

Where Barraclough saw no room for compromise, Irving Kristol feared the outcome of any concessions by the United States. Indeed, he found "very worrisome" the "apparent willingness of many State Department officials to reformulate American foreign economic policy in the hope of achieving a more amiable 'dialog' with the so-called Third World."[26] From Kristol's perspective, the "new cold war" was in essence "a conflict of political ideologies. What the 'Third World' is saying is not that it needs our help but that their poverty is the fault of our capitalism—that they are 'exploited' nations while we are a 'guilty' people."[27] Kristol added that "these governments are ideologically committed to the redistribution of wealth and to the frustration of business enterprise which creates wealth. Since the wealth they wish to redistribute does not exist in their own countries, they have decided to redistribute the wealth of the United States and the nations of Western Europe."[28] Ascribing these motives and behavior patterns to all developing-country governments, Kristol expressed a fear that any attempts at North-South negotiation of the rules and norms of the international economic system would inevitably undermine the institutions and the strengths of liberal capitalist societies while (presumably) contributing little, if anything, to the developmental capabilities of the South.

A much more nuanced analysis of the present "crisis" was presented by Robert W. Tucker in a series of articles published by *Commentary* magazine during the course of 1975.[29] While many of the issues raised by Tucker merit extended analysis, two interrelated themes are of particular significance to the assessment of the policy options before the United States. The first theme concerns what Tucker posits as a growing disjunction between power and order in international relations. The second involves the potential conflict between a) the "new political sensibility" of Western elites (essentially a commitment to closing the income gaps between rich and poor *people* throughout the world), and b) the "new egalitarianism" of most Southern governments (which aims at a new distribution of wealth and power among *states* in the present international system but *not* at a change in the state-centric nature of the system itself). Let us analyze these two themes in turn.

---

[26]Kristol, *Wall Street Journal,* op. cit.

[27]Ibid.

[28]Ibid. Individuals living in *most* of the world's developing countries will certainly be surprised to read that their governments are ideologically, or in any other respect, committed to the domestic redistribution of wealth.

[29]See particularly Tucker, "Egalitarianism and International Politics," op. cit., and Tucker, "A New International Order?" op. cit.

Tucker's examination of the thesis that continued crises will attend the growing degree of global interdependence leads him to argue, on the one hand, that the need for varying forms of international order will be greater than in the past "because interdependence creates relationships . . . which, if not somehow resolved may easily lead to chaos."[30] At the same time, however, he notes the growing number of constraints on the use of force in international relations, and particularly the apparent unwillingness of large segments of Western elites imbued with the "new political sensibility" to consider the use of force in North-South conflicts.[31] In his words, the period of the cold war

> was the last great manifestation of the old politics with its parochial interests, its obsession with national power, its hierarchical ordering of states, and its reliance on forcible methods. By contrast, the new political sensibility proclaims a politics of interdependence for a world that must cope with problems the nature and dimensions of which will no longer yield to particularistic methods of the past, and surely not the forcible methods of the past. In place of a world in which the hierarchical ordering of states seemed natural and inevitable, interdependence holds out the promise—as one sanguine analyst puts it—of "a world in which nobody is in charge."[32]

But what will emerge from a global context in which "nobody is in charge," in which the powerful states begin to suffer from a conjunction of moral and national-interest constraints on action, and in which the less powerful states begin to view interdependence as an opportunity to obtain maximum concessions from the developed states? This, in highly simplified form, is what Tucker views as the growing dilemma of the disjunction between power and order in the international system; it is a partial but insightful view of the potential crisis of interdependence as it relates to North-South relations.

One astute political analyst, Bruce Russett, commented in the spring of 1975 that achieving a balance between order and justice would be the major problem of international politics over the coming decade.[33] If Tucker's first theme is concerned almost exclusively with the "order" ingredient in Russett's balance, his second theme—the inherent potential for major contradictions between the "new political sensibility" within the North and the "new egalitarianism" within the South—is directly focused on the second ingredient, i.e., the issue of justice.

---

[30]"A New International Order?" ibid., p. 49.

[31]For a more detailed presentation of these constraints, see Roger D. Hansen, "The Political Economy of North-South Relations: How Much Change?" *International Organization,* Autumn 1975.

[32]Tucker, "Egalitarianism and International Politics," op. cit., pp. 27–28.

[33]Bruce Russett, *Foreign Policy*, No. 18 (Spring 1975), p. 108.

The new political sensibility of Northern elites and the new egalitarian-ism of Southern power holders share the objective of changing present international economic norms and rules in order to effect major transfers of income and economic opportunity to the South. But thereafter, as Tucker sees it, they part company. "While the order we have today is an order of states, the *justice* sought by the new political sensibility is, for the most part, a justice for individuals which can be guaranteed only by the atrophy of the sovereign powers states continue to claim."[34] Thus Northern elites exhibit a deep ambivalence regarding the nation-state. They recognize that for the present moment it is the only effective instrument available to begin the processes of income transfer and the restructuring of economic opportunity; they also recognize that the state is "the principle obstacle by virtue of its reluctance to act save on the basis of demonstrable self-interest and its resistance to yield any functions identified with its sovereignty."[35]

Tucker sees no such ambivalence in Southern thinking. "In a word, it is *not the essential structure* of the international system that the new egalitar-ianism has challenged, *but the distribution of wealth and power within this system.* . . . It is not *individual inequality* then, that forms the gravamen of the indictment brought by the new egalitarianism against the present order, but *collective inequality,* and above all the *inequality of states* at very different stages of development."[36]

In summary, it can be seen that members of the second, more pessimistic school are in agreement that a "crisis of interdependence" exists but are much less sanguine than others about the potential results of such a crisis. Some feel that ideological battle lines have been drawn, that there is no room for compromise, and that most probably military conflict of some sort is inevitable. Others share the view that the North-South struggle is essentially political and ideological in nature but are less certain about "inevitable" outcomes. Some presumably feel that if the United States leads a Northern coalition that refuses any compromise involving changes in present international economic regimes, the Southern challenge can be "overcome"—to the benefit of liberal capitalist societies in particular and of economic growth in general.

But the two major issues raised by Tucker remain the most salient ones identified by this school. First, can the present international system avoid the legion of problems which increasing interdependence is potentially capable of producing when "no one is in charge"—no one *either* in the sense of recognized status hierarchies typical of a more-or-less traditional state system *or* in the sense of newly agreed rules and norms of behavior among states which slowly come to replace the more traditional forms of statecraft? *If* Tucker's judgment of present Southern statecraft is correct, i.e., that its desire is simply to alter the present balance of power in a more-or-less

---

[34]Tucker, "Egalitarianism and International Politics," op. cit., p. 35.
[35]Ibid.
[36]Ibid., p. 30. Emphasis added.

traditional fashion, then the question of whether the present problems or those that will inevitably follow can be surmounted without resort to force will depend to a great degree on the actors, the motives, and the contextual elements of each crisis.

Tucker's second issue raises in a most fundamental manner the following question: What is the "new international economic order" all about? Is it proposed as an international effort to improve the standards of living and the economic opportunities of *people* within developing countries, or is it an effort to improve the economic and political power of Southern *states* within the international system? While the two goals are not in essence mutually exclusive, the degree to which they overlap will vary tremendously from state to state. Developing countries whose governing elites are committed to domestic reforms aimed at increasing economic opportunities for the least privileged groups in their societies could use all the potential benefits of a "new international economic order" to enhance such developmental efforts. On the other hand, however, developing countries governed by elites less interested in development strategies and economic reforms supportive of the underfed, underemployed, undereducated, and ill-housed could channel all the benefits of international economic reforms into strengthening inequitable patterns of development and into other programs (e.g., certain foreign policies) which enhance present forms of social stratification within their states and which experiment with new forms of regional stratification abroad.

Whether or not Tucker is correct in his assessment of Southern motives—and we will return to this point later—the issue he indirectly raises is crucial in two senses. First, if he is correct, then Northerners who generally support efforts to assist the process of economic development should ponder very seriously the degree to which a "new international economic order" will enhance development efforts. At the very least they should recognize that there is no simple one-to-one correlation between elements of a new international economic order and development prospects within developing countries, *particularly* if in their minds the concept of development is tied to benefiting the least privileged members—the "forgotten 40 per cent"—of the Third and Fourth Worlds. And second, again provided that he is correct in his judgments, can support for a new economic order which is *not* tied to development efforts affecting the poor majorities in developing countries be sustained within Northern electorates? If it should become clear that in many developing countries the results of a new international economic order are simply to strengthen present structures of social stratification and to enhance the demands of Southern countries in round after round of North-South bargaining, what will be the consequences for the Northern political bases of support for global economic development? And what will be the trade-off between domestic and foreign priorities? For example, will the U.S. Congress come to the aid of Zaire before it helps the city of New York? Little empirical work has been done on this type of question, and it is always possible that Northern political and economic interest groups with goals unrelated to economic and social development will find that incremental responses to Southern demands are worth the price of continued North-South "cooperation." Nevertheless, in the longer term this may be one of the most important issues raised by the host of questions surrounding the creation of a new international economic order.

The Seventh Special Session of the U.N. General Assembly

All of the governmental and unofficial assessments of the "crisis of interdependence" analyzed above were products of the events of the two-year period prior to the September 1975 Special Session of the U.N. General Assembly convened to discuss development and international economic cooperation. To what extent did the activity of that Special Session itself, including the resolution adopted in its final hours, tend to confirm or cast doubt upon this analysis? And what course of action does it suggest for U.S. foreign policy as it impinges, directly or indirectly, upon North-South relations?

In terms of the issues being examined in this chapter, the most prominent aspect of the Seventh Special Session might be termed the "reemergence of the moderates" within the Group of 77 developing countries. From beginning to end, those Third World countries least interested in scoring empty rhetorical victories and most interested in producing a resolution on international economic reforms acceptable to the industrialized countries prevailed within the Southern bloc. Three actions on the part of the Group of 77 support this interpretation. First, the Group nominated a minister from an OECD country to serve as chairman of the ad hoc committee that was given the task of attempting to produce a draft resolution acceptable to both North and South. Second, most countries of the Group greeted Secretary of State Kissinger's speech and proposals with marked courtesy and with an apparently genuine willingness to suspend criticism of it over the short term—despite the fact that the speech contained few concrete concessions to the Group's demands. Indeed, all that the speech and the proposals contained therein amounted to in reality was an apparent willingness on the part of the United States a) to recognize that the Southern demand for serious negotiations was in itself a legitimate request, and b) to begin that process of negotiation in a series of different venues.[37] And third, the fact that the Special Session produced a consensus resolution which is a very diluted statement of Southern views as they have appeared over the past two years testifies to the preponderant voice of the "moderates" within the Group.

---

[37]If the United States were to take positive action to deliver upon most of the *contingent promises* in the speech—particularly those related to such non-resource-transfer areas as trade liberalization, where major assistance to development efforts could be rendered—then the above characterization of the Kissinger proposals would prove to be too harsh.

A second striking aspect follows directly from the first. If it took so little actual commitment on the part of the United States to produce such a shift of influence within the Group of 77 (for example, in the area of actual resource transfers, the total contingent financial commitments in the U.S. proposals were so small, and each one of them so hedged in presentation, that new potential commitments can hardly exceed $400-$500 million), it is obviously necessary to consider the possibility that "Southern solidarity" and the prominence of the radical voices within the Group of 77's activities over the past two years have been to a considerable extent a function of U.S. diplomacy. As long as the United States responded negatively to almost all developing-country requests in almost all international conferences, the moderates within the Group of 77 had no hand to play; the radical voices assumed a forcefulness far out of proportion to their number and their influence within the Group.

It is of course true that many of the developing countries were, by the fall of 1975, facing very serious economic difficulties. Thus there was a far more urgent need for Northern assistance of one form or another than existed in the first eighteen months after the quadrupling of oil prices. Therefore the all but total lack of nuance in U.S. policy toward the demands of the developing countries prior to the presentation of the new U.S. position in September of 1975 is certainly not solely responsible for the rapid escalation of Southern demands over the past two years. But if the two are causally correlated to any significant degree, predictions of "irreconcilable" political-ideological struggles will prove to be accurate only if U.S. intransigence makes them self-fulfilling prophecies.

A final aspect of the Seventh Special Session that merits noting in the context of this chapter concerns the putative "strength" of the developing countries "in an interdependent world." Time and again over the past two years, attention has been called to the rapidly growing "strength" of the world's developing countries. And the more most analysts have considered the altering perceptions of strength, growing global interdependencies, and increasing constraints on the use of force in North-South confrontations, the more impressed they have been by the potential capacity of the South to create global economic chaos, and therefore to be able to bargain much more aggressively with developed countries for changes in present international economic (and political) "rules of the game," e.g., in present trade, monetary, foreign investment, technology, and aid regimes.

Yet the overriding desire of the great majority of the developing countries at the Seventh Special Session was to move rapidly from a posture of confrontation with the North to one of negotiation. The fact that they accepted the U.S. opening statement in good faith despite its strong tendency to opt for a reformed and refurbished "old" international economic order, and that they accepted the diluted version of their own goals in the Session's final resolution appears to bear testimony to their present weaknesses, not strengths. This may be a cyclical phenomenon; in the midst of a global depression, developing countries find themselves at the nadir of their bargaining position vis-a-vis the North. Nevertheless, as will be noted below, it suggests that Southern "power," like Southern "solidarity," may have been considerably exaggerated—even after cyclical variations are taken into account.[38]

North-South Relations in 1976 and Beyond: A Tentative Reading

Predicting the course of North-South relations over the next several months, let alone the next several years, is a risk-prone operation. The parameters of the problems involved are changing rapidly—particularly in their *perceptual* aspects. The goals of the major actors in the game are at times highly divergent, and most actors are in a position to force a confrontation in the various negotiating forums (the Paris talks, the Interim Committee of the International Monetary Fund, the World Food Council, etc.) that are likely to be active during 1976. Beyond these obvious potential settings for North-South negotiations to suceed or fail, the course of events in the Middle East or in U.S.-Soviet negotiations over the entire range of detente issues could heavily influence the outcome of "the crisis of interdependence" in its North-South context.[39] With these caveats, four general observations on the probable course of North-South negotiations over a new international economic order in the coming months seem worth mention.

1. The first concerns the putative *willingness to negotiate on the part of the United States and some other leading Northern countries*. It is simply too early to tell whether the apparent breakthrough at the 1975 General Assembly Special Session will be followed by the development of a Northern negotiating strategy that is committed to at least the minimum degree of reform necessary to produce a series of constructive dialogues with the developing countries in Paris, in the IMF Interim Committee, in the IMF-IBRD Development Committee, at the fourth session of the United Nations Conference for Trade and Development, and elsewhere. Measured either by the dollar value of new U.S. commitments or by the relinquishing of "liberal-capitalist" efficiency concepts, the U.S. package of proposals made at the

---

[38]The issue of Southern "strengths" and "weaknesses" is of course a difficult one to analyze with any degree of certainty. Strength will vary not only over business cycles, but with regard to issue area (in some of which a "solid" South may be in a position to exercise a veto power), existing degrees of Southern "solidarity" and Northern "solidarity," and everyone's perceptions of the opportunity costs involved in each potential confrontation. Furthermore, "weaknesses" were probably not the sole explanation of the moderation in the Group of 77 activity at the Special Session. Another partial explanation could be that the moderates felt that there was nothing further to be gained from continued confrontation and that a tactical switch was therefore appropriate.

[39]For example, a resurgence of conflict in the Middle East could link the OPEC countries more tightly to the South and rekindle the more radical demands of the Group of 77. Likewise, issues like the November 1975 U.N. vote condemning Zionism could rekindle Northern intransigence. Further steps toward detente, particularly a step which would even marginally help to break the OPEC oil price through Soviet oil sales to the United States at a lower price, could, on the other hand, lead to a weakening of "Southern solidarity" in the face of a *perceived* East-West accommodation that could further debilitate many Southern bargaining strategies.

United Nations was marginal. Yet it proved acceptable to Southern states as an initial offer to begin serious negotiations. However, if the conceptual, organizational, and financial implications of those proposals are not made more concrete in discussions over the coming year, the opportunity to reach mutually accommodative solutions to a host of North-South economic and political problems presented by the Seventh Special Session could be lost. If the United States continues to attempt to break the OPEC oil price to the exclusion of entering serious negotiations with non-oil-exporting developing countries, "Southern solidarity" and radical leadership of the Group of 77 may reemerge if and as global economic conditions improve. But a close reading of the past six months suggests that the "price" to the North of North-South efforts at cooperation will prove to be far less than many have suggested, and that a genuine Northern commitment to negotiate through-out 1976 could produce some very substantial gains—political as well as economic and Northern as well as Southern—at a very marginal cost.

Indeed, optimists might well argue that in "properly" negotiated agreements, the gains would considerably *outweigh* the costs. Their conclusion would be based on the following types of observations. Increased trade liberalization would benefit the Northern consumer as well as the Southern producer. Recent estimates suggest that U.S. import restrictions alone cost the United States over $2 billion per year (excluding the petroleum sector). Even if the costs of a generous and effective domestic trade adjustment-assistance program were subtracted from this total, U.S. consumers would still be major beneficiaries of a trade liberalization program specifically responsive to the "demands" of the developing countries. Moreover, the same pattern of *mutual gains* might also evolve in the areas of international monetary reform, foreign direct investment, and some commodity buffer stocks. In the first case, a reform measure linking the supply of international liquidity more directly than the Bretton Woods system to the needs for financing international trade could produce mutual benefits (e.g., lower rates of inflation). In the second case, international agreement on the activities of multinational corporations that reached agreement on both *host*-country and *home*-country policies affecting foreign direct investment flows could benefit both sides by harmonizing the contradictory goals that now influence the allocation of foreign direct investment. In the third case, some buffer-stock arrangements—for example, food reserves—could increase rather than decrease efficiency of *global* production, enhance global "equity" goals, and increase the pace of economic development.

One could list many other areas in which mutually beneficial outcomes would be possible. The trouble is, of course, that one cannot *guarantee* such outcomes for several reasons. One cannot guarantee that goals will always be reconcilable, that "positive-sum" solutions will always result, that agreement can be reached on the division of the gains where such solutions are found, or that initially negotiated agreements will exhibit a great deal of endurance. Finally, there remains the gap between international agreements that can potentially increase the aggregate welfare of both developed and developing nations and the domestic reforms needed to spread the domestic costs and benefits in an "equitable" manner.

On balance, therefore, it is impossible to demonstrate that the economic benefits of a yet-to-be-completed negotiation will outweigh the costs entailed. But the improved negotiating prospect suggested by the reemergence of the Group of 77's "moderates" does suggest that optimism is more appropriate than pessimism at the present stage of North-South relations.

2. The second observation concerns *trends within the Group of 77*. As noted above, the reemergence of the moderates at the Seventh Special Session suggests at least two tentative conclusions. The first is that serious analysis should apply a rather high discount to much of the rhetoric which characterized the eighteen months preceding the Special Session. The successful example of OPEC, U.S. diplomatic intransigence, and global economic conditions all help to account for the pronouncements of this period, and a repetition of that particular conjunction of factors is unlikely to recur. The second tentative conclusion is that a large majority of the world's developing countries are in a weaker bargaining position than has generally been recognized and are therefore more willing and anxious to continue with the process of *moderate reforms*—many of which can be formulated so as to benefit both developed and developing countries—than with pressing holy wars over "irreconcilable conceptions of a just world order."[40]

To the degree that this observation is accurate, the views of those analysts who have emphasized the irreconcilability of developed- and developing-country values, norms, and policies would appear to be overstated reactions to the most hyperbolic of developing-country statements, generally emanating from a small and most probably nonrepresentative group within the larger framework of the Southern bloc (be it the Group of 77 or the nonaligned nations). In Kristol's case, room for error is magnified by a tendency to dismiss all Southern demands as ideological attacks on a "free enterprise" system which, if responded to affirmatively, would lead to "intervening massively" in our domestic economies. Furthermore, Kristol seems to view the present international economic system as a classic free market model. Not only can one take issue with his initial premises regarding the condition of "free market competition" both domestically and internationally; one can also question the "either-or" element of his analysis.[41] In a world where almost all nonsocialist economies are "mixed," it is difficult to believe that carefully negotiated schemes which might involve some international forecasting, planning, and possibly some buffer-stock

---

[40] It is easy to conceptualize reforms of the international trade, monetary, and investment regimes that would be of benefit to both groups of states. For an excellent analysis of many potential reforms of this nature, see *International Organization,* Vol. 29, No. 1 (Winter 1975), passim.

[41] For an extremely insightful critique of Northern views of "the free market system" at the international level, see Carlos Díaz Alejandro, "North-South Relations: The Economic Component," *International Organization,* Vol. 29, No. 1 (Winter 1975), pp. 213–42.

arrangements would dramatically change the character of Northern economies *except* in very specific product sectors (food production is one such possible area) where serious global discussions demonstrated *to all parties* the need for more global planning.

A final trend within the Group of 77 underscores one aspect of the potential for fragmentation of the Southern bloc that has been evident from the outset.[42] This is the apparently increasing degree of tension between the oil-exporting nations and the rest of the developing world. For close to eighteen months, there was almost no *public* criticism within developing countries concerning OPEC's oil-price rises. But in the fall of 1975, an increasing number of Southern states, led by Tanzania and other black African countries, broke their silence to criticize the OPEC countries for doing so little to ease the effects of oil-price rises on non-oil-exporting developing countries; the first Southern mutterings about "Arab imperialism" became prevalent.

This is only the most obvious example of the delicate and fragile nature of the "Southern bloc." Its reification over the past several years, again beginning with the OPEC oil-price rises of 1973-74, has concealed at least as much as it has revealed about the course of political, social, and economic developments within the developing countries of the world. In particular, it has concealed the growing strain within a group of countries that has little in common save the issues created by Northern patterns of responding negatively to Southern requests for often marginal (and often appropriate from both an efficiency and an equity calculus) reforms of the present international economic system.

3. The third observation concerns *the varying judgments passed on the outcome of the General Assembly Special Session and the framework for North-South negotiations over the coming year.* It is probably accurate to characterize both of the major schools of thought analyzed earlier in this chapter as being disappointed with the Special Session and the subsequent efforts at negotiation. The "egalitarian" school, which has viewed the "crisis of interdependence" as an opportunity to permanently alter major aspects of the present international economic and political systems, seems generally disillusioned with the U.S. presentation at the United Nations, with the contents of the Session's final resolution, and with the limited (in its view) opportunities that the presently scheduled international negotiating sessions are likely to allow for major systemic changes. This school is disappointed with the continued weakness of the Southern bargaining position relative to the strong position (perceived if not real) of the United States. Proponents of this view are likely to characterize the successful U.S. efforts to resuscitate negotiations late in 1975 as the "last gasp" of the trickle down theory of development.

On the other hand, most spokesmen of the second school feel that the United States in particular and the North in general compromised too much

---

[42]Hansen, "The Political Economy of North-South Relations," op. cit.

at the Special Session. Agreements to discuss development issues, raw materials other than petroleum, and international financial issues in the Paris meetings; agreements to discuss particular commodity arrangements within the U.N. system; and other gestures suggesting a willingness to examine developing-country problems, prospects, and requests for systemic reforms are viewed as so many Trojan horses carrying with them the potential for an unending series of demands that will not be satiated until the "liberal-capitalist" system as we now know it ceases to exist, and until the developed countries have lost all will and/or capacity to withstand the course of change.

At present, the burden of the evidence suggests that the worries of the second school appear to be far less justified than those of the first. The reasons for this judgment have been noted in analyzing the results of the Seventh Special Session, and need not be repeated here.

4. The final observation concerns the two dilemmas posed by Robert Tucker: 1) *the disjunction between power and order;* and 2)*the interaction between the "new political sensibility" in the North and the "new egalitarianism" in the South.* One can speak with little sense of finality about either dilemma and cannot look for a quick consensus to emerge on either topic. Nevertheless, the following speculation seems appropriate at this point in the policy debates that will of necessity consider these dilemmas, directly or indirectly.

Concerning the first dilemma—the disjunction between power and order, and the danger that this disjunction engenders for an interdependent international system—it seems fair to suggest that perhaps the disjunction has been overstated from the very beginning. Tucker's portrait of the dilemma rests on the assumption that the industrialized states are increasingly unwilling to resort to "power" when fundamental national interests are challenged by "weaker" countries. But Tucker defines power very much in the traditional strategic-diplomatic sense, rather than in terms which seek measurements of power and its usefulness in an "interdependent" world.[43] Interdependencies are not symmetrical; in the aggregate some countries are much more vulnerable to nonmilitary actions of foreign states than others. Furthermore, because of their different levels of economic development and access to technology and capital markets, some countries have a much greater capacity to withstand potentially harmful foreign actions (of a nonmilitary character) than others. Again speaking in the aggregate, interdependencies between developed and developing nations are asymmetrical in favor of the former. Oil and *perhaps* a few other minerals aside, Southern bargaining strategies are limited by the number of arrows in their quiver.

---

[43]For an early attempt at the latter type of analysis see Robert O. Keohane and Joseph S. Nye, Jr., "World Politics and the International Economic System," in C. Fred Bergsten, ed., *The Future of the International Economic Order: An Agenda for Research* (Lexington, Mass.: D.C. Health and Company, 1973), pp. 115–79. They suggested that "where actors are asymmetrically interdependent, we expect the less dependent to be able to manipulate the relationship as a source of power within the issue-area and perhaps in other issue-areas as well" (p. 122).

Moreover, these countries generally are still dependent on developed countries for capital, technology, markets, and (for those increasingly interested in them) weapons and weapons technology. Given this aggregate asymmetry in bargaining positions, it seems plausible to conclude that the world's developed countries have a broad "power" potential that can be brought into play in determining the degree of "order" that will characterize the international system.[44] This general point is strengthened when one recognizes that Tucker seldom if ever disaggregates his consideration of "developing countries" in discussing North-South relations. He speaks of the ability of the poorer countries to bring "chaos" to "the system"; except for OPEC, however, one wonders just how much chaos (except, perhaps, of a self-immolative nature) most other developing countries can create. The self-immolative scenario cannot be ruled out entirely, though it probably deserves a low-probability assessment for the medium term. Perhaps more important over the same time period is the ability of a "solid" South to "veto" certain systemic reforms (e.g., monetary reform) desired by developed-country governments. The use of the "veto" would certainly increase Southern bargaining leverage somewhat, but it also might, if pushed too far, lead to the reconstitution of "rich club" institutional responses. While this result would be costly to both North and South, the developing countries would pay the larger relative price.

Had Tucker paid a bit more attention to the changing essence of power in the present state of international relations and to the heterogeneity that lurks beneath the label "South," he might have been somewhat less concerned about the apparent disjunction between power and order (initially dramatized by the actions of OPEC in 1973-74). It is true, however, that Tucker was also speaking about perceptions and values within Northern elite groups; and if these have changed *permanently* as dramatically as Tucker suggests, then the *fact* that any disjunction between power and order can generally be sharply limited without resort to traditional modes of power becomes less relevant than the perceptions and the values of Northern elite groups.

With regard to Tucker's second dilemma, the evidence is even less conclusive. As noted above, an issue crucial to the purposes of this essay is posed by the question: What is supposed to be the essence of a "new international economic order"? Is it an order that accords high priority to human developmental needs, with particular emphasis on the poorest 40 per cent of the world's population? This seems to be what many Northerners, imbued with Tucker's "new political sensibility," would like to promote. Yet in the aggregate, as noted by two Northerners at The Hague Symposium last summer, the concept of a "new international economic order" as developed

---

[44]However, the outcomes of individual bargains are likely to vary broadly with the number and *variety* of actors involved—nation-states, transnational corporations, international organizations, etc.—and, in the economic area, the phasing of global business cycles and varying actor perceptions of the opportunity costs of conflict versus accommodation. To give but one concrete example, "resource-scarcity" issues are bound to be more salient to Japan and the European Community than to the United States, given present levels of resource endowments of these different developed countries.

within the Group of 77 and the nonaligned nations had little if anything to do with distributive justice *within* Southern countries, let alone *among* them.[45]

This raises a crucial issue for Northern supporters of further efforts to aid the development process. Will the apparent lack of concern for distributional issues within developing countries characteristic of most new international economic order proposals pose a significant hurdle to further efforts at North-South accommodation? Some partial evidence from U.S. congressional initiatives over the past three years suggests that within Congress only those programs related to economic development that are formulated to raise the standard of living of the "forgotten 40 per cent" can sustain significant support. This potential issue could be finessed, of course, if Northern and Southern governmental and business groups were to quietly compromise on an updated version of old development strategies and to portray the compromise as the result of a reasonable negotiation. In fact, this outcome would probably satisfy most Northern and Southern governmental and business groups, which would prefer marginal to major changes in both perceptions and practices affecting the issues of social and economic and political stratification. If this result does occur, then a new international economic order may prove to have been purchased at a very significant price when measured in terms of "justice" and "environmental integrity."

With many Southern governments looking to alter the structure of power internationally; with far fewer of them looking to the needed altering of domestic structures; and with major Northern governments concerned almost solely with the restoration of "order," what source can we expect to provide the impetus for programs aimed at those most in need of a more equitable distribution of income and economic opportunity? Can such concerns be made an integral part of the process of negotiations begun after the Seventh Special Session? That effort would appear to be the major task of those Northern and Southern governments, institutions, and individuals dissatisfied with the results of the more traditional approaches to economic and social development. If the effort is not successfully undertaken, even the most fruitful negotiations may produce ephemeral results for the development process (including "peace, justice, and environmental integrity") except in the very long run.[46]

---

[45]See the papers by Hollis Chenery and Sidney Weintraub in The Hague *Symposium Report,* op. cit., pp. 5–11 and 26–30, respectively.

[46]Those members of the development economics profession who continue to believe in the values of the "trickle-down" theory of development—political and social as well as economic values—will dispute need for a more "poverty-oriented" approach. So may those who assume that the latter approach necessarily entails a vigorous emphasis on the redistribution of income and wealth, and who argue that such policies are highly impractical in most developing-country settings. However, a reformed approach need not emphasize the *redistribtuion of wealth.* It can focus upon a *redistribution of economic opportunities* through programs of land reform, rural education and health reforms, reforms in the structure of factor prices in the industrial sector, and many others which do *not* involve direct income and wealth redistribution. To label all attempts to introduce substantial reforms into the "standard" development strategies of the past twenty-five years as "redistribution strategies" is to introduce a false and contentious dichotomy into an already complex subject.

The basic ingredients for such a shift in emphasis within the present attempts at reform are not entirely missing. First, a major portion of the Kissinger proposals to the Seventh Special Session dealt specifically with the problems of the least privileged. Second, not all Southern countries are as disinterested in this set of problems as analysts who do not apply the proper degree of disaggregation to the world's developing countries suggest. The percentage may be small, but a significant number of developing countries recently have been experimenting with less traditional and more "poverty-oriented" approaches to growth. Furthermore, even regimes whose hearts are not in the effort are beginning to rethink development policies in light of rapidly rising unemployment, growing internal income inequality, and the inherent potential for political instability which such trends entail. Finally, within the North, the idea of a *global* minimum standard of living and attendant economic opportunity is spreading. The movement is reaching the point where institutions and organizations—public and private—are conceiving blueprints for such an effort, beginning to approximate its costs, and giving increasing thought to the problem of implementation. How can such a program be instituted in a manner that minimizes perceived threats to state sovereignty within developing countries while guaranteeing that the forgotten 40 per cent are reached by the policies shaped to meet their development needs?

Shortly after the conclusion of the Seventh Special Session, Zbigniew Brzezinski suggested that "what is now needed is a sustained and serious follow-through, based on congressional support and broad popular understanding of the need for a truly historical effort to update and reform the international system."[47] Unless the U.S. Congress and the American people are convinced that efforts at reform will be directed at least as much to problems of equalizing economic opportunities for those least privileged within the South as they are to altering status and hierarchy among and between collectives in the present international state system, prospects for "a truly historical effort" will remain somewhat less than overwhelming.

---

[47]*New York Times*, October 5, 1975.

CHAPTER II

The World Food Situation and the U.S. Role

Martin M. McLaughlin

The improved climate of discussion at the Seventh Special Session of the U.N. General Assembly was in some measure prefigured by the unanimity with which the ministers of 134 nations, meeting at the World Food Conference in Rome in November 1974, had adopted twenty-one substantive resolutions and a solemn declaration that every man, woman, and child has a right to an adequate diet.[1] The world has fallen far short of securing that right for an intolerably large number of people but has acknowledged it in principle. If, as the Seventh Special Session indicated may be the case, the World Food Conference spirit of problem solving carries over into the fields that so far have been marked by more confrontational postures, one can hope that the relatively cooperative international approach to the world food problem gradually may cease to be the exceptional case and may even become the prototype.

This possibility makes progress in the food area—and the avoidance of "U.S. food power" rhetoric[2]—even more important; if we cannot move forward in this area, where the United States wields predominant power because of its agricultural productivity and its share of the world grain trade, the possibility of progress in other sectors seems considerably more doubtful. On the other hand, some success on this set of issues could open the way to further agreement on some of the even more fundamental, long-range

---

[1]*World Food Conference: Note by the Secretary-General*, U.N. Doc. No. E/5587, November 22, 1974, p. 57.

[2]Emma Rothschild, "Food Politics," *Foreign Affairs*, Vol. 54, No. 2 (January 1976). Ms. Rothschild describes very perceptively both the danger and the illusion that the food power advocates are attempting to promote. For another view, see "U.S. Food Power: Ultimate Weapon in World Politics?" *Business Week*, December 15, 1975, pp. 54-60.

problems of international economic systems. What is needed is a coherent U.S. food policy.

Although the food predicament of the 460 million people who were acknowledged by the World Food Conference to be malnourished or facing starvation has not yet improved markedly,[3] their short- and long-term prospects appear slightly more hopeful now. Two factors—in addition to the improved atmosphere—contribute to this judgment of cautious optimism: a) the 1976 crop prospect, and b) the slow but steady progress toward building the institutions called for by the World Food Conference.

The 1976 Crop

Although U.S. Department of Agriculture (USDA) predictions about the 1976 U.S. crop have been scaled down from "record" to "bumper," it is clear that agricultural production worldwide has increased significantly.[4]

In 1975 U.S. farmers produced just over 200 million metric tons of cereal grains (wheat, rice, and feedgrains) out of a world total of 1.25 billion tons. The United States exported about a third of its production, accounting for about 50 per cent of the world grain trade. Reserves that were carried over into 1976 totaled just over 100 million tons worldwide.[5] With consumption slightly outrunning production, this carry-over figure represents a thirty-day world supply—a reserve that is 10 per cent better than that of last year, but still far below what world food security would require.[6] In 1976, world cereal production is expected to increase to nearly 1.3 billion tons; almost all of this gain reflects the anticipated North American crop, of which the United States is expected to harvest more than 250 million tons. About 80 million tons will be exported, making up 50 per cent of the expected total world grain trade of 161 million tons.[7]

---

[3]See Table A-1, p. 128.

[4]Throughout this section, "1975 crop" and "1976 crop" refer, respectively, to the harvests of the 1974/75 and 1975/76 crop year. It should be noted that while USDA figures are the best available, the General Accounting Office called attention to serious inaccuracies in the 1971/72 and 1974/75 projections, pointing out especially that "the Department has noted that forecasting is particularly difficult in times of economic change and turbulence." From U.S. General Accounting Office, *What the Department of Agriculture Has Done and Needs to Do to Improve Agricultural Commodity Forecasting and Reports*, Report to the Congress by the Comptroller General (RED-76-6), August 27, 1975, pp. i-ii.

[5]U.S. Department of Agriculture, Foreign Agricultural Service, *World Grain Situation: Outlook for 1975/76*, Foreign Agriculture Circular (FG 12-75), October 7, 1975, p. 2. However, the U.N. Food and Agriculture Organization (FAO) estimated the reserve levels at 93 million tons (excluding the U.S.S.R. and China). U.N. Food and Agriculture Organization, *The State of Food and Agriculture, 1975*, Item 6 of the Provisional Agenda of the November 1975 FAO Conference, U.N. Doc. C 75/2, August 1975, p. 2.

[6]No objection has been voiced, either at the World Food Conference or during the follow-up period, to the generally agreed minimum food security figure of 60 million tons in reserve in addition to the normal carry-over from year to year of 100 million tons. The 60-million-ton figure could add about 18 days'supply to the present reserve, making the total 48 days' supply, or just about half the 1961 effective world reserve of 95 days' supply. For a survey of world grain reserves, 1961-1976, see Table B-1, p. 152.

[7]Since only about two thirds of this total—about 108 million tons—moves from one *region* to another, the United States accounts for roughly 80 per cent of interregional grain exports. U.S. agricultural exports are expected to gross nearly $26 billion in 1976. For data on net grain trade in recent crop years, see Table B-2, p. 153.

Elsewhere in the world, the 1975 harvest results were also much improved. The rains came in the Sahel, and India experienced a very good monsoon. Canada shared in the good weather that produced the American harvest; and Australia, too, had a good crop. Western Europe's crops were normal, and no unusually adverse conditions were experienced in Latin America or Southeast Asia. Only in the Soviet Union was there a severe shortfall, largely due to bad weather.

But at the same time that production has risen, so have the claims of consumers. World population grew in 1975 by about 75 million people —roughly the equivalent of the combined population of France and Canada—and the demand for indirect consumption of grain in the form of animal products in the old rich and newly rich nations has shown no tendency to deviate from its rising curve. The decision of the Soviet Union to repeat its action of 1972 and buy heavily in the North American market—in the face of its crop shortfall (less than 140 million tons of production compared with a target of 215 million)—has reduced the availability of that bumper crop to meet the immediate needs of the most vulnerable people to a level no better than what was achieved last year.[8]

Even with a good crop, however, the world remains dangerously dependent on the weather alone to safeguard it from a plunge into famine. And well over a year after the World Food Conference, the United States, the world's largest exporter of food in a world where half a billion people are facing starvation, continues to lack a coherent food policy—a lack which has contributed to great uncertainty and instability in the world food economy in recent years.

World Food Conference Follow-Up

In addition to adopting a unanimous declaration of intention to eradicate hunger and reduce malnutrition during the decade of 1975-1985 and passing twenty-one resolutions on world food policy, the World Food Conference called for the creation of several new institutions and broadened the scope of some existing ones. This network of institutions appears to be making significant, if gradual, progress. With promises of $200 million each from the United States and the European Community; the expectation of an additional $100 million from Australia, Japan, Canada, and others; and a further conference scheduled for late January 1976 in Rome, the International Fund for Agricultural Development (IFAD) seems off to a reasonable start toward its SDR 1 billion (about $1.2 billion) capitalization—provided that the Organization of Petroleum Exporting Countries, mainly Saudi Arabia and Iran, can sort out their differences and match the $500 million expected from the OECD countries. The Consultative Group on Food Production and Investment in Developing Countries (CGFPI)—established in February 1975 under the joint auspices of the World Bank, the FAO, and the U.N.

---

[8]It can be hoped that the new U.S.-U.S.S.R. grain agreement will help to modify the sharp fluctuations of the past when it goes into effect in October 1976; but it is more likely that its impact on systematizing trade will be mainly psychological.

Figure 1. Major Intergovernmental Bodies in the Food Field

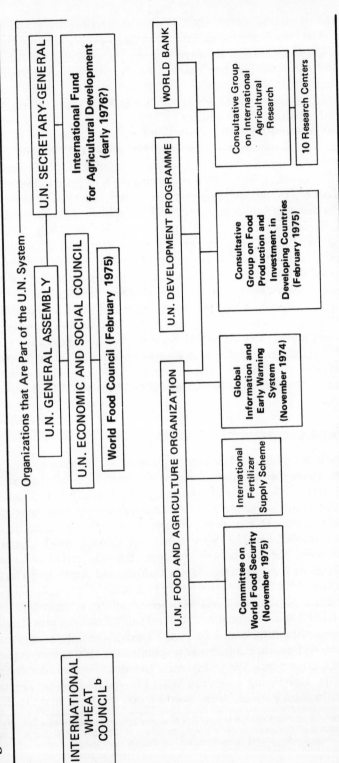

aBold type indicates new institutions established (or yet to be established) on the recommendation of the World Food Conference.
bThis loosely-organized but important London-based consultative mechanism—which is outside the U.N. system of organizations and therefore has no official responsibility for implementing the recommendations of the World Food Conference—now involves some sixty countries, including the Soviet Union. It is the body within which international wheat agreements have been negotiated since the late 1940s.

Development Programme (UNDP)—has identified the following production and investment priorities to guide IFAD and other investment in the food-deficit countries: 1) to encourage small landholders and poor farmers in general, 2) to increase yields and improve nutrition, 3) to shift emphasis from export crops to those for local consumption, and 4) to emphasize the production of chemical fertilizers. Yet another new institution, the Global Information and Early Warning System, has been set up under the aegis of the U.N. Food and Agriculture Organization (FAO), with the U.S.S.R. and China remaining notable nonparticipants. Discussions leading (it is hoped) toward the creation of a world food reserve unfortunately are moving at a deliberate and exasperating pace in the International Wheat Council.

Previously existing organizations also have responded to the initiatives of the Conference. The Consultative Group on International Agricultural Research (CGIAR), founded in 1971, has increased its budget from $34 million in 1974 to $64 million in 1976—with emphasis to be placed on tropical and arid-lands agriculture and on crops for local use in those regions rather than for cash exports. The new International Food Policy Research Institute, associated with CGIAR, began operations at its Washington headquarters in July 1975. The International Fertilizer Supply Scheme (IFS) of the FAO, financed partly by the U.N. Emergency Office and partly through special funding appeals by the Director General of the FAO, has made 73,000 additional tons of fertilizer available to the food-importing countries most seriously affected by food and energy price rises and has raised nearly $200 million in pledges and funds.

All of these activities and arrangements are monitored by the new World Food Council, established by the U.N. General Assembly in February 1975. The Council's thirty-six-country membership[9] is a careful blend of food exporters, food importers, food-deficit countries, rich countries, poor countries, large countries, and small countries; the membership composition also provides for representation of all world regions (except China) and of a wide spectrum of political and economic systems. The Council's first meeting in June 1975 provided an occasion for reassessing the current world food situation as well as for confirming the Council's mandate to monitor and encourage action on all phases of the World Food Conference resolutions and to make recommendations for action to other U.N. bodies.

Despite this encouraging, gradual progress—still largely on the institutional side—one cannot help wondering why it takes so long to proceed forward along an agreed track toward an agreed destination, and what would have happened this year if the weather had not been favorable and the

---

[9]Members of the World Food Council are: Argentina, Australia, Bangladesh, Canada, Chad, Colombia, Cuba, Egypt, France, Gabon, Germany (Fed. Rep. of), Guatemala, Guinea, Hungary, India, Indonesia, Iran, Iraq, Italy, Japan, Kenya, Libyan Arab Republic, Mali, Mexico, Pakistan, Romania, Sri Lanka, Sweden, Togo, Trinidad and Tobago, Union of Soviet Socialist Republics, United Kingdom, United States, Venezuela, Yugoslavia, and Zambia.

harvests plentiful. The temporary fading of the specter of famine leaves relatively untouched the major food problems that have been building up over the years and that were recognized by the World Food Conference.

Major World Food Problems

The central problems in the world food picture can be conveniently classified—as was done by the World Food Conference—into three main categories: food production, food security, and food trade.[10] Resolutions concerning all three areas were passed without dissent at the Conference, and action to implement them needs to be assigned priority at both national and international levels.

Food Production. The Conference called on all governments and international development agencies to increase substantially their official development assistance to agriculture, especially to the least developed and most-seriously-affected countries (World Food Conference Resolution I) and to the poorest population groups. The Conference also approved specific resolutions on the problem of fertilizer supplies and on agricultural research; emphasized assistance to small farmers and landless peasants; and proposed the creation of the already mentioned International Fund for Agricultural Development, which would operate through existing multilateral funding institutions.

Action along these lines is under way at both the national and multilateral levels. The foreign aid legislation passed by the U.S. Congress in December 1975 increases the authorization for food and nutrition programs from the $300 million appropriated in the previous year to $618.8 million.[11] In addition, the legislation provides $200 million for IFAD and calls for increased agricultural research focusing on tropical, small-farm agriculture. The language of both the bill and the accompanying congressional committee reports reflects the intent of Congress to promote action on the special problems encountered by poor farmers and the need to ensure their participation in the development process. The new legislation accepts the basic premise that agricultural production needs to be increased in the areas where food shortages exist (as does the income of the poor so that they can buy it) for the following reasons:

(a) Production increases can be achieved more cheaply in relatively underdeveloped areas;
(b) High shipping costs and the attendant energy costs can thus be avoided;
(c) Most of the underutilized crop land (both in acreage and in yield) is located in such areas;

---

[10]*World Food Conference*, op. cit., passim. References to Conference resolution numbers will appear in parentheses in roman numerals in the text.

[11]International Development and Food Assistance Act of 1975, Public Law 94-161, section 103.

(d) The incremental gain from increased use of agricultural inputs (seeds, fertilizer, energy, pesticides, training) is very much greater in the developing than in the industrialized countries;

(e) The dependency relationship often fostered by food-transfer programs can be largely avoided; and

(f) Undue food-price rises in the industrialized countries, as well as in the poorer parts of the world, can be prevented.

Although not every country can be or needs to be *self-sufficient* in food, all could become *self-reliant* (i.e., able to purchase their food, if not grow it). This point, of course, relates not so much to food policy as to development policy—especially to rural development policy, which, since it deals with the quality of life of the rural poor and with their health, education, employment, and income, has a much broader scope than merely increasing agricultural production. If people cannot buy food, it makes little sense to stress all-out production. The world food problem is at least as much one of *distribution* as of production; and small farmers in the poor countries—as the World Food Conference repeatedly emphasized—are the principal victims. These farmers—who constitute 80 per cent of the population in many Third World countries—desperately need agricultural inputs such as tools, fuel for pumps and tractors, fertilizer, seeds, and pesticides. In order to acquire these items, they need a great many things, among them credit on reasonable terms; more equitable patterns of land holding; and storage facilities, roads, transport, and a marketing system that assures them a fair return on their investment and their labor. They also need extension services that fit their situation; education and training (including management skills); low-cost effective health care; nutrition programs and access to family-planning services; and environmental sanitation and water purification programs. Nor can they gain any headway without risk-minimizing, incentive-stimulating assistance from their governments, or without a sense of dignity—a sense that agriculture is not the least desirable way of life—and some voice in the decisions that affect their lives.

The United States and other industrialized countries should 1) increase assistance to small-farm agriculture, 2) attempt to ensure that this assistance in fact does reach the small farmer, 3) emphasize research that will benefit the small farmer, and 4) use whatever opportunities their development relationships with cooperating governments provide to encourage them to improve the lot of their rural poor.

Food Security. Consideration of this issue by the World Food Conference encompassed nutrition programs, food aid, and food reserves. The Conference recommended that governments "initiate new or strengthen existing food and nutrition intervention programmes"—especially with respect to protein/calorie malnutrition among the most vulnerable groups.

With regard to food aid, the Conference stressed that a minimum level must continue "in order to insulate food aid programmes from the effects of excessive fluctuations in production and prices"; it also urged greater advance planning of food aid, a larger grant component, and a minimum target of 10 million tons a year, starting from 1975 (Resolution XVIII).

For the intermediate time frame, the Conference called for accelerated implementation of the proposed International Undertaking on World Food Security,[12] the establishment of grain reserves, and the creation of the Global Information and Early Warning System on Food and Agriculture (established in November 1974) with full international participation and cooperation (Resolution XVI).

Except for the directives on *food aid*, the implementation of these requests has been considerably less effective than that of decisions in the production area. Even with an increase in U.S. food aid from a projected 3.3 million tons to a little less than 5 million tons actually shipped, the world community was able to reach only 8 million of the target of 10 million tons of food aid in 1975; pledges for 1976 total 9 million tons. U.S. action in this area is critical, since more than half the food aid will come from the United States. This year's foreign aid bill establishes a minimum for donated food aid under the program.[13] The legislation also modifies the operation of the program in several ways consistent with the thinking of the World Food Conference. It provides for food-aid commitments to be made earlier in the year to enable better planning; it links food aid to the support of rural development in the recipient countries by not requiring repayment of up to 15 per cent of loaned funds (provided they are used for rural development projects); and it separates food aid from short-run political considerations by requiring that the bulk of it (75 per cent) be allocated to low-income countries with an annual per capita gross national product below $300.

The United States has participated in discussions in both the International Wheat Council and the FAO concerning a possible world *food reserve* consisting of national grain reserves administered according to internationally agreed guidelines. Why is such a reserve system needed? Its common-sense rationale follows Joseph's advice to Pharaoh (in the Book of Genesis) to store up grain in the seven years of plenty in order to be able to feed the people in the seven lean years that were to follow. A second major reason is the economic consideration that—given the forecast that the world food supply for at least the next decade will be chronically tight with intermittent periods of surplus—substantial and well-managed food reserves would make

---

[12] Annex to resolution 3/73 on World Food Security, Draft International Undertaking on World Food Security. Reprinted in U.S. Senate, Committee on Agriculture and Forestry, Subcommittee on Foreign Agricultural Policy, *The World Food Conference— Selected Materials for the Use of the U.S. Congressional Delegation to the World Food Conference,* October 30, 1974, pp. 214-17.

[13] The President's increased food-aid budget of $1.519 billion for 1976 will buy a little more than 6 million tons of food. A minimum of 1.3 million tons of this is required for the donation program (P.L. 480, Title II) by the terms of the new foreign assistance bill (P.L. 94-161). The remainder will be made available under the long-term low-interest "concessional" sales program (P.L. 480, Title I). The grant element thus accounts for about one fourth of U.S. food aid—which is probably no less concessional than other countries' similar programs.

it possible to meet shortfalls and improve nutrition as well as stabilize prices. Such a system of food reserves also would help avoid the practice of the world's billion affluent people of using their greater purchasing power to preempt available food from the world's poorest billion people. The richest billion have been eating more each year, while the poorest billion have been eating less.

The problem of the world food reserve might be viewed as only technical, but deep political questions underlie virtually all the "technical" issues that are still in serious dispute:

(1) At what level should such a system of reserves be maintained? Is the World Food Council's proposal of 60 million tons, including feedgrains, more appropriate than the U.S. proposal of 30 million tons (25 million tons of wheat and 5 million tons of rice)?

(2) Who should pay for the reserve? Should it be funded by the United States alone (as in the past) or by the United States in partnership with rich food-importing countries, such as Japan and the U.S.S.R., and countries with large financial surpluses, such as the OPEC countries?

(3) How should it be managed—through government-held stocks, as in the United States until recently, or privately, as urged by U.S. Secretary of Agriculture Earl Butz, agribusiness, and most farm organizations?

(4) Should price or quantity be the trigger for stockpiling or release of stocks—i.e., should action to increase or draw down reserve holdings be activated by indicators including stock levels and deviations from production trends, or by price-fixing agreements?

(5) Who should "hold the key" to the reserve system? Should it be tapped at the decision of a World Food Authority—as originally proposed by World Food Conference Secretary-General Sayed A. Marei —or at the decision of individual nations, acting according to internationally agreed guidelines?

Even in the face of the World Food Conference's consensus on the *need* for a system of reserves, there is still little evidence of cooperation to bring about its actual establishment. The United States seems almost alone in pressing others toward joint action on this major Conference recommendation; and even the U.S. proposal that was put forward in September 1975 at the International Wheat Council meeting is a lowest-common-denominator trade-off between the U.S. State Department's desire to fulfill commitments made at the World Food Conference and the U.S. Agriculture Department's determination to hold government "intervention" in the market to a minimum. The U.S. proposal for quantity triggers runs counter to the European Community's effort to sustain its Common Agricultural Policy, which is marked by the explicit setting of price ranges for agricultural commodities. The Europeans—and the developing countries—would prefer to discuss the reserve as an issue in the multilateral *trade* negotiations, where the food issue would be related to other commodity issues. It should be remembered, however, that the World Food Conference placed at least equal stress on the reserve as a food *security* issue. Moreover, the probable purchase of more than 30 million tons of grain on the world market by the U.S.S.R. this year has effectively postponed the beginning of any stockpiling effort until the next harvest. According to the FAO, "these sales mean that it is no longer likely that world wheat stocks can be replenished to any marked extent in the present season."[14]

Food Trade. This was the area in which the Conference was least effective. The industrialized countries (particularly the United States) were not interested in considering resolutions that would in any way restrict them in future trade negotiations. It was equally clear that the developing countries felt an urgent need for improving their terms of trade and increasing their access to developed-country markets. Because of the intractability of this issue, the Conference avoided the real question, simply noting "the interrelationship between the world food problems and international trade," and calling for "a steady and increasing expansion and liberalization of world trade with special reference to food products" (Resolution XIX).

Thus while a significant measure of agreement exists on the longer-range goals of assistance to agricultural development in food-deficit countries, and while the areas of disagreement on the food-reserve question, though difficult, are fairly well delineated, the agricultural trade situation presents a much less hopeful picture. Since most resource transfers between developed and developing countries—in agriculture as in other fields—are commercial transactions, the character of agricultural trade is very important. The less developed countries find themselves at a disadvantage in some areas of the international food trade, as in many trade areas. "Only non-competing tropical food products maintained their position in the 1960s and early 1970s, but even here advances in one developing region have often been at the expense of others."[15] At the same time, the most rapid growth in *processed* agricultural products has taken place in developed countries. It is in this context that the developing countries have found it necessary to increase their food imports, mainly cereals (due to a variety of factors, including population growth and a series of bad harvests), but have lacked the foreign exchange to outbid the food-importing rich countries. The poor countries also have been adversely affected by higher maritime freight rates and the unstable trade conditions of the past three years—beginning with the Soviet purchase of almost 20 million tons of grain from the United States in 1972.

---

[14]U.N. FAO, *The State of Food and Agriculture, 1975,* U.N. Doc. C 75/2, op. cit., p. 2.
[15]U.N. Food and Agriculture Organization, *Mid-Term Review and Appraisal of Progress in the Food and Agricultural Sector during the Second United Nations Development Decade,* Item 7 of the Provisional Agenda of the November 1975 FAO Conference, U.N. Doc. C 75/16, August 1975.

Moreover, the agricultural market in the United States, which is the major world power in food trade, is dominated by half a dozen large companies whose operations are largely beyond public scrutiny (only one is a public corporation).[16] They own grain elevators, storage facilities at delivery points and market terminals, containers, railroad cars, barges, and ocean-going vessels and exercise very strong influence on the operations of the commodity exchanges (located mainly in the American Midwest). The present market structure, dominated by the five companies, not only opens the possibility of an undesirable concentration of economic power in a food market where demand is characterized by low elasticity,[17] but—in the absence of a national food policy also—permits a wealthy outside purchaser to move in and out at his own time and pace, even though these movements may be very disruptive. The free market may work well if all large purchasers act in the general interest, as in the case of Japan's agreement to buy about 14 million tons of grain annually over a three-year period. But when a large purchaser, e.g., the U.S.S.R., takes advantage of the situation and the U.S. government is unwilling to exercise control in the public interest, both the American consumer and the American farmer are disadvantaged —as are the thus preempted half a billion hungry people abroad, whom both the United States and the Soviet Union (and all other World Food Conference participants) have pledged to help. The most urgent need, therefore, is for *a national food policy dealing with all major aspects of U.S. agriculture (and nutrition).* Once such a policy exists, the structure of the market becomes a question of its appropriateness to that policy's implementation.

Corollaries to the Major Food Problems

One of the dangers of focusing on a single problem such as food, even for the purpose of analysis, is that its place in the network of development problems may be obscured. Significant related problems include at least those discussed below.

Nutrition. Studies of the food problem often restrict themselves to quantitative considerations of supply and delivery, omitting the qualitative question of how food is used, i.e., nutrition. The World Food Conference

---

[16]"Five firms dominate the U.S. grain export industry, accounting for 85 percent of total exports. Since 1971, Cargill and Continental each have had about 25 percent of the U.S. exports; Cook Industries, 15 percent; and Bunge and Louis Dreyfus corporations, 10 percent each. . . . Of the remaining 15 percent of the market, 8 percent is divided among five small export companies and the remaining 7 percent among four producer-owned cooperatives." Michael J. Phillips, "The Status of Cooperatives in the Imperfectly Competitive Grain Export Market" (Speech before the American Agricultural Economists Association, summer 1975), reprinted in *Congressional Record*, December 17, 1975, p. S 22613. See also Dan Morgan, "Merchants of Grain" (a four-article series), *Washington Post*, January 2-5, 1976.

[17]"Because of the inelastic demand for food, the absence of stocks will result in major fluctuations in prices whenever the growth in supply departs much from the growth in demand." Economic Research Service, U.S. Department of Agriculture, *The World Food Situation and Prospects to 1985*, Foreign Agricultural Economic Report No. 98 (Washington, D.C.: U.S. Department of Agriculture, 1974), p. viii.

recognized that nearly half a billion people were *malnourished* or facing starvation. This is not a purely quantitative question, but one of quality of diet as well. Malnutrition is the endemic disease of the socially and economically disadvantaged. Although during the past year the actions of international bodies, national governments, and private agencies have probably reduced the number of deaths due directly to malnutrition, this area has seen very little concerted action toward improvement, despite the frequent past resolutions of the FAO and the one adopted by the World Food Conference (Resolution V).

In the developing countries, which contain nearly two thirds of the world's people, the average calorie intake is still below the nutritional minimum for normal activity and growth; 700 million of the world's people also have impaired work capability because of iron-deficiency anemia. If calorie intake falls below requirements, the utilization of protein is impaired —since it must first provide energy for which calories normally account. The problem of chronic hunger is far from solved—and continues to prevent the elimination of infectious diseases, which were brought under control in the industrialized world long ago but still ravage the populations of the poor countries because malnutrition makes them vulnerable. Because of poor sanitation, adverse climate, some traditional health practices, lack of basic information and health facilities, and a disproportionate emphasis on curative and high-technology medicine for the urban elites, nutrition education and nutrition practices are much worse in the poor countries than in the developed world, where they are acknowledged to be inadequate. Moreover, nutrition programs that concentrate on the symptoms rather than the underlying systemic causes (poor income distribution, low agricultural productivity, the preemption of good agricultural land for cash crops by local or foreign commercial interests)[18] cannot make much lasting impact and often compete for funding with what the developing-country governments perceive as their (economic) development goals.

Population Growth. At its present annual rate of growth of roughly 2.6 per cent, the world's population of 3.8 billion is expected to double by the end of the first decade of the twenty-first century. Since the global food supply can keep pace during that period only through increased yields at constantly rising costs (unless there are technological breakthroughs or great production increases in the developing countries), the possibility of a Malthusian solution is ever present. Equilibrium is inevitable; the main question is whether it will come through low or high birth and death rates. The rate of population growth must be slowed, and the basic question is how to decrease the number of *wanted* children.

The motivation to have numerous children springs from personal, social, and economic considerations relatively untouched by the education and commodities that family-planning programs customarily provide. But

---

[18]It is possible, of course, that in certain places and at certain stages of development, cash-crop agriculture can be contributory to development.

there is no single or simple answer. At the 1974 U.N. World Population Conference, John D. Rockefeller III, a life-long supporter of population programs, acknowledged that

> the only viable course is to place population policy solidly within the context of general economic and social development. . . . This approach recognizes that rapid population growth is only one among many problems facing most countries, that it is a multiplier and intensifier of other problems rather than the cause of them. . . . It recognizes that motivation for family planning is best stimulated by hope that living conditions and opportunities in general will improve.[19]

The commonly cited food-population equation posed by the pessimists of the "triage" or "lifeboat" school[20] is a gross oversimplification. Population growth is not the only factor affecting the food problem from the demand side; affluent consumption patterns constitute an increasingly large percentage of the pressure, and disparities in income distribution are also reflected in disparities of food availability. In any case, birth-control policies can have no significant short- or even medium-term impact on food supply.

Fertilizer. The single agricultural input that received greatest attention at the World Food Conference and that is often thought to be the distinguishing feature of modern agriculture is fertilizer, whose vital role in production was emphasized at the Conference and has occupied the attention of such Conference follow-up bodies as the CGFPI since that time. While world production of fertilizer steadily advanced over the past few years, its use increased even more sharply, driving the price far beyond what farmers in the poor countries could pay. This remains the case even though international prices for nitrogenous fertilizers have dropped off by more than 50 per cent from the high points of mid- and late 1974.[21] This recent supply/price development severely and adversely affected several large importing countries, notably India, because farmers drastically cut their use of fertilizer. This was especially unfortunate given the fact that a unit of fertilizer applied to the soil in most less developed agricultural economies could produce more than twice the grain increment that it could in the industrialized agricultural economies. Recognition of this fertilizer dilemma by the World Food Conference resulted in a stepping-up of the International Fertilizer Supply Scheme of the FAO, greater efforts to improve the operating efficiency of fertilizer plants in the developing world, and

---

[19]John D. Rockefeller III, "Population Growth: The Role of the Developed World" (Speech before the Tribune, World Population Conference, Bucharest, Romania, August 1974), p. 4.

[20]See James W. Howe and John W. Sewell, "Let's Sink the Lifeboat Ethics," *Worldview*, October 1975.

[21]The price of the main nitrogenous fertilizer, urea, which had increased from $70 a ton in 1972 to more than $350 a ton in mid-1974, was quoted at $102 a ton at Gulf of Mexico ports at the end of 1975.

increased emphasis on investment in new capacity for fertilizer production in the developing countries—where both feedstocks and investment capital were expected to become more readily available from the OPEC countries. However, the sharp drop in prices is expected to discourage further investment for at least the next decade, unless the three major agricultural producers outside of North America—China, the Soviet Union, and India —suffer severe crop shortfalls at the same time.[22]

The above discussion by no means covers the full range of problems linked to the world's food predicament. Other related matters that deserve more extensive treatment than can be given here include: *environment* (the impact of developing-country agricultural practices on the ecosystems that sustain agriculture)[23]; *employment* (whether the "pull" of demand stemming from more jobs is more likely to increase the supply of food than the "push" of policy); *urbanization* (the stake of the growing numbers of urban poor in rural development); and *waste* (of both human and physical resources).

Hunger and Development

The world food crisis that burst into view in 1973 as a dramatic and compelling event simply masks the underlying and continually worsening problems of malnutrition, starvation, and hunger that are the essence of "underdevelopment." This permanent misery is more a matter for concern than the occasional disaster, for the latter tends to get handled, even if inadequately, while the former, being much more difficult, tends to get postponed. But how long can the world live on this knife-edge margin?

Hunger ultimately can be understood only in the context of development. While an essay on the world food situation may attempt to provide a calm analysis, it cannot escape becoming to some degree an outraged plea for action to alleviate the suffering of half a billion people—a task which is difficult but *feasible*, given the knowledge and resources at the disposal of the international "community." Food is, after all, a unique commodity; people eat or they die. They are hungry because they are poor; and they are poor mainly because they are relatively powerless. Most poor farmers already know how to farm better than they do; but they cannot afford the risk of failure frequently inherent in trying improved methods. A man at the margin of existence can only gamble with his own life—and the lives of his family. Until the poor farmer can protect himself against that risk (and others), until he participates effectively in the decisions that affect him, the quality of life of the rural poor—not to be equated with "productivity"—will not improve significantly.

---

[22]Fertilizer industry sources indicate that both China and the Soviet Union are expected to be self-sufficient in nitrogen fertilizer by 1980, which will remove them from the import market and may further depress prices.

[23]For a comprehensive treatment of the ecological problems that bear upon the food system, see Erik P. Eckholm, *Losing Ground* (New York: W. W. Norton & Co., Inc., 1976).

At root, the problem of hunger is a moral one. Hunger is a symptom; the disease is injustice or, if one prefers, underdevelopment. The problem of development is not solely, or even mainly, one of resource transfers or economic growth; it is ultimately a problem of human dignity, of having the power to decide *whether* and *in what way* one wishes to "develop." Those of us who live in the so-called developed world are "developed" to the extent that we are free and equal; development is not appropriately measured in terms of material possessions, but in terms of the quality of life. The genius of the founding fathers of the United States, whose rhetoric will be heard repeatedly during this bicentennial year, lay in their effort to make effective the philosophical principle that "all men are created equal." The basic equality is the equality to become what one's individual nature permits one to become. The person who is chronically hungry, chronically poor, chronically sick, chronically powerless—or "underdeveloped" in the sense in which we use it—does not have the possibility of realizing that equality to which we say he is entitled by nature. He is therefore the victim of injustice, and those of us who have the power to rectify that injustice also have the responsibility to do so. This is the meaning of morality with regard to world hunger. For the time being we have to feed the hungry; food aid buys us that time. Over the longer run, however, we have to help create the conditions that will make it possible for the hungry to feed themselves. This is what a well-conceived and wisely administered development assistance program—in conjunction with global economic reforms—would try to do.[25]

But not all the remedial action has to come from the industrialized world. One of the discontinuities of this age is the inadequate sharing of income *within* countries as well as between the developing countries and the industrialized world. To change that sharing by providing greater financial and policy support for the rural poor is the task of the governments of those countries. Nearly every World Food Conference resolution called upon governments to move toward land reform and changes in the power structure that would bring the small farmer into the decision-making process in both economic and political (social) matters (Resolutions I and II). It is increasingly clear that many developing-country governmental policies—on pricing, taxes, exchange rates, credit, movement of food in-country, research and extension, and land tenure—have a disincentive effect on the small farmer.[26]

---

[25]It should be noted that the United States has its own "less developed country" at home, consisting of the disadvantaged of all kinds—the poor, the minorities, the elderly; in our attention to the problems of the poor abroad, we cannot afford to ignore similar injustices at home. The bicentennial rhetoric should not blind us to the evidence of how far we fall short in the United States of fulfilling these noble principles.

[26]U.S. General Accounting Office, *Disincentives to Agricultural Production in Developing Countries*, Report to the Congress, Comptroller General of the United States (ID-76-2), November 26, 1975.

Even though it is probably not within the mandate—and is increasingly rarely within the power—of the industrialized world to effect inside the developing countries themselves the kinds of changes needed to solve the problem of world hunger, there are some steps that the United States and other developed countries need to take, both domestically and internationally, to legitimize the moral leadership that is still possible and that is desperately required if the world is to move toward securing the right to eat for everyone.

What should we do in the face of injustices abroad that we cannot ourselves correct? One response surely would be to put our own house in order—to correct the inequitable sharing of our common patrimony and our economic growth *within* the United States, which creates semi-colonial conditions for the thirty million poor and hungry who collectively constitute "the other America." A second would be to adjust our international trading practices so as to help increase the earning power of the rural poor abroad and thus move toward releasing them and their countries from increasing dependence on the "developed" world. A third would be to insist that the priorities we and other development "donors" have set for our programs be strictly applied so that the benefits actually accrue to the poorest segments of society, especially the small farmers. For the short run, a fourth might be to respond more affirmatively and generously to the central ethical question of whether we who have more than enough food should share it with those who do not—and to use our powers of persuasion in the marketplace of ideas to move others to that response.

What U.S. Food Policy?

Spokesmen for the Administration have claimed that the United States is serious about following up the recommendations of the World Food Conference and does have a coherent international food policy, consisting of 1) maximum production, 2) food aid, and 3) free trade. But there is some doubt attached to each of these planks. When *maximum production* threatens to produce a surplus over immediate consumption (which could replenish the world's depleted food stocks), the call to maximize is quickly muted. *Food aid* was reduced in 1973 and 1974 below previous levels—in fact to less than 3 per cent of all agricultural exports—and then was raised in 1975, but only after strong congressional and public pressure (and mainly to get a larger total out of which to supply the Indochina operation). Can it really be claimed that "*free trade*" is operative when soybeans are embargoed, when fertilizer shipments overseas are stopped for over half a year, and when the market is suspended while grain deals are negotiated with the U.S.S.R. and Poland?

As far as World Food Conference follow-up is concerned, the Office of Technology Assessment of the U.S. Congress noted on December 10, 1975, the difficulty of coordinating policy among the twenty-six Executive Branch offices and bureaus that have "some significant responsibility" in regard to food.[27] It is not difficult to understand why U.S. delegates to the bilateral grain negotiations in Moscow in September 1975, the eighteenth FAO Conference in Rome in November 1975, the Conference on International Economic Cooperation in Paris in December 1975, the multinational trade negotiations in Geneva and Tokyo, the periodic International Wheat Council meetings in London, and the upcoming fourth session of UNCTAD that is to convene in Nairobi in May 1976 do not have consistent guidelines to follow on food policy.

In the Congress, too, several committees and subcommittees have jurisdiction over or interest in food policy: the House Agriculture Committee, the House International Relations Committee, the Senate Agriculture and Forestry Committee, the Senate Foreign Relations Committee, the House and Senate Appropriations Committees, the Senate Banking, Housing, and Urban Affairs Committee, etc. Here, too, constituency representation often puts members of Congress at cross-purposes. A sorting out of these various policy inputs in both the Executive and the Legislative Branches is urgently needed.

Indeed, some steps already are being taken on both coordination and policy. On December 3, 1974, President Ford wrote to the president of the National Academy of Sciences enlisting its aid "in a major effort to lessen the grim prospect that future generations of peoples around the world will be confronted with chronic shortages of food and with the debilitating effects of malnutrition." The Academy responded by contracting with the National Science Foundation for a study by the National Research Council (to be submitted in June 1977), establishing a Steering Committee, and by presenting two interim studies to the President on November 10, 1975.[28]

In the absence of an organizing mechanism or a clear statement of priorities in the government, it is difficult either to forecast or to advocate a coherent, comprehensive U.S. food policy. Nevertheless, it would seem that a sensible policy should include at least the following elements:

1. U.S. food *production* should be maximized within reasonable ecological limits and its quality maintained and improved; restraints on food crops, such as rice, should be eliminated; a floor should be put under the prices the farmer receives for his products; range-fed livestock should be favored over grain-fed; no land should be held out of production as long as world food stocks have not been replenished to a point where there is global protection from any reasonable coincidence of bad harvests; availability of agricultural inputs should be increased and improved; and funds for agricultural research should go up sharply, with less emphasis on energy-

---

[27]E.A. Jaenke & Associates, Inc., *A National Food Policy: Requirements and Alternatives* (Paper presented to the U.S. Congress, Office of Technology Assessment Board Hearings, Washington, D.C., December 10, 1975) pp. 23-28.

[28]National Research Council, Commission on International Relations, *World Food and Nutrition Study: Interim Report* (Washington, D.C.: National Academy of Sciences, 1975); and National Research Council, Commission on Natural Resources, *World Food and Nutrition Study: Enhancement of Food Production for the United States* (Washington, D.C.: National Academy of Sciences, 1975).

intensive, nonnutritious "fast foods," synthetics, and marketing; and more on agricultural practices and processes (photosynthesis and nitrogen fixation).

2. While production is, of course, a prerequisite of having anything to distribute, *distribution* is more difficult to handle because it moves us even more deeply into the realm of politics; differences of opinion among politicians, economists, scientists, and technicians about production pale before the political debates on who gets what, when, where, how, and why. Yet both the priorities and the mechanisms for the distribution of U.S. food need to be reviewed to ensure that the needs of the malnourished and starving are given consideration before the total satisfaction of commercial market demand. The marketing of food should be improved by opening American markets to developing-country exports generally, and to agricultural products in particular; by monitoring financial transactions of U.S. grain-trading companies; by tightening the regulation of commodity markets and the supervision of shippers; and, if necessary, by considering the establishment of a national grain board.

This last issue raises a number of difficult problems for U.S. agricultural policy in general because of American dominance of the world's food supply. If the current U.S. grain marketing system were abolished or substantially changed, how would world grain prices be set? How could high production costs and surpluses from overproduction be avoided? Would a governmental marketing mechanism become dominated by parochial political interests to the detriment of producers and consumers, both here and abroad? Could it operate efficiently? The history of U.S. and other regulatory agencies over the past century does not lead to optimism about the ability of government to regulate private enterprise. There is, therefore, a need for a great deal more research and analysis on new mechanisms by which the price benefits of competition can be combined with the need to allocate grain supplies on some basis other than sheer ability to pay.

3. In the *development assistance* area, the United States should increase funds for technical assistance, training, and research in food, nutrition, and rural development; take the lead in building up a world food-reserve system; work actively in the World Food Council, the Consultative Groups, and other institutions attempting to implement the recommendations of the World Food Conference; support strongly the multilateral institutions and programs directed at genuine rural development and assistance to the small farmer; and cease to promote the export of high-technology, resource-depleting American agricultural practices to the less developed countries. It should also, in the short run, improve the Food for Peace Program (P.L. 480) as the new aid bill now provides,[29] particularly by increasing the grant component. The President should designate a significant share of this year's abundant harvest for people in need, either as food aid or as a food reserve. Doubling U.S. food aid would take less than 2 per cent of the expected crop. The ultimate determinant of food *aid*

---

[29]Public Law 94-161, op. cit., Title II.

has to be need, not ability to pay. If we can earmark 8 million tons of grain for the U.S.S.R., we should be able to do it for the poor as well.

4. Turning from public policy to *individual action*, the emphasis among Americans should be on the consumption habits generated by affluence. We out-eat Indians and others more than 5:1, and we out-consume the entire developing world by a much larger per capita ratio in energy, food, and natural resources.[30] This consumption pattern, which is putting a significant incremental strain on resources—perhaps even greater than the population growth rate—is essentially a problem we share with the rest of the industrialized world as well as with the small but growing emulative elites in the less developed countries. What is required is a reduction of consumption not only of food, but of other items as well, particularly energy—first, through a "war on waste," which should be a global priority; second, through improved nutrition education; and third, through a stress on the quality of life rather than the quantity of material goods amassed or consumed in the name of economic growth. We are also often reminded that more modest consumption is better for us in terms of reduced pollution of land, water, and air; a lower level of cholesterol from less grain-fed beef; a lessened incidence of diet-related illnesses, and a less frenetic life generally.

Conclusion

The achievement record in implementing the decisions of the World Food Conference is mixed; clearly there is a long way to go in this area and a need for continued vigorous private support. Global institutional organization for action has been improved; and, as noted at the beginning of this chapter, there is some basis for hope that the apparent mellowing of the atmosphere for the international discussion of these issues between the 1974 and 1975 Special Sessions of the U.N. General Assembly will pave the way for effective action. The World Food Council and the Consultative Group on Food Production and Investment have now launched their operations; there is some encouraging movement in the direction of establishing the International Fund for Agricultural Development; negotiations concerning a world food reserve are ongoing, if slow; the international food-aid target for 1975 was almost met; and the crop prospects for 1976 are good, with much more favorable weather in such critical regions as South Asia and the Sahel. The new U.S. foreign aid legislation represents a move toward fulfilling the prescriptions of both the World Food Conference and the Seventh Special Session of the U.N. General Assembly for a rapid increase in food production in developing countries.[31]

None of these hopeful developments, however, should provide cause for complacency. The world's performance clearly has not yet matched

---

[30]See Table B-19, p. 173.

[31]U.N. General Assembly, Seventh Special Session, Resolution 3362 (S-VII), September 16, 1975, section V.

the rhetoric of its leaders. We still have no clear indication that those leaders have the commitment to move actively toward reducing any of the glaring disparities between life in the developed and developing countries; and the food outlook for the long term is especially difficult.[32] The need to attack the food problem has changed little since the President's Science Advisory Committee analyzed the situation nearly a decade ago: "The scale, severity, and duration of the world food problem are so great that a massive, long-range, innovative effort unprecedented in human history will be required to master it."[33] Certainly there is an important and continuing role for congressional and private watchfulness and pressure.

U.S. action on the food issue—perhaps even more than on other development issues—is critical. The United States accounts for more than half the world's trade in grain. Our production in 1975 was roughly 200 million tons, and we fed more than 150 million tons of it to animals either in the United States or abroad through commercial sales. Yet we have not increased our food-aid pledge for the relief of the immediate human hunger problem, nor have we established a food-aid minimum sufficiently far ahead to permit recipient countries—or our own farmers—to plan ahead for distribution and use. We have not established a food reserve either nationally or internationally; and although negotiations on this particular issue currently are proceeding in various forums, we do not appear to be very far down the road. While the *authorized* funding level for long-term development aid a) is higher than in recent years, b) was passed by significant majorities in both houses of Congress, and c) incorporates many of the right reasons for providing assistance and the preferred modalities for allocating it, no funds have yet been appropriated for these purposes. Even if all these already authorized funds are made available and are expended effectively, the official development assistance of the United States will be hovering around 0.2 per cent of GNP, or less than a third of the development assistance target of 0.7 per cent set for the 1970s by the International U.N. Strategy for the Second Development Decade.

In the final analysis, the implementation of recommendations of the World Food Conference—which could go a long way toward solving the global food problem and the underlying "development" problem—is a test of the real commitment of *all* countries to this objective. Speaking to delegates from all over the world at the first World Food Congress in Washington in 1963—more as a world public figure than as an American president—John F. Kennedy said: "We have the means, we have the capacity, to eliminate hunger from the face of the earth in our lifetime. We need only the will." This essential policy component still appears to be missing on the part of the leaders of both the rich and the poor countries.

---

[32]U.N. FAO, *Mid-Term Review and Appraisal*, U.N. Doc. C 75/16, op. cit., p. 3.

[33]A Report of the President's Science Advisory Committee, May 1967, excerpted in Annex A of Douglas N. Ross, *Food and Population: The Next Crisis*, Conference Board Report No. 639 (New York: The Conference Board, Inc., 1974), p. 23.

CHAPTER III

Toward a Global Approach to the Energy Problem

James W. Howe

Two years ago, the United States embarked on a course that was intended by former President Nixon to achieve energy independence by 1985. His action was triggered by the oil embargo of the Organization of Petroleum Exporting Countries—an event that was viewed as so great a threat to U.S. security that the instinctive reaction of many Americans was to want independence from oil imports. Since then, however, it has become evident that, without new technological breakthroughs, complete oil independence would be prohibitively expensive even for the United States. It is clear, moreover, that such independence of oil imports simply is not feasible for the other industrial countries that are the allies and chief trading partners of the United States. Therefore, the U.S. energy policy debate is now focusing on *how much* energy independence should be sought—considering its high costs and considering the feasibility of making foreign sources more dependable, thereby decreasing the risks inherent in continued partial reliance on imports.

The central theme of this chapter is that the problem of human use of energy is intrinsically global; that a sound response to this challenge can best be developed on a global basis; and that if nations continue to attempt to solve the problem independently, they will all lose much time and capital. The need for such a shift in perspective on the energy question was recently highlighted by U.S. Senator Edward Kennedy:

> The time has come for a global approach to energy—in the development of energy resources *wherever* they are found, and

Note: This chapter was prepared with the assistance of James Bever, ODC research assistant, who contributed especially to the preparation of the technical section on the range of energy options available to the developing countries.

wherever the greatest economic benefit can come to mankind. We need to survey the world's energy needs for the future, and worldwide possibilities for development. For in the final analysis, there is no basic confrontation between today's producers and consumers. Rather there is a shared need for a long-term energy strategy that will meet global needs for the indefinite future.[1]

It is important to recognize that a global response could be effected at two levels—through *national* planning and actions undertaken with full regard for their global implications, and through *international* planning and actions. Currently decisions about energy are being made primarily at the national level—although much more can and should be done by existing (and yet to be created) international institutions. Action should be taken at both levels to help ensure adequate supplies of energy at reasonable prices to all nations. The costs of achieving that goal would be lower for all parties if they worked toward it cooperatively than if they persisted in "going it alone." Unfortunately, such a global approach is not now being followed.

To be sure, U.S. pursuit of independence would benefit the rest of the world to the extent that it reduced U.S. demands on foreign energy supplies or resulted in scientific discoveries that helped other countries produce or conserve energy. However, the risk of such a policy is that the United States might devote enormous resources to developing domestic energy sources which would not be economical from a global perspective, given the availability of lower-cost alternative foreign sources. In the long run, the whole world would suffer from the inefficient use of scarce resources and time if a less than globally optimal course of action were pursued solely because one nation had opted for independence.

As already noted, however, energy decisions at present are not made from such a global perspective but from a narrowly national one, and the two are often very different. In the short run, of course, it might actually pay the United States to develop a given source of energy whose cost of production was higher than that of a foreign source. Extracting oil by expensive means from a dying U.S. oil field might, for example, cost $9 a barrel, whereas a new field abroad might be developed to produce oil for one third of that amount; yet the cost of importing the latter into the United States might in fact exceed that of oil from its own high-cost well because the Organization of Petroleum Exporting Countries (OPEC) had succeeded in keeping world oil prices high. However, any assessment of the efficiency of resource use from a global point of view would find both U.S. investment in its own high-cost oil and the oil producers' cartel irrational. Given the potential importance of U.S. technology in helping to solve the world's energy problem, it is regrettable for all parties that the U.S. and global interests at present often are not perceived as convergent.

---

[1]Edward M. Kennedy (Address at the American Academy of Arts and Sciences Symposium on Arid Zone Development, Boston, Massachusetts, October 23, 1975).

The current mix of globally inefficient national energy policies is a part of the price the world pays for the oil cartel—a price that must be weighed against the value of the cartel in redressing—albeit very unevenly—previous inequities in global income distribution. In the longer run, if a more rational international economic order were to emerge (e.g., if energy were sold at prices reasonably close to costs), there would be an inherent compatibility of national and global energy interests, from which the entire world would benefit.

These observations are not offered as a condemnation of the goal of energy independence. In fact, it would be ideal if the technology were developed to permit nations and even localities to be truly energy-independent—i.e., to draw their energy needs from safe, clean, cheap, and renewable *local* sources such as sunshine, wind, waste products, or flowing water. However, the route to such eventual independence (if it is indeed technologically and economically feasible) is a cooperative international approach—without which a) there will be needless and costly duplication of research, and b) the potential of developing countries to make use of their unexploited petroleum, solar energy, and research capability will remain neglected.

Three multilateral approaches to energy are now under way. One is represented by OPEC, another by the International Energy Agency of the Organisation for Economic Co-operation and Development (OECD), and a third by the Energy Commission established by the Conference on International Economic Cooperation in December 1975. Neither of the first two efforts is global, and the danger of confrontation between them imperils the entire world economy. One ingredient missing in both is the participation of the oil-importing developing countries which, to be sure, do not now consume much commercial energy, but which contain most of the world's people—all dependent on energy. (Indeed, developing countries need as much help in obtaining an adequate energy supply as they do in obtaining an adequate food supply, yet there is no effort in sight in the energy field that is on a scale with international aid in the food field.) The third effort—the Energy Commission—does offer the possibility of a global approach. It remains to be seen, however, how fruitful the work of that group will be.

This chapter argues for a cooperative global approach to the subject of energy by both national and international institutions. For the United States, such an approach would have several advantages:

1. To the extent that it resulted in developing the least expensive sources of energy in the world, a global approach could reduce investments in energy alternatives; for the United States, which is currently heavily involved in such an effort, this could mean the saving of significant amounts of capital.

2. By increasing global supplies of energy and by developing sources in many nations, a global approach could make the international energy trading system much more dependable and help keep the price of energy close to its cost of production.

3. Similarly, by increasing the local production of energy in many oil-importing countries, a global approach could reduce these countries' demand on oil supplies elsewhere in the world. It makes sense to attempt to hold down U.S. energy prices by helping oil-importing countries develop economical domestic sources of energy, just as it does to try to restrain U.S. food prices by helping the poor countries grow more of their own food supply—a course of action the United States has adopted.

4. Because the poor countries must have energy to develop and because the United States has a stake in their development, it serves U.S. purposes to follow a global approach that does not neglect this large part of the world.

5. Whereas the route of confrontation between the OPEC and the OECD countries provokes retaliation and currently is one factor that encourages the numerous oil-importing poor countries to line up with OPEC to avoid further damage to their economies, the global approach offers the poor countries an alternative to lining up with either side. Because OPEC has relied on poor-country political support for its actions, strong disapproval by these countries of further sharp price rises could discourage further OPEC price actions. This restraining influence would also benefit large oil importers such as the United States.

Any advocacy of a global approach eventually must also deal with the socialist countries—which, as a group, are relatively well-supplied with energy (in contrast to food), and which traditionally have been reluctant to take part in global systems.[2] Is a "global" energy approach possible without them? Should it be deferred until their cooperation is assured, or should other countries go ahead without them? Probably the prudent course is to encourage their participation in global energy cooperation and to keep the door open, but not to delay cooperation while awaiting their entry.

A global approach also must take account of the current world energy-use picture. Several facts are salient in this connection. First, current global rates of use of several energy forms (oil, gas, wood, uranium) are such that supplies will be depleted within a few decades. This is a planetary problem calling for a planetary response. Second, the distribution of commercial energy use is very uneven—with the OECD countries (which account for only 18 per cent of the world's population) consuming some 60 per cent,[3] and the oil-importing developing countries (with close to half the world's population) consuming only 10-15 per cent.[4] Third, there is little concern for

---

[2] For example, most socialist countries do not belong to the World Bank, the General Agreement on Tariffs and Trade, the International Monetary Fund, or the U.N. Food and Agriculture Organization.

[3] See Table B-14, p. 166.

[4] One of the most notable defenses of this distribution pattern was made by former President Nixon in his 1973 speech to the Seafarers International Union: "There are only seven per cent of the people of the world living in the United States, and we use thirty per cent of all the energy. That isn't bad; that is good. That means we are the richest, strongest people in the world, and that we have the highest standard living in the world. That is why we need so much energy, and may it always be that way." (Quoted in *New Yorker*, December 15, 1975, p. 33.)

or understanding of the energy situation in poor countries, where about half of the energy used comes from noncommercial sources that are either directly available or traded at the village level (e.g., wood, crop debris, draft animals, and dung). The vast bulk of research on and development of new energy sources is related to such commercial forms as fusion, breeder reactors, and enhanced oil recovery, which have little applicability in many of the poorest countries.

The bulk of this chapter will be devoted to a discussion of six lines of action essential to a comprehensive, cooperative international approach to the world energy problem: 1) initiation of global planning and analysis, 2) improvement of the global effectiveness of energy research and development, 3) cooperative action to close the oil- and gas-drilling gap, 4) collective consideration of the nuclear option, 5) identification of other energy options available to developing countries and assistance with their energy policy choices, and 6) balance-of-payments assistance to the oil-importing developing countries. In order to take stock of the present energy condition of the planet and to stimulate a global approach to these six lines of action, it will be argued in the final pages of this chapter that a World Energy Conference should be convened in a few years, for which detailed preliminary work needs to be launched now. Each of these six points is discussed in the sections that follow.

1. Initiation of Global Planning and Analysis

One of the most useful results to emerge from the cooperative approach to the world food problem has been the development of a global food "balance sheet." Thanks to the work of the U.N. Food and Agriculture Organization (FAO), the U.S. Department of Agriculture, and others, statistics now are available on the current global volumes of food (using grain as the basic source of food), on total demand for food (both in market terms and in terms of human need), on the growth of supply and demand over time, and on the projected food deficit (as of certain future dates under varying assumptions as to grain production, population growth, and levels of affluence).

In the case of energy, a similar kind of global analysis is needed. We need to know current global consumption of energy. We need global projections under varying scenarios of affluence and poverty much like the projections of future U.S. energy consumption that were prepared by the Ford Foundation Energy Policy Project.[5] And we need global consideration of the disadvantages and advantages of several energy technologies—much like the analysis of U.S. energy options carried out by the Energy Research and Development Administration.[6] Each energy technology has enthusias-

[5]Energy Policy Project of the Ford Foundation, *A Time to Choose: America's Energy Future,* final report (Cambridge, Mass.: Ballinger Publishing Company, 1974).

[6]Energy Research and Development Administration (ERDA), *Creating Energy Choices for the Future,* Vols. 1 and 2 (Washington, D.C.: U.S. Government Printing Office, 1975).

tic—in some cases passionate—supporters. This is true of oil, coal, solar electricity, solar heating and cooling, wind, and nuclear sources. Few popular current-events magazines can be found that do not carry a story of a promising new solution. Yet global estimates on the productive potential and cost of each are lacking. For example, we are told that large windmill towers could be rigged off the Atlantic that could meet the power needs of New England. But we need to know more: What is the total global offshore or inland potential of wind (at a level that does not despoil the earth's lovelier vistas)? What would windmill-tower construction cost in money? In raw material supplies? In time? We need the same information about nuclear fission, nuclear fusion, geothermal energy, biogasification, solar heating and cooling, solar electricity, etc. Some analytical work of this kind is now being conducted by individual nations or groups of nations.[7] What is generally missing from these studies, however, is the global context, and for that reason they also are seriously deficient from the point of national interests. A global perspective should not be limited to analysis; as in the case of food (nearly a decade ago), an indicative world plan should be undertaken for energy that speculates knowledgeably about the advantages and disadvantages of the several technologies. How would various energy scenarios affect the global energy balance sheet? What implications would each technology have for other global and national problems (e.g., the ecosystem, income distribution, rural development, human fertility, urban decay, depletion of raw materials, soil erosion, etc.)?

Some tentative estimates should be prepared in the next few years as a kind of approximation of where the planet stands on energy. More reliable analysis and indicative planning would, however, require a permanent institution working on a year-round basis. That institution also could play a useful role by preparing energy policy studies and stimulating discussion and debate among nations, international bodies, and private experts on both international and national energy policy topics. Such discussion would be especially valuable to developing countries, which thus far have little expertise in energy policy.

2. Improvement of the Global Effectiveness of Energy Research and Development

Essentially all of the research and development of new energy technology is in the hands of the industrialized countries.[8] There have been some preliminary efforts to coordinate—or at least compare notes on—energy research

---

[7]For a sampling, see the reports prepared under the auspices of the Energy Policy Project of the Ford Foundation, as well as Organisation for Economic Co-operation and Development, *Energy Prospects to 1985* (Paris: OECD, 1974); Organisation for Economic Co-operation and Development, *Energy R & D* (Paris: OECD, 1975); ERDA, *Creating Energy Choices*, op. cit.; and Federal Energy Administration, *Project Independence Report* (Washington, D.C.: U.S. Government Printing Office, November 1974).

[8]OECD, *Energy R & D*, op. cit. This publication reviews the great volume and variety of energy research and development in the OECD countries.

and development among the OECD countries. These countries understandably see energy technology as a means of helping to solve their particular energy problems. The danger is that not enough research and development will be devoted to approaches that are of particular importance to developing countries. A further danger is that by leaving developing countries out of this sphere, some opportunities to gain from the research potential of these countries will be lost.

The approach used in the case of food again may be instructive in this connection. A formal network has emerged in that field which links the research and development efforts of a number of developed and developing countries on several crops, including corn, wheat, rice, and sorghum. Such linkages include, for example, joint research projects, advisory and training services, and exchanges of information, materials, personnel, and research results.[9] They focus widely dispersed research activities on a single goal, thus achieving great economy of effort. In the case of corn, for example, an international institute located in Mexico helps to coordinate the efforts of researchers in more than two hundred agricultural research stations throughout the world in pursuit of greater production of higher-quality corn.[10] Such a network, which would also be useful in the energy field, permits each participating country to put into the research effort as much as it can afford and to draw from it as much as it is capable of using.

The analogy between food and energy is, like all analogies, imperfect. For example, most of the world's food is produced and consumed in the developing countries, which is not true of energy. On the other hand, some of the most promising opportunities to produce more food exist in developing countries—which is also true of energy. The research facilities of the developing countries are not great in either food or energy, but because of natural factors, the optimal location for food research in some cases is in these countries. The same also may prove to be true in the case of certain energy sources, such as wind, ocean thermal differences, and sunshine. Particularly in the tropics, where those forms of energy that depend on sunshine are especially abundant, energy research probably would be especially beneficial. Because of that abundance, together with the relatively low costs of labor and in some areas also of land and local building materials, it might be cheaper to locate certain research facilities in the tropics. This would be particularly true if the facilities were operated jointly with the host country, which would put up part of the local costs of the project—much like the solar energy projects conducted in Niger with French assistance.[11]

---

[9]National Research Council, Commission on International Relations, *World Food and Nutrition Study: Interim Report* (Washington, D.C.: National Academy of Sciences, 1975), p. 13.

[10]Ibid., p. 15.

[11]These include solar water heaters, solar thermal electric stations, and solar-cell-powered television reception. See National Academy of Sciences (NAS), Ad Hoc Panel on Alternative Energy Sources for Developing Countries, *Renewable Energy Resources for Developing Countries*, draft 1975, sections IV-1, IV-2 (Washington, D.C.: National Academy of Sciences, forthcoming 1976).

Each of the developing countries needs to have an indigenous energy analytical capability to keep abreast of technological developments in the field, to advise its government on the formulation of a long-range energy policy, and to cooperate selectively with technologically advanced foreign institutions in local research on particular approaches that appear to have promise. Opportunities for cooperation within the network exist at several levels: a) between bilateral and multilateral aid programs and recipient governments on matters involving training and capital transfers, b) between energy research and development agencies in industrialized countries and specific projects or counterpart institutions in the developing countries, and c) between scientific institutes and institutions of higher learning in developed and developing countries. In addition, again following the model of food, institutions are needed to help coordinate and stimulate activities on given energy topics—such as wind, biogasification, coal liquefaction, solar heating and cooling, solar electricity, and energy conservation—either throughout a region or throughout the world. In some cases, *existing* institutions might undertake such roles either on their own initiative or at the request of technical conferences of experts on particular subjects.[12] In other cases, it might be warranted to create a *new* international organization—much as the International Maize and Wheat Improvement Center was established by private foundations in Mexico to serve as a research headquarters for corn and wheat and subsequently has come to be recognized as the leading institution on these topics. As the network of cooperative energy activities around the world proliferates, a need may arise for additional formal assignments of specific international leadership roles to existing international or globally recognized national institutions.

An international institution also will be needed to provide an overview of and financial support for the entire network. Such an institution could call attention to gaps, overlaps, and other imbalances in world energy research efforts. Perhaps the global planning institution recommended on p. 92 could also perform this overview.

A question may arise as to why the OECD, with much of the world's research and development capability in energy, should complicate matters for itself by extending its network to include the rest of the world. Would it not have to give to the extended network more than it gets back from it? This would undoubtedly be true while the network is being established and while the new research and analytical institutions of developing countries are gaining experience. But if the experience with the food research network is a reliable guide, there would come a time when the network began to pay back handsome dividends to the industrialized and developing countries alike. And even if repayment did not in every case justify the investment in terms of the energy research and development budgets of industrialized countries,

---

[12]Such conferences abound. For example, under U.S. government auspices, the Washington Center for Metropolitan Studies is convening a conference on bioconversion techniques in spring 1976.

it would repay them amply when their wider interests in world development were taken into account—for there can be no adequate development in the poor countries unless their long-term energy needs are met.

In any event, the cost of enabling the developing countries to partici-pate in the global energy research network—by supporting the capacity of their energy research institutions through the provision of technicians, training, and materials—would not be great in comparison with projected developed-country energy research and development outlays. The OECD estimates (on the basis of 1972 prices) that, over the next ten years, its member countries will spend between $1.3 and $1.8 trillion, from both private and public sources, on energy research and development.[13] In the context of these expenditures, it probably would be a prudent step to spend the relatively minor amounts needed to include the developing countries in the global energy research network. The socialist countries also should be encouraged to participate—although their relative affluence should enable them to finance their own research and development efforts.

3. Cooperation in Closing the Oil- and Gas-Drilling Gap

The exploitation of oil and natural gas involves very capital-intensive exploration, production, and transportation methods. Both oil and natural gas require centralized processing, marketing, and distribution systems, and can be distributed to consumers by pipeline or truck.[14] Natural gas is more difficult, dangerous, and costly to process and transport overseas than oil, although it can be converted (presently only at high cost) into safer, more convenient fuel forms such as methanol or methane gas. Unlike oil, natural gas is the cleanest and most flexible fossil fuel; it can be found associated with oil fields or in independent fields; and it also can be generated (at high cost) from oil or coal. Some developing countries which produce natural gas (in oil-associated fields) at present market less than half of it; they flare away the rest because of their present inability to utilize it in their domestic markets and because of the high costs and danger involved in exporting it. In other developing countries which could presently use more natural gas, the exploitation of domestic gas reserves has been limited by the low level of discovery and development.

It is estimated that oil and gas fields discovered to date are sufficient to last the world for two to three decades at present consumption rates. Proved oil reserves are heavily concentrated in the Middle East, North Africa, Venezuela, the United States, and the Soviet Union.[15] But this may be due to the fact that most of the exploratory drilling also has been concen-trated in these areas. For example, the United States, with only 5 per cent of the geologically oil-favorable area of the world, nevertheless has been the

[13]OECD, *Energy Prospects to 1985,* op. cit., p. 22.
[14]OECD, *Energy R & D,* op. cit., p. 31.
[15]OECD, *Energy Prospects to 1985,* op. cit., p. 89.

site of two thirds of all the world's oil wells to date, 8 times the number drilled in the U.S.S.R., and up to 300 times the number drilled so far in the geologically promising regions of Africa. Based on a comparison of geological conditions, the amount of potentially undiscovered oil and gas may equal or even exceed by several times the amount that has been discovered to date. The most promising regions for future exploration are located outside the OECD countries and the Middle East in a range of developing countries in Latin America, South Asia, and Africa (and their offshore areas).[16]

If it is true that such potential exists, an obvious priority is to drill more exploratory wells in these underexplored promising areas. Much of the drilling can be done by agreements between oil and gas companies and host governments—including service contracts, joint ventures, and other arrangements that hold a better prospect for enduring than the concessional agreements that are collapsing in so many parts of the world.

Many developing countries do not yet have the expertise to bargain effectively with oil and gas companies to obtain contracts that will not break down quickly once oil or gas is discovered because the contracting government feels it has gotten the worst of the bargain. It is in the interest of the host governments supplying the oil and gas, the private oil- or gas-drilling companies, and the home governments of the drilling companies that contracts be stable and therefore mutually satisfactory. Thus it is in the interest of all three parties (and of the potential consumers) that developing-country engineers, economists, scientists, and other experts be trained to help host governments arrive at acceptable contracts.

A great deal of innovation has been introduced in private contracting arrangements in recent years—much of it in the direction of ensuring the host country control of its oil resources and of the bulk of the profits from their exploitation. At the same time, these contracts leave room for the private oil companies to make a profit. One of the more common arrangements outside the OPEC area, for example, is a production-sharing contract, in which the private company puts up the risk capital and is repaid in oil for all its capital plus an agreed profit.

A climate of mutual trust must be created if the oil and gas companies and host countries are to cooperate in exploiting known geological potential. Host countries must be technically able to assure themselves that companies are living up to their contracts (e.g., actually producing those quantities which—given the capacity of the oil and gas basins and market conditions—will optimize earnings for the host country). Companies must have confidence that the host countries will adhere to the contract over a reasonable period of time. Otherwise they either may not be willing to agree

---

[16]Bernardo F. Grossling, *In Search of a Statistical Probability Model for Petroleum Resource Assessment,* U.S. Department of the Interior, Geological Survey Circular 724 (Washington, D.C.: U.S. Government Printing Office, 1975), pp. 3, 4. A publication to be released by the U.S. Geological Survey in spring 1976 will provide detailed data on the oil- and gas-drilling gap.

to a contract, or they may insist on a contract that will let them get their money back in a hurry, out of fear that it soon may be abrogated.

Moreover, the possibility of providing financing for some aspects of exploration through multilateral institutions—perhaps the World Bank or the U.N. Fund for Natural Resources (operating under U.N. Development Programme auspices)—should be considered. One possible specific use of such funds would be to finance geological work, including geophysical exploration, in those developing countries where so little data is available at present that private oil or gas companies are not likely to be interested in exploring. Whether a limited amount of exploratory drilling should also be financed by multilateral public sources is a topic that should also be considered. The services of oil and gas companies already are in great demand to explore in areas that are *known* to be promising. Now that the former lucrative arrangements based on concessions to private companies are no longer provided, however, these companies are not as willing to make large investments in geologically unknown terrain. In many African countries, for example, general geological conditions suggest oil or gas potential, but governments have virtually no data to pinpoint where exploratory drilling should be done. Once such preliminary work has been completed, private companies could be invited to undertake exploration. Multilateral financing is needed not only for loans, but also for technical advice, since many developing countries have little expertise in geology or any of the other aspects of petroleum discovery and production. In some cases a multilateral financing agency might be asked by a borrower to act on its behalf in contracting to get the geological work done. A second potential use of multilateral financing would be for insuring oil drillers against the above-mentioned political risk of having their contracts abrogated once oil has been struck. If such insurance could be purchased, oil drillers might become much more active in underexplored but geologically promising countries.

One mechanism for providing multilateral financing for these purposes might be a separate new fund, possibly located in an existing institution such as the World Bank or the U.N. Development Programme. A capitalization of $1 billion—or even less—for the next ten-year period probably would be adequate, even though the total cost of locating and learning something about the world's undiscovered oil and gas basins might be many times that figure. However, it does not all have to be discovered and proven at once. Nor does all of it have to be supported with multilateral government sources. If the facility operated as a revolving fund in making loans available to countries for exploration, it would eventually finance a great deal of essential exploration. To be attractive to the borrowing governments, the fund would have to be prepared to postpone or even write off repayment of exploration loans that did not discover oil or gas, but it would have to share in the windfalls where its loans struck it rich. The fund also could sell insurance to oil drillers against the risk of arbitrary contract abrogation in the wake of an oil discovery. Presumably such insurance would only be available for activities in member countries. Both the drillers and the member countries would be required to give the fund assurances against violations of contract. Only member countries would be eligible for assistance with geophysical exploration.

4. Collective Consideration of the Nuclear Option

In the near and medium term, nuclear energy, together with coal and hydroelectricity, are the chief alternatives to oil and gas as sources of power. Nuclear energy production in 1974 accounted for only 5 per cent of the world's installed electric generating capacity.[17] By 1985, however, nuclear reactors are projected to account for 25 per cent of worldwide total electrical energy, and by the year 2000, for 55 per cent.[18] At the end of 1973, there were 130 nuclear reactors in the world with a capacity of 50,000 megawatts (Mw), yet only 7 of these, totaling 2,000 Mw, were in operation in three of the world's low-income countries—India, Pakistan, and Spain. Over 250 nuclear plants on order or under construction for 1980 should contribute at least 220,000 Mw of energy and 20 per cent of total installed electric power. This total includes 23 reactors, totaling 15,000 Mw, ordered by ten low-income countries (Argentina, Brazil, Taiwan, the Republic of Korea, India, Mexico, Romania, Spain, Pakistan, and Yugoslavia).

Nuclear plants are extremely capital-intensive, with fixed charges on the capital costs of plants comprising the principal part of nuclear electric costs. Although nuclear plants have 1.5 to 2.5 times the capital costs of oil- and coal-powered electric plants, their fuel costs are one half to one sixth those of oil- or coal-powered plants, and they benefit from greater economies of scale. Their fuel-cost input, however, is dependent on the stability of world uranium prices and the availability and advent of new nuclear fuel technologies, which may occur as early as the 1980s. However, if new resources (or new technologies such as the breeder reactor, which uses fuel 50-70 times more efficiently than the currently used fission process) are not developed, then nuclear fuel costs may well rise sharply by the year 2000.[19] Without the breeder reactor, uranium supplies may not last much longer than oil.

The availability of the nuclear option to developing countries will be limited by lack of capital, the shortages and high costs of skilled manpower and management, shortages of global plant manufacturing capacity, and the fact that most plants, including those manufactured and marketed overseas by the United States, have at least a 600 Mw capacity, which is too large to be cost-effective for the small national electrical grid systems used in most developing countries. However, a 200-300 Mw heavy-water reactor has been developed in Canada that may be preferred by many countries not only

---

[17]Arthur D. Little, Inc., *An Overview of Alternative Energy Sources for LDCs,* Report to the U.S. Agency for International Development, Technical Assistance Bureau, Office of Science and Technology (Report No. C-77105, August 7, 1974), p. I-H-1.

[18]Obtained informally from World Bank sources.

[19]Obtained informally from World Bank sources.

because of its capacity, but also because it is not dependent upon enriched uranium fuels (which are produced only in a few countries, including the United States), as it can directly utilize local uranium resources instead.[20]

Officials of the World Bank estimate that fifteen to twenty low-income countries have national electrical grid systems large enough to economically use the 500-600 megawatt-range reactors. These countries account for the majority of the gross national product and population of the world's poorer countries. The fifteen are: India (which already has a nearly autonomous program), Brazil, Pakistan, Israel, Spain, Argentina, Egypt—none of which have ratified the Nuclear Non-Proliferation Treaty—and Taiwan, Greece, the Republic of Korea, Mexico, the Philippines, Romania, Thailand, and Yugoslavia.[21]

The spread of nuclear power plants will make the establishment and operation of an international safeguard system extremely complex and difficult. Nuclear technology has brought the world new problems to be solved and higher risks to be borne: the management of radioactive fuels and materials; the disposal of radioactive wastes; the dependence of many countries on foreign sources of technology, uranium, and fuel; the hazard of an accident or theft of fissionable material; the obligation to comply with international environmental and performance regulations and to submit to international monitoring; and the high requirements for manpower training and public education which go hand in hand with the introduction of such a new, potentially dangerous technology. The dilemma with nuclear energy is that *without* the breeder reactor to multiply the amount of fuel, uranium may be depleted in a few decades; but *with* the breeder, even greater quantities will be produced of the nuclear by-product plutonium—a material that is suitable for constructing nuclear weapons without very high technology and that is a serious security problem even at current low levels of production without the breeder. Forty-five countries are already known to possess 346 research reactors; the nuclear device which India exploded in 1974 was produced from such a reactor.[22] It is frightening to contemplate a world in which even more countries and perhaps even a number of private terrorist groups have nuclear weapons.

A major policy issue for developing countries is whether—and how far—to pursue the nuclear option, given all of these new problems. A major policy issue for the nuclear powers, on the other hand, is whether to encourage the developing countries to do so and what kinds of international constraints to impose on the use of nuclear power to minimize the dangers. For these reasons, the world's major nuclear materials exporters—the United States, the U.S.S.R., France, Germany, Britain, Canada, and Japan—met in London in November 1975 to agree on tighter safeguards to prevent purchasers of nuclear technology from diverting it to military uses.

---

[20]Little, Inc., *Alternative Energy Sources,* op. cit., p. I-H-17.
[21]Obtained informally from World Bank sources.
[22]"Accord Reported in Nuclear Sales," *New York Times,* January 4, 1976.

However, with every year that the present emphasis on the nuclear option continues, vast additional capital will have been invested in that technology, thus slowly committing the world to it. By the time the breeder becomes commercially available (if it does), the temptation to deploy it may be overpowering. A high-level international review of this course should be conducted as soon as possible and certainly long before the breeder is ready to be deployed. A World Energy Conference, which is called for later in this chapter, should be one of the forums involved in that review.

The possibility of utilizing nuclear fusion as a source of energy is a far longer-term option now under intensive study. Using virtually inexhaustible raw materials such as deuterium (an isotope of hydrogen found in abundance in sea water), nuclear fusion might one day produce vast quantities of energy. It is believed, but not confirmed, that the process, although certainly very capital-intensive, will be low in pollution and could also conceivably have low production costs. At best, the process will be proven technologically possible by the latter part of this century; thus it is not likely to become commercially significant for many decades.

5. Identification of Other Energy Options Available to Developing Countries and Assistance with Their Energy Policy Choices

Two years after the oil embargo, the United States is still struggling to decide what its long-term energy policy should be. The process is painful for the United States, despite its unparalleled advantages in the forms of enormous capital resources, possession of the world's most advanced technological capability, a stable government, and a wealth of natural energy resources. For most oil-importing developing countries—which do not have all of these advantages but do face a similar problem of formulating a long-term energy policy—the problem is more complex than for the United States. Most of these countries must consider two energy sectors: a) *commercial* energy (such as oil, gas, and electricity, which are bought and sold in large regional or national marketing and distribution networks), and b) *traditional or noncommercial* energy (such as firewood and draft animals, which are used on the spot by the producer or gatherer or traded only within the traditional village context).

Although the noncommercial energy sector has largely disappeared in the industrial countries, it is still very important in developing countries—a fact that is often neglected by both energy researchers and policy makers in developing countries. In much of the developing world, the traditional sector represents by far the larger share of the total energy consumed. One source estimates that it is comparable to the entire flow of crude oil among nations (about 30 million barrels a day).[23] In India, for example, the noncommercial

---

[23]Arjun Makhijani with Alan Poole, *Energy and Agriculture in the Third World,* A Report to the Energy Policy Project of the Ford Foundation (Cambridge, Mass.: Ballinger Publishing Company, 1975), p. 1.

sector provides about twice as much energy as commercial sources.[24] Energy from draft-animal power in India provided more than one third of all energy consumed in 1965-66—or more than the amounts provided by all commercial sources or all other noncommercial sources.[25] Other important sources of noncommercial energy used in developing countries include noncommercial fuels (mainly firewood, dung, and crop debris), use of the sun for crop drying, use of flowing water for small homemade hydropower units, and the use of wind for windmill-powered pumps.

The next several pages briefly examine a range of nonpetroleum, nonnuclear energy options that are a part of the total energy picture confronting the developing countries. For these (and other) countries, some of these options—most of which involve the use of renewable energy sources—provide short-run and/or long-run alternatives to costly, rapidly depletable petroleum, and to costly, potentially dangerous nuclear power. Another important option open to these countries (although, of course, on a smaller scale than in the developed countries) is the conservation of energy sources in both the commercial and traditional sectors.

The following survey, while necessarily superficial, nevertheless illustrates the urgent need of oil-importing developing countries for assistance in evaluating their energy options and in actually developing the selected options; it also assesses the potential of these countries to obtain needed energy supplies at a cost that would not—as it does in the case of imported oil at present—imperil or arrest their development progress. Of course, the successful application of any of these technologies in the developing countries would add to the global store of knowledge of energy alternatives, thus potentially benefiting rich countries as well.

The Coal and Geothermal Options. Two currently abundant but eventually depletable energy resources whose potential in the developing countries remains largely untapped are coal and geothermal sources.

Coal has been identified as a significant potential substitute for petroleum in many parts of the developing world, including some African countries, Brazil, Argentina, Chile, Turkey, Indonesia, Korea, and Taiwan. Botswana, Colombia, and Swaziland even show a possibility of export potential. To date, however, only India has made notable efforts to exploit its coal reserves.[26] Although the environmental and ecological problems that arise from coal burning, processing, and mining must be borne in mind, and control and corrective measures still need more research and application, coal lends itself well to a multitude of energy uses. Aside from its use for space heating, it may become competitive with petroleum as a source for

[24]Ibid., p. 23.

[25]International Bank for Reconstruction and Development, *Economic Situation and Prospects of India,* 3 Vols. (Report No. 402-1N, Asia Region, South Asia Department, May 7, 1974), Vol. 2, p. 20.

[26]Efrain Friedmann, "Energy Supply and Demand Outlook" (Paper presented at the meeting of the U.N. Economic Commission for Latin America, Santiago, Chile, September 2-6, 1974), p. 20.

A General Review of Global Energy Resources[a]

Energy Resource	Duration of Resource	Scale of Application[b]	Capital Costs[c]	Environmental Costs	Present Use of Resource in:		Potential Use of Resource in:	
					Industrialized Countries	Developing Countries	Industrialized Countries	Developing Countries
Oil	Depletable	Large	High	High	High	High	High[d]	High[d]
Natural Gas	Depletable	Large	High	Low	High	High	High[d]	High[d]
Nuclear (Fission)	Depletable	Large	High	High	Low	Low	High	Low[e]
Nuclear (Breeder)	Depletable[f]	Large	High	Unknown[g]	Pilot Projects	None	High	Low[e]
Nuclear (Fusion)	Unlimited[h]	Large	High	Unknown[i]	Experimental	None	High	Low[e]
Coal	Depletable	Large	High	High	High	Low	High	High
Geothermal (Surface)	Depletable	Large	High	High[j]	Low	Low	Low[k]	Low[k]
Geothermal (Subsurface)	Depletable	Large	High	High[j]	Experimental	None	High	High
Solar (Electric Cell)[l]	Renewable	Small	High[m]	Low	Specialized	Specialized	High	High
Solar (Thermal Electric)[l]	Renewable	Small	High[m]	Low	Pilot Projects	Pilot Projects	High	High
Solar (Flat Plate Collector)	Renewable	Small	Low	Low	Low	Low	High	High
Firewood (No Reforestation)	Depletable	Small	Low	High	Low	High	Low	High
Firewood (Reforestation)	Renewable	Small	Low	Low	Low	Low	Low	High
Dung and Crop Debris (Traditional Use)	Renewable	Small	Low	Low[n]	Low	High	Low	High
Dung and Crop Debris (Biogasification)	Renewable	Small	Low	Low[n]	Low	Low	High	High
Draft Animal	Renewable	Small	Low	Low[o]	Low	High	Low	High
Solar (Farming)	Renewable	Small	Low[p]	Low	Pilot Projects	Pilot Projects	High	High

	Renewable	Large/Small						
Rivers (Large Hydroelectric Projects)	Renewable	Large	High	High	High	High	High	High
Rivers (Small Hydroelectric Projects)[l]	Renewable	Small	High[m]	Low[q]	Low	Low	Low	High
Wind (Mechanical)	Renewable	Small	Low	Low	Low	Low	Low	High
Wind (Electric)[l]	Renewable	Small	High[m]	Low[r]	Low	Low	High	High
Ocean Thermal Difference	Renewable	Large	High	Unknown[g]	None	Pilot Projects	Low[s]	Low[s]
Tides	Renewable	Large	High	Unknown[g]	None	Pilot Projects	Low[s]	Low[s]

a Energy conservation is excluded from this table but is nevertheless subject to consideration as an important policy option, as are the recycling or processing of refuse, sewage, and industrial wastes for material recovery, fertilizer production, or generation of heat, gas, alcohol fuels, or electricity.

b Does the energy resource lend itself to small-scale, localized application for power production and distribution at the farm, village, or multi-village level, or does it necessitate large-scale collection, processing, production, and distribution systems on the regional or national level?

c Do the resource's exploitation, operation, and maintenance lend themselves to low cost, labor-intensive methods using local materials or domestic manufactures and local manpower, or do they require high capital cost, capital-intensive, high technology methods using highly trained manpower?

d Continued use expected to remain high although resource is threatened by depletion.

e Expected that 15-20 developing countries will be able to apply these technologies in a cost-effective manner in the foreseeable future.

f Breeder reactor, if developed, will use nuclear fuel 50-70 times more efficiently than conventional fission.

g Probably high.

h Assuming deuterium or similarly abundant isotope is used in the process.

i Probably low.

j Disposal of chemical by-products may be dangerous to local environment.

k Assumes most of world's geothermal steam resources to be tapped already.

l Assumes integration into large regional or national electric grid will not be cost-effective in the foreseeable future.

m Takes into account that manufacture of specialized photovoltaic devices and electric generators is a capital-intensive process.

n Assumes that residual of processing these for fuel is returned as fertilizer to the soil.

o Overgrazing could result if uncontrolled.

p Does not take into account some anticipated techniques such as hydrolysis, which is likely to be capital intensive.

q Many small hydroelectric units do not require dams, which may be damaging to the environment, since they can utilize naturally flowing or falling water.

r Large windmill towers might spoil the scenic beauty of some areas.

s Available only to coastal countries with appropriate coastal features.

ammonia-fertilizer production, for electric-power generation, for fuel and heating oils, and for pipeline- or tank-quality gas. The competitive advantages of coal-burning electrical plants over oil-burning plants depend upon the quantity and quality of coal reserves available and locational factors. Coal liquefaction into heating and fuel oils and gasoline, as well as coal gasification into either low-quality or pipeline-quality gas, are not currently economically feasible, but may become competitive by the 1980s with further technological development and higher petroleum and gas prices.[27]

Given current technology, however, the increased use of coal carries with it major dangers. These are in the first instance the dangers to the miners involved in coal extraction—as was dramatically illustrated by the recent disaster in India, in which hundreds of miners lost their lives—and second, the more widespread dangers to the ecology and the health of the consumer nations. For example, the phenomenon of acid rain, apparently associated with coal burning, needs to be understood better before the use of coal is intensified in highly populated areas.[28]

Geothermal sources of energy—steam, hot brine, and hot rocks—are available in areas of current or recent volcanic or earthquake activity. The exposed forms of these sources—such as hot springs and geysers—are easier to detect and exploit, but are localized in only a few widely distributed areas in the world. Subsurface sources of steam, hot brine, and hot rocks are available in greater abundance throughout the world but are far more costly and difficult to detect and exploit. Hot springs, hot- or moderate-temperature brine water, and steam can be utilized for electricity generation, indoor space heating, refrigeration, mechanical energy to operate manufacturing processes, and agricultural uses such as soil heating; they also are sources of potable mineral water and chemicals. Geothermal steam-turbine systems for electricity generation are currently available or under construction for commercial or experimental use in China, Mexico, the Philippines, Zaire, and El Salvador, as well as in some OECD countries.[29]

While most of the world's known exposed supplies of hot steam and hot brine water already are under exploitation, more exploration is needed in promising areas in many developing countries, especially in areas that are thought to be potential sources of hot rock formations. Such subsurface exploration at present involves very capital-intensive operations that clearly are beyond the means of some developing countries; less expensive exploration and drilling techniques are under investigation in the United States, but will not be available in the short run. Nevertheless, despite the costs inherent in exploration and drilling, which may range from $100,000 to $1 million per well, it appears that geothermal-generated electricity and steam heating can

---

[27]Little, Inc., *Alternative Energy Sources,* op. cit., p. I-F-12; also, Friedmann, "Energy Supply and Demand Outlook," op. cit., pp. 16, 17.

[28]National Academy of Sciences (NAS), *Mineral Resources and the Environment* (Washington, D.C.: National Academy of Sciences, 1975), pp. 237–51.

[29]Little, Inc., *Alternative Energy Sources,* op. cit., p. I-C-4.

be made available in selected areas at lower cost than conventional fossil-fuel-generated electricity and space heating, and in some areas could be competitive with hydroelectricity, largely due to lower capital costs, lower operating costs, and no fuel costs for the geothermal power facilities.[30] Thus the cost-effectiveness of geothermal energy exploitation can only be determined on a case-by-case basis.

The Renewable Solar Energy Options. For millions of years, the earth has received a daily supply of energy from the sun, some of which over time has been stored in fossil-fuel form as oil, gas, and coal. Until recent times, man's exploitation of these fuels has been so minimal as to not threaten the existing stock. For the past two hundred years, however, and especially since World War II, these resources have been used at such a quickening pace that concern is increasing that they soon will be depleted. Yet the sun continuously supplies the earth with various forms of renewable energy that are adequate to meet human needs many times over. Obviously, sooner or later human energy needs, now drawn mostly from stored energy—often at high economic, environmental, and even political costs—will have to turn to renewable solar energy. Unfortunately, most of the current U.S. government proposals for energy research and development would merely accelerate the use of stored energy, although attention to the renewable and inexhaustible sources is increasing.

Direct solar energy in the form of sunlight is the most abundant renewable source of energy available to the many developing countries located in the earth's torrid regions, where the intensity of sunshine is greatest.[31] It can be utilized for 1) generating electricity—by the action of sunlight on specially treated chemical plates or by focusing sunlight on water boilers to produce steam to turn electric generators; as well as for 2) water heating, space heating, and crop drying—by concentrating and conducting the heat in the sun's rays. Although the technologies for using solar energy directly for the generation of electricity still are in various stages of development and generally are characterized by limited economic applicability at the present time, technologies for water and space heating and crop drying are simpler and have already demonstrated a growing commercial appeal in a number of countries, for example the United States and Japan.

The direct conversion of sunlight into electricity by means of silicon solar cells is currently employed in the United States for outer space applications, and in the United States, Japan, and some other countries for a variety of highly specialized purposes, such as lights on floating ocean buoys, for which other sources are inapplicable or less efficient. However, the production and application of solar cells is too expensive for widespread applicability at the present time.[32] Furthermore, the amount of electricity

[30]NAS, *Renewable Energy Resources,* op. cit., sections II-7, VI-7.

[31]Ibid., section IV-1, p. I-G-1; also, Makhijani with Poole, *Energy and Agriculture,* op. cit., p. 96.

[32]Friedmann, "Energy Supply and Demand Outlook," op. cit., p. 23.

generated by each cell is so low that large surfaces must be covered with these cells to generate any significant amounts of energy. Finally, the problem of storage of electrical energy for use at night and on cloudy days limits the ability of solar cells to replace other sources of energy even for household appliances such as pumps and stoves.[33] It is likely, however, that the economic competitiveness and adaptability of solar cells will be greatly improved with further research and development efforts. Moreover, if there were greater demand for solar cells by large governmental institutions, such as the military and the civil service, it would help to cut costs of production.[34]

Electricity also can be generated by a solar-thermal electric process—by focusing direct or mirror-reflected sunlight onto a water boiler. The boiler then produces steam to operate a turbine generator, which in turn yields electricity. This method is being experimented with in the Soviet Union, the United States, Israel, and West Africa. However, the costs of solar-power units such as these are currently very high, limiting their economic application to areas where the only alternatives are short-lived and high-priced conventional engines requiring expensive fossil fuel.[35]

The development of a device known as the solar flat plate collector to absorb direct sunlight and conduct the heat via air or water has made it possible to use solar energy for a wide variety of purposes other than the generation of electricity. Solar crop dryers using the flat-plate-collector technique have been designed for use in the United States, Turkey, Canada, Brazil, Australia, India, and Trinidad. Technologies for using solar energy to heat water for domestic household application are undergoing growing commercial use in Japan and, to a much lesser extent, in Australia, the United States, Israel, and a number of other countries. Likewise, the flat-plate-collector technology has served as the basis for designs and experimental applications for space heating and cooling, household refrigeration, and rather capital-intensive desalination processes.[36] Although these technologies currently are at the pilot-project or experimental stage—or only in embryonic stages of commercial use—they eventually may become applicable at the village or agro-industrial level in the developing world.

In addition to the above uses of direct solar energy, there are a number of *indirect solar energy* sources—some of which are already economical while others are still in various stages of experimentation. These renewable energy sources include several that are dependent on nature's process of photosynthesis (firewood, crop residues, animal dung, and algae and other

---

[33]Some of these problems could be solved by situating the production unit in space and beaming electricity to earth as microwave power. Proposals to do so are now being discussed by scientists. See, for example, Gerard K. O'Neill, "Space Colonies and Energy Supply to Earth," *Science*, Vol. 190, No. 4218 (December 5, 1975), pp. 943–47.

[34]David Morris, "Solar Cell Energy," *Washington Post,* November 11, 1975.

[35]NAS, *Renewable Energy Resources*, op. cit., section IV-1.

[36]Ibid.

green plants), as well as wind, ocean thermal differences, rivers, and tides.[37] Except for the last two sources, these indirect forms of solar energy are most plentiful in the many developing countries located in the earth's torrid zone. The potential for deriving usuable energy from each of these sources is discussed in the sections that follow.

A little-known energy crisis exists in the noncommercial sector in many developing countries as a result of the ever growing demand for and shortage of *firewood*, which is used by 90 per cent of the population of the developing world as the chief fuel for warmth, cooking, household chores, and cottage industries. Wood is different from many other energy sources in that it is a rapidly renewable resource that lends itself well to local adaptation. Fast-growing varieties have been developed to be economically usable within ten years after planting.[38] Expanded reforestation programs for firewood are desperately needed, together with increased control, protection, and public-information measures to preserve and monitor the economic use of this increasingly valuable resource. Reforestation has a low-to-negligible capital cost, no fuel cost, and a low cost per unit; lends itself well to labor-intensive methods and decentralized application; and offers a renewable source of energy for a large part of the developing world.

Biogasification of agricultural *crop residues* and *animal dung* is an important technology for the conversion of green plants and the waste of animals that have eaten green plants into useful forms of energy in the villages and farms of the developing world. The technology that is currently available for this process appears to be economical and to have great potential for widespread application throughout the developing world; its special advantage is that it produces not only a quality gas fuel but also an organic fertilizer in readily usable form. The biogasification process involves the breaking down of crop residues and animal dung by anaerobic bacteria into simple organic compounds which are then eventually converted to a mixture of methane gas and carbon dioxide which, in turn, can be further processed into methane gas similar to pipeline-quality natural gas. Biogasification units have been built by the thousands on individual farms in India, where they have provided a cheap source of energy for household purposes. The gas derived from this process can be stored in tanks and used either for electricity generation or (in bottled gas form) as a fuel for farm machinery, cooking, or refrigeration. Furthermore, biogasification units reduce the costs of importing natural gas and transporting it from ports to rural areas.

---

[37]These diverse sources are all forms of renewable *solar* energy because of the sun's crucial role in their availability. Firewood, crop debris, animal dung, and algae and other green plants are all products of the photosynthesis process, for which sunshine is essential. The wind is a product of differences in solar intensity on various parts of the earth. The heat of the sun's rays is responsible for the thermal differences between the warm surface waters and the cold deep waters of the oceans. The sun also causes the atmospheric evaporation of water, which contributes to its continuous recycling on land in the form of rivers and supplements the moon's influence on the ocean's tidal movements.

[38]Erik P. Eckholm, *The Other Energy Crisis: Firewood* (Washington, D.C.: Worldwatch Institute, 1975), pp. 5, 14.

The residue of undigested materials serves as an excellent organic fertilizer which can be used for high-yielding seed varieties, especially when mixed with phophorus and potassium from local mining, wood ashes, or imported sources.[39]

Solar farming, which involves the growing, harvesting, and processing of certain *high-energy-content species of green plants,* including various algae, is another potentially inexpensive and ecologically harmless source of energy for human use. Although it is still in an experimental phase, current testing indicates that in some cases these techniques can be applied successfully on land, in inland water bodies, the sea, and special man-made ponds without competing for available land with food crops or timber. Some experiments have involved harvesting, drying, and either a) burning the plants to produce heat or steam-generated electricity, or b) fermenting the plants in anaerobic tanks by using biogasification or similar techniques to yield methane gas and alcohol fuels. Other lines of experimentation have involved either the growth of anaerobic microorganisms and the processing of their metabolic by-products into alcohol fuels, or the growth of photosynthetic algae capable of producing molecular hydrogen, which can be collected and used as fuel.[40] In Israel, scientists have succeeded in their experimental efforts to produce high-grade fuel oil from algae grown in saline pools.

Currently, hydroelectricity generated by the flowing water in *rivers* accounts for about 44 per cent of the electricity needs of the developing countries and for 24 per cent of those of the industrialized nations.[41] Moreover, the developing countries have a greater untapped potential of hydroelectric power than the developed countries, especially in Africa, but also in Latin America and south central Asia. The hydraulic turbine is now used extensively for generating electricity and lends itself well to use in both large-scale projects, such as the Aswan Dam, or small-scale local village projects, such as those introduced widely throughout China. The costs of the small-scale projects can be kept down by using reinforced concrete, wood, and local materials wherever possible.

In some areas of the developing world, potential sources of cheap hydroelectric power remain untapped. Some of the global implications of this potential—as well as the implications of the lack of a global approach to energy development and use—are illustrated by present distribution patterns of aluminum production. Africa, for example, has one third of the world's hydroelectric potential (but only 2 per cent of the world's installed capacity); it also has 50 per cent of the world's known reserves of bauxite, a raw material essential to aluminum production. In many African countries—for example, Guinea, Ghana, Tanzania, Mozambique, Cameroon, Malagasy,

[39]Makhijani with Poole, *Energy and Agriculture,* op. cit., p. 111.

[40]The above discussion is largely taken from NAS, *Renewable Energy Resources,* op. cit., sections V-5, V-6.

[41]Friedmann, "Energy Supply and Demand Outlook," op. cit., p. 22.

and Zaire—bauxite deposits are located near existing or potential sources of very cheap hydroelectricity. Yet for many years the United States, for example, has subsidized its domestic aluminum industry with electricity at rates of as little as one third the cost of production in an effort to keep the industry located in the United States. This, of course, has increased the cost to the U.S. taxpayer and (from a global perspective) wasted scarce energy. Many of the African countries mentioned above have the potential to make hydroelectric energy available at rates as low as one seventh the costs of electrical energy used in the U.S. aluminum industry.[42] Thus the African countries with this potential and the industrialized countries might well explore ways to make the most of these differences in comparative advantage—by, for example, encouraging the relocation of these energy-intensive aluminum plants on mutually beneficial terms.

The age-old technique of harnessing *wind* through the windmill is still an underutilized option in the developing world. Yet the windmill is well suited to the needs of many developing countries because it is a relatively cheap and simple technology designed for small-scale local construction and use; because it requires little repair or maintenance and has a ten- to twenty-year lifetime; because it can be built mostly of local materials; and because it lends itself well to use for electric generation or mechanical energy for compressing air, for cottage industries, and for agricultural uses such as pumping water for irrigation, land reclamation, or watering livestock.[43] Moreover, wind activity tends to be greater in the land and sea areas between 10 and 20 degrees north and south of the equator, especially near coastal regions—an area encompassing a large number of the world's developing countries. Although the technology for large-scale wind-power systems for use in nationwide electrical grids is within the realm of possibility, it appears that such a large-scale grid application is still not economically competitive with conventional energy sources.[44]

Certain ocean areas of the world have been identified as suitable for the generation of electricity through a process that depends upon *ocean thermal differences* between surface water warmed by the sun and cold water in the deep ocean clefts directly below. The surface water is pumped into low-pressure boiler tanks (in which water boils at low temperatures) to produce steam, which in turn operates turbines to produce electricity. The cold water is pumped up from below and used to condense the steam back into liquid form. Since the cold water is also rich in nutrients, including phosphate-bearing organisms, it can be stored in pools on land to grow nutritious shellfish and to produce phosphates for fertilizers.

---

[42]Stanton Smith, "Equity for Africa's Raw Materials Producers" (Paper prepared for the Symposium on Changing Vistas in U.S./African Economic Relations, Washington, D.C., March 21, 1975).

[43]NAS, *Renewable Energy Resources,* op. cit., section V-3.

[44]J. Peter LeBoff, "Wind Power Feasibility," *Energy Sources,* forthcoming; and Ernest Peterson, "Wind Power," *Science,* Vol. 185, No. 4150 (August 9, 1974), p. 480.

Coastal or island regions in which both warm-water currents and deep water or deep crevices in the ocean bottom are located close to shore—the Caribbean, the east coast of Africa, South Asia, the South Pacific except west and south Australia, and East Asia south of Japan—would be potential sites for adaptation of such a technology. Although some experimentation with this capital-intensive technology was conducted in the 1930s in Cuba, in the 1950s in the Ivory Coast, and is currently in progress in the U.S. Virgin Islands, the process is still only in the pilot-project stage.[45]

Improved technology for harnessing the energy of the flow of *tides* in and out of estuaries has made tidal energy a somewhat less expensive resource, although not even the recent increases in oil prices make it competitive with conventional power sources, due to the high costs of plant construction. Machinery is now available that overcomes the time-dependent nature of tides by pumping water into a storage reservoir, making it feasible to meet electricity demand as needed. A reversible turbine generator has been designed to harness both tidal inflow and outflow. Together with the development of high-voltage transmission lines, these advances enable electrical energy to be produced and distributed with this continually renewable energy source in those areas where topography is suitable and electric-line grid systems can be developed to reach the market. Tidal energy projects now exist in France and the Soviet Union, and studies indicate that potential for tidal-power development may exist in many coastal developing countries, although its cost-effectiveness can only be determined after much more intensive study at the individual country level.[46]

The Option to Conserve Energy by Avoiding Wasteful Processes. In addition to considering the nonpetroleum and nonnuclear sources identified above (including the options involving increased use of coal, geothermal sources, direct solar energy, and the range of indirect solar energy sources), the developing countries could benefit by adopting a more rational approach to energy conservation at their present stage of energy use—rather than later, as is being done belatedly in the developed countries. It should be noted at the start that conservation steps in the oil-importing developing countries would not involve limiting the expansion of efficient uses of energy (for transportation, production, comfort, etc.), but rather the avoidance of waste.

Little is known about opportunities to conserve energy in developing countries, but some observations on this subject can be made on the basis of work that has been done in the United States. The four basic areas in which energy can be conserved are the residential, business, transportation, and industrial sectors.[47] Most oil-importing developing countries are located in

[45]Roland D. Paine, Jr., "Power without Pollution," U.S. National Oceanic and Atmospheric Administration Reprint, Vol. 1, No. 1, January 1971.

[46]Little, Inc., *Alternative Energy Sources,* op. cit., section I-B.

[47]Energy Policy Project of the Ford Foundation, *A Time to Choose,* op. cit., p. 46. The "business" sector is generally referred to as the "commercial" sector. However, since the term "commercial" in the context of this chapter also refers to any energy that is bought and sold as part of a large-scale marketing distribution system, the term "business" is used here instead.

the tropics, where the heating of private dwellings is limited to a wood fire a few times of the year, and where the heating and cooling of buildings still is mostly confined to modern hotels and retail businesses in large cities. Thus, with the exception of some developing areas that lie outside the torrid zone or at high altitudes (e.g., Korea, Argentina, and Chile) and some modern cities (e.g., Sao Paulo), there are few opportunities for decreasing the use of commercial energy in residences and businesses. However, where the use of noncommerical energy still predominates—as in the villages of the developing world—there are some potential long-term opportunities for energy savings through, for example, the substitution of stoves for fireplaces or open fires for cooking purposes.[48]

In most developing countries, the large automobile is not an important energy consumer, and hence a large saving is not available in the transportation area. Other opportunities to save energy in the transportation sector without taking a toll on development vary among developing countries but are small in comparison to, for example, those of the United States.

In the United States, the greatest energy savings are possible in industry—through more efficient steam generation,[49] especially at electrical power plants; better recuperation and reuse of heat now discharged as exhaust gases or waste materials; more efficient industrial processes (especially in the manufacturing of paper, steel, aluminum, plastics, and cement); and greater recycling of material waste.[50] It may be assumed that industrial processes in developing countries are no less inefficient than in the United States, and that the opportunities for energy savings, relative to output, are at least as great. Thus a major effort to achieve such savings would include a) making sure that any new industrial plants take advantage of the latest energy-saving processes; b) reducing waste at power plants by locating them, when feasible, at the site where industrial process steam is needed; and c) using human labor in place of equipment whenever this is judged desirable after careful assessment of all the costs—social as well as economic. Many developing countries are not yet committed extensively to an existing industrial infrastructure, and this gives them the opportunity to profit from the energy-wasting mistakes made by the industrialized countries over the years.

Choosing the Best Options. In choosing the most desirable mix of energy resource options and conservation alternatives, the governments of the developing countries must, like all nations, weigh both short-term and long-term considerations. They must decide the difficult questions of what importance to assign to the commercial energy needs of the modern sector of their economies relative to the energy needs of the traditional rural sector,

---

[48]Makhijani with Poole, *Energy and Agriculture,* op. cit., p. 71.

[49]Energy Policy Project of the Ford Foundation, *A Time to Choose,* op. cit., p. 66.

[50]In both the developed and developing world, especially in areas of population concentration, some energy could be saved through greater recycling of refuse and sewage into usable materials (e.g., recycled paper, metals, and fertilizer), and some energy could be generated by processing refuse and sewage to produce heat, gas, alcohol fuels, and electricity.

where most of their people still live. And they must weigh these choices in the light of domestic as well as international economic, environmental, and (inevitably) political considerations.

A partial list of the kinds of energy policy choices facing a typical developing country might include the following:

1. To what extent should it permit its economy to follow the footsteps of the rich countries (toward further dependency on liquid fuel and the internal combustion engine), and to what extent should it take what might require very disruptive steps to begin to direct it along different lines?

2. How much of its limited managerial and policy attention should it devote to commercial energy problems, and how much to the noncommercial, traditional energy arena?

3. Similarly, to what degree should it rely on a national power grid (with its advantages of scale of power generation and its disadvantages of heavy cost of transmission lines), as compared with diffused generating sources closer to the point of consumption?

4. How much should it emphasize the needs of rural areas and agriculture versus urban areas and industry in the allocation and pricing of energy?

5. To what degree should it seek to conserve energy by avoiding certain types of capital-intensive (and therefore to a certain extent energy-intensive) "modernization"?

6. In which cases is it economically warranted and feasible—from a management and capital point of view—to pursue the option of nuclear power generation?

7. Under what circumstances should it undertake those energy-intensive stages of processing raw materials—e.g., bauxite into aluminum —now performed in developed countries which, under the pressure of energy shortages, are considering exporting such stages?

8. What should be its policy on working with oil companies to explore for petroleum within its jurisdiction?

9. How should it approach the myriad of energy-use choices that abound at the local level? The complexity of possible alternatives can be illustrated by a brief look at the use of dung and crop residues in rural areas. A country, a community, or even an individual might be presented with the following kinds of decisions: Should it feed crop residues to animals, burn them directly for heat or power generation, or process them to produce methane gas? If the latter, should it use the gas directly for heat and internal combustion power, or indirectly for generating electricity? If it feeds the crop residues to draft animals, the latter produce more dung and more draft power. Dung, like crop residues, can be burned, used as fertilizer, or processed for methane. After residues or dung produce methane, the resulting slurry is in some ways a more valuable (chemically available more quickly) fertilizer than it was before the methane was drawn off. Burning residues for electricity produces electricity more cheaply than going through the methane process, but it does not leave anything for fertilizer. These are

not unimportant questions, since crop debris, dung, and draft-animal power constitute the largest source of energy available to many developing countries.

The above list only hints at the complexity of the choices confronting the developing countries. Moreover, these countries have little or no capacity to develop new technological solutions, which, after all, are the great hope for solving energy problems. This is indeed a severe constraint which, together with their lack of capital, underscores the extreme dependence of most of the oil-poor developing countries on the rest of the world.

A great deal of research needs to be done to identify and put into perspective the elements of sound energy strategies for developing countries. There is room for work by individual scholars, by research institutions and governmental bodies in developing countries, by energy research agencies in developed countries, by bilateral and international aid agencies, and by new energy institutions yet to be created at the international level. The U.S. Energy Research and Development Agency (ERDA)—among others —should launch a vigorous program of support for such policy research.

But the basic task is one for the governments of developing countries. To design a sound energy policy, such countries will need to have a great deal of expertise in energy technology, energy economics, and energy planning. Given the current shortage of such expertise in the developing countries, bilateral and multilateral development assistance agencies may find no higher priority in many countries than to respond to requests for such training. In some cases it might be useful for aid agencies to furnish teams of experts to do an initial energy survey with action recommendations.

This review of new sources of energy and opportunities to conserve it suggests that it may be possible for many developing countries to avoid the blind alley in which the OECD countries find themselves. According to ERDA, the United States is largely dependent on oil and gas and must eventually change to another basic technology in order to be able to use inexhaustible sources of energy when they become available. That will require large-scale and hopefully gradual conversion of much of the industrial, commercial, and agricultural infrastructure of the developed countries. If the developing countries could bypass at least some of this oil and gas dependency, they (and the entire world) would profit from the savings thus achieved.

6. Balance-of-Payments Assistance to the Oil-Importing Developing Countries

The chief victims of the world's energy crisis have been the developing countries—about 80 of which are dependent on imported oil. And for most of these countries, less energy means slower development. At the beginning of the decade of the 1970s, it was hoped that the 6 per cent growth rate achieved by most of the developing countries in the 1960s could be maintained. This hope would have been jeopardized by the energy crisis alone, even if the latter had not been accompanied by a drop in developing-country export earnings and by continued increases in the cost of their other imports. This convergence of adverse circumstances greatly weakened the already poor development prospects of these countries. The payments and development crisis of the poorer oil-importing developing countries is more fully summarized in the overview essay of this volume (pp. 5-7).[51]

In the short run, developing countries must balance their energy imports (mostly oil) with their means of payment. In the long run, they must make investments in energy sources that will keep imports of energy from costing more than they can afford. The balance-of-payments deficit unfortunately may prevent them from making the investments to achieve energy viability in the long run.

The OPEC countries have expressed concern about the crushing burden inflicted by their actions on the poorest countries, and some of them have sought to alleviate the damage by increasing their flows of aid.[52] In 1974 these flows reached an estimated $2.2 billion, and in 1975 they may have reached $4.5 billion, still far short of matching the $10 to $15 billion oil-price burden on oil-importing developing countries[53]—especially since much of the aid went to Egypt and Syria, which are net oil exporters.

The richer OPEC nations may wish to consider action analogous to the precedent set by the United States in selling some of its food to poor countries under the P.L. 480 program. Under that program, food is sold at market prices to needy countries on low-interest terms that allow the purchaser a long time to repay. Such an approach to oil sales would have the following advantages: a) it would provide immediate relief (in fact, it would prevent the damage from occurring in the first place), whereas regular aid programs would take years to deliver after the damage had taken place; b) it would give relief to the oil-importing developing countries in exactly the amounts needed to prevent damage; c) it would not be as difficult to administer as an aid program; and d) OPEC would eventually be paid for its oil, but on terms suitable to the capability of the purchaser.

Of course, not all of the deficit of the oil-importing developing countries is caused by the rise in the price of oil.[54] Much of it is due to the price rises of imports from industrialized countries and to the loss of sales to their recession-hit industrialized customers. Industrialized countries, like the OPEC countries, have an obligation to undo the damage caused by their price rises. Many of the proposals discussed at the Special Session of the U.N. General Assembly in September 1975—proposals that are under con-

---

[51]See Tables B-7, p. 158, and E-2, p. 194.

[52]Aid is here defined as those resource transfers that have a 25 per cent grant element comparable to "official development assistance" as defined by the Development Assistance Committee of the Organisation for Economic Co-operation and Development. See Tables E-16, p. 212, and E-17, p. 213.

[53]Robert S. McNamara, "Address to the Board of Governors," September 1, 1975 (Washington, D.C.: World Bank, 1975), p. 6.

[54]See Tables B-5, p. 156, and B-6, p. 157.

sideration in the World Bank, the IMF, the Paris Conference on International Economic Cooperation, UNCTAD, and other forums—are intended to bring such relief; they are analyzed in the overview essay to this volume (pp. 8-9, passim) and are not taken up here. The actions needed by OPEC are discussed in this chapter because they are appropriate to its topic of energy.

Proposal for a Global Review of Energy: A World Energy Conference

The challenges presented to all countries by the global energy situation are highly complex. This brief examination raises a number of questions and makes a few suggestions, but offers a firm answer to one question only: Should nations seek to resolve their energy problems singly, or should they approach the problem cooperatively, looking for answers that serve each nation by meeting the needs of all of humanity? The latter approach, although it may entail some short-run sacrifices, is the surest and most economical way for every nation to achieve its energy goals.

To stimulate and symbolize the need for such cooperation, a World Energy Conference[55] should be held within the next few years. Here again, the food field may serve as a model. As Chapter II shows, the World Food Conference held in Rome in late 1974 succeeded in focusing world attention on the global food problem and reached some significant agreements. Part of the reason for the success of the Conference was its comprehensive preparatory work, which was carried out over a period of several years and included pioneering work not only by international institutions but also by national agencies, notably the U.S. Department of Agriculture. One or two years of comparable intensive work by international and national agencies are needed in preparation for a World Energy Conference.

What results might one expect from such a Conference? Several topics are suggested for its consideration and action.

Examination of the Elements of a World Energy "Balance Sheet." How much energy might the world need to consume in 1985? In the year 2000? Beyond? Under what alternative scenarios with respect to distribution, extremes of austerity and luxury, and ecological and public health risks? How can these energy needs best be met? How much longer will it be prudent to live on *stored* energy—the "debit" side of the global energy "budget"? What steps are necessary, and when, to move toward the use of solar or other *inexhaustible* energy sources—the "current income" side of the global energy "budget"? The balance sheet should include global calculations on how much of human energy needs could be supplied by, for example, wind, thermal gradients, solar electricity, solar heating, and biogasification; it should also summarize the capital and time requirements for each.

---

[55]"World Energy Conference" should not be confused with the private organization of the same name, with headquarters in London, which meets every three years and focuses attention largely on technologically oriented topics.

Consideration of Whether Any New International Energy Institutions Are Needed. Secretary of State Kissinger in his statement to the Seventh Special Session of the U.N. General Assembly (and later in his December 16, 1975 speech to the Conference on International Economic Cooperation) proposed the creation of an International Energy Institute. Its duties have not yet been clarified in detail but evidently would include the training of personnel from developing countries in energy analysis and policy studies. One can identify at least five kinds of tasks that need to be performed by one or more international energy authorities:

(a) Global energy analysis and indicative planning (the energy balance sheet);

(b) International energy policy studies and the stimulation of international energy policy discussions and debates on such topics;

(c) Studies of national energy policy options and the stimulation of international discussion on such topics;

(d) The monitoring, support, and coordination of the global network of energy research and development; and

(e) The training of energy policy experts from developing countries.

International discussion and debate is needed to resolve the issue of what institutions are needed. For example, should all five of these tasks be performed by one agency—e.g., the International Energy Institute proposed by the U.S. Secretary of State? Or should they be divided between two agencies—e.g., a World Energy Council for the first three policy-oriented tasks and another institution, such as an International Energy Institute, for the last two technical and research-oriented tasks?

Discussion of Global Research and Development Efforts on Energy. The Conference should have before it a competent review of the energy research priorities of industrialized countries that comments on whether or not those priorities are optimal from a global point of view. It should undertake to agree on a resolution stating the changes which it believes the industrialized countries should make in their energy research and development programs—e.g., whether they should give increased attention to unconventional sources of energy or to other sources of particular applicability to developing countries (such as solar energy) and whether they should physically locate more of their research efforts in the developing countries, perhaps undertaking them jointly with host governments or host-country institutions of higher learning. The Conference should review the status of the international energy research network described earlier in this chapter and debate whether additional research topics should be added to the network; whether those already in the network are adequately dealt with; and whether any basic changes of approach are needed in the network.

Discussion of the Need for Special Measures to Close the Petroleum-Drilling Gap. In preparation for the Conference, there should be a series of meetings among petroleum experts, drilling companies, oil companies, government representatives, and others to debate and build a consensus on what can be done to ensure that the oil and gas resources of those countries with geologically promising terrain are indeed developed. If those meetings develop a consensus, the Conference should review, debate, change (if necessary), and adopt that consensus as a global policy objective. If no consensus is presented to the Conference, it should spell out a new process for developing and reaching agreement on a consensus among these groups and should give guidelines to the participants in that process.

Discussion of the Problems Involved in the Use of Nuclear Energy. If the Conference is held within the next two years, this probably will be too early for it to also have before it a document representing a consensus of interested nations on the many difficult problems of nuclear energy. However, it should have an unofficial agenda of the elements of the problem. The Conference could perform a useful role by debating the problems and agreeing on a forum or a process and a timetable for further consideration and resolution of these problems. One of the specific questions the Conference will need to consider is how the work of the International Atomic Energy Agency fits into the process.

Discussion of Aid Efforts Related to Energy. The Conference should consider several questions in this area. First, should the OECD, OPEC, and socialist countries be doing more to alleviate the effects on developing countries of recent economic trends? Second, are the policies of the several bilateral and multilateral aid agencies giving adequate support to developing countries on their long-range energy problems? Should they finance more research on new sources of energy? Is more training needed? Third, what can aid agencies and multilateral organizations do to help poor countries develop effective and orderly energy policies? Would aid-financed international study and debate of the several energy options be useful to developing countries? Would aid-financed energy surveys be useful? The Conference also should attempt to agree on a resolution summarizing any changes recommended in the energy activities of the several aid agencies.

This chapter has urged that nations treat the energy problem as a global one that will best be solved through a global approach. That approach must seek to extend financial support to the energy-poor nations most burdened by the associated problems of inflation and recession; to help them develop coherent energy policy choices; to help them find and develop petroleum resources in underexplored areas; to work cooperatively in evolving a safe global policy on nuclear energy; to develop a world network of research and development efforts that will take advantage of all of the world's human and natural resources; and to nurture the intellectual and institutional capabilities to think about and plan *globally* for the human use of energy on this planet.

STATISTICAL ANNEXES

Florizelle B. Liser

Contents

NOTE TO THE ANNEXES

Some Facts of Interest

Annex A: The Global Poverty-Affluence Spectrum. The gap between the world's poor and its affluent is wide and growing wider. It is a gap in wealth and opportunity that exists between nations as well as within nations. The discrepancies in the distribution of global wealth are depicted in a number of ways and from a variety of perspectives by the tables in Annex A.

1. While the developing countries' share of world population has increased, their share of the world's wealth, export earnings, and expenditures on health and education has declined in the period 1960 to 1972 (Table A-9).

2. In 1973, over one hundred developing countries (with 50 per cent of world population) accounted for 14 per cent of the global gross national product; some twenty-five developed countries (with only 18 per cent of world population) accounted for 66 per cent of global GNP; and the centrally planned economies (including both developed and developing countries and having 32 per cent of world population) accounted for 20 per cent of global GNP (Table A-2).

3. Of the world's 3.8 billion people, over half (54 per cent)—all living in Africa, Asia, and Latin America—have per capita incomes under $200 per annum; hundreds of millions of these people exist on annual incomes of less than $75. In contrast, most of the 15 per cent of the world's population with incomes over $3,000 a year live in Europe and North America (Tables A-10 and A-11).

4. World Bank estimates indicate that the prospects for increasing the income of the world's poorest people during the present decade are bleak: over the ten-year period 1970-1980, the per capita income of the billion people living in the poorest nations is expected to increase by only $3, from $105 to $108. During this same period, the per capita income of the 725 million people living in the middle-income developing countries (excluding the OPEC countries) will have increased by $130 (from $410 to $540), and per capita income in the developed countries will have increased by some $900, from $3,100 to $4,000 (Table A-12).

5. Table A-13 shows the distribution of wealth *within* a number of countries; it indicates that neither high income inequality nor low income inequality is restricted to rich or poor countries alone. Moreover, tables A-4 through A-7 show that some of the low- and middle-income developing countries that have attained a relatively low level of inequality have also been far more successful than others in meeting the essential physical needs of their populations. Among these countries are the People's Republic of China, Sri Lanka, the Republic of Korea, and China (Taiwan).

6. Per capita and national income figures alone are not adequate indicators of the gap existing between the world's affluent and its poor. Other considerations such as birth and death rates, average levels of literacy and education, life expectancy, availability of natural resources, and access to trade with other countries must also enter into any assessment of relative advantage and disadvantage. For example, while Gabon's petroleum revenues have rapidly raised its per capita income from $880 in 1972 to $1,310 in 1973, only 12 per cent of its population is literate and its child mortality rate is high (24 per cent of its annual deaths are children under five years of age). Similarly, although both have annual per capita incomes of $120, Sri Lanka and India have markedly different literacy rates: 76 per cent in Sri Lanka compared with 34 per cent in India (Tables A-3 through A-7).

Annex B: Food, Fertilizer, Energy, and Minerals. In an increasingly interdependent world, a rapidly growing world population as well as affluent consumption patterns affect both present and future generations. Each person added to the world's population, as well as any one person's excessive consumption, exerts an increasing claim and burden on the world's scarce food, energy, minerals, and other resources. Worldwide recession and inflation and unexpected increases in the prices of such essential items as grain, fertilizer, oil, and minerals have adversely affected both developed and developing nations and have been particularly debilitating for the latter.

1. In 1975, world grain reserves (measured in terms of daily world consumption requirements at present population and consumption levels) amounted to a food supply of 35 days for the entire world. The preliminary estimate for 1976 is that reserves will decline to 31

days' supply. These recent reserve levels contrast sharply with those of the past; in 1961, for example, world grain reserves amounted to 105 days' supply (Table B-1).

2. While U.S. earnings from its agricultural exports rose from $6.1 billion in 1965 to $21.3 billion in 1974, the proportion of food assistance under Public Law 480 (the Food for Peace Program) as a percentage of total U.S. agricultural exports has dropped over the same ten years from 26 per cent to 4 per cent. In 1975, U.S. food assistance as a percentage of total agricultural exports increased to 5 per cent (Table B-3).

3. In 1974, developing countries imported approximately the same amounts of grain and oil as in 1973 and slightly lesser amounts of manufactured fertilizer; yet they paid $575 million more for fertilizer imports, $5 billion more for grain imports, and $10-$12 billion more for oil imports (Tables B-5, B-6, B-7, and B-8).

4. The developed nations also have been hard-hit by the rise in oil prices. Although the United States depends on imports for only 37 per cent of its oil needs, the European Community countries depend on imports for 98 per cent of their needs and Japan for 100 per cent of its needs. The worldwide additional cost of oil imports as a result of recent price rises has been estimated to be $65.7 billion (Tables B-8 and B-11).

5. North America, Western Europe, and Japan—which together comprise 18 per cent of the world's population—consume over 55 per cent of the world's energy and (except for the United States) are dependent on imports for over half of that consumption (Tables B-11 and B-14).

6. The United States is somewhat more advantaged than other developed countries in the minerals area as well. While the European Community and Japan are completely dependent on imports of such crucial industrial raw materials as nickel, tungsten, and to a lesser degree copper, the United States depends on imports for 72 per cent of its nickel needs, 68 per cent of its tungsten needs, and only 6 per cent of its copper needs (Table B-18).

7. Tables B-16 and B-17 show that the developing countries are the major world suppliers of vital raw materials (often supplying over 90 per cent of world exports of a commodity) and that world prices of these unprocessed raw materials tend to fluctuate; in the past three years, these fluctuations have been particularly extreme.

8. Because average per capita consumption of foods, energy, and raw materials is higher in developed than in developing countries, the costs in 1970 of fulfilling the natural resource requirements of the 7.7 million population increase in developed market economies were equal to those of fulfilling the requirements of the more than five times greater population increase (43.2 million) in developing countries (Table B-19).

Annex C: World Trade. The developing countries today obtain almost 80 per cent of their foreign exchange from export earnings; 10 per cent is made available through official flows of aid; and another 10 per cent comes from private capital and investment—making trade a more crucial factor in the development prospects of the poor nations than aid or investment. The tables in Annex C reflect the importance of trade to the developing countries, as well as the differences among these countries in the amount of foreign exchange available to them as a result of their different resource endowments and export capabilities.

1. In 1974, the total exports of the industrial market economies amounted to $526.1 billion and represented 62 per cent of the value of world exports. In contrast, the exports of developing countries in 1974 amounted to $232.8 billion and represented only 27 per cent of the value of world exports; this was more than double the 1973 value of developing-country exports, which amounted to $109.4 billion or 19 per cent of the world total (Table C-1).

2. In 1975, the oil-exporting developing countries, which account for about 58 per cent of the value of total developing-country exports, had a trade surplus of $98.5 billion. The exporters of other minerals accounted for about 5 per cent of total developing-country exports and had a trade surplus of $2.4 billion. All other developing countries accounted for approximately 38 per cent of the value of total developing-country exports and had a combined trade deficit of $28.3 billion (Table C-4).

3. The composition of trade differs among various groups of countries: exports of manufactured products comprise 74 per cent of the total exports of developed market economies and 60 per cent of those of the centrally planned economies; in contrast, 74 per cent of the exports of developing countries are primary products. Yet more than 60 per cent of the total imports of both developed and developing countries are manufactured products (Table C-3).

4. The effect of developed-country trade barriers on exports is suggested by the estimate that if the barriers to nine selected primary commodity exports were removed immediately, the

annual export earnings of developing countries would increase by some $7 billion by the end of the decade (Table C-5).

5. In its trade with other countries, the United States in 1975 had a $6 billion deficit with the OPEC countries, a $2 billion surplus with the Fourth World countries, and a $3 billion surplus with all other developing countries (Table C-7).

Annex D: World Military Transactions. World military and arms expenditures have risen from $142 billion in 1963 to $270 billion in 1973.

1. Even at a time when they have been severely affected by increases in the cost of essential imports and/or foreign exchange shortages, many nations are allocating 1-5 per cent (and often more) of their GNP for military expenditures (Table D-2). In some cases, per capita public military expenditures exceed those for education (Table A-7).

2. Between 1968 and 1973, the countries of the Middle East and North Africa increased their share of total world major weapons purchased from 16.8 per cent to 47.4 per cent; the Far East share declined from 36.5 per cent to 22.4 per cent. In 1973, the United States provided 54.5 per cent of all major weapons sold (Table D-3).

3. In 1975, the United States provided $1.3 billion in military aid (a drop from the 1973 military aid level of $4.6 billion, due mainly to the end of U.S. involvement in Indochina) and received weapons sales orders of $9.5 billion (of which $6.2 billion were from developing countries) for future delivery. The United States is the predominant supplier in this area (Table D-1).

Annex E: Resource Flows. The deterioration of their external financial position in 1974 has caused many developing countries to become increasingly reliant on external inflows of capital (Table E-2).

1. The current account deficit of the non-OPEC developing countries in 1974 totaled $30.6 billion (more than three times the 1973 deficit of $9.4 billion). Of that amount, the countries designated by the United Nations as "most seriously affected" (MSA) by balance-of-payments difficulties accounted for $8.7 billion. The estimated 1975 deficit is $45 billion, of which $12.7 billion is attributable to the MSA countries (Tables E-3 and E-4).

2. Of all non-OPEC developing countries, only 29 borrowed in Euro-currency and international and foreign bond markets to ease balance-of-payments difficulties in 1974, and only three of these were countries having per capita incomes under $200. Euro-currency borrowing amounted to $6.7 billion; borrowing in international and foreign bond markets (both public and private) totaled $162 million (Tables E-5 and E-6).

3. Of the seventeen OECD Development Assistance Committee (DAC) members, only Sweden has met the Second U.N. Development Decade target of providing official development assistance equal to 0.7 per cent of its GNP a year. Total official development assistance from all DAC members in 1974 was $11.3 billion, or 0.33 per cent of their combined GNP (Tables E-7, E-8, E-10, and E-11).

4. In 1974, U.S. disbursements of official development assistance equaled $3.4 billion, representing 0.25 per cent of GNP and ranking the United States thirteenth among the seventeen DAC members; this contrasted with $4.2 billion spent on barbershop, beauty-parlor, and bath services; $12 billion spent on household cleaning and polishing preparations; and $22.9 billion spent on alcoholic beverages (Tables E-8 and E-12).

5. Since DAC began to record levels of private voluntary assistance in 1970, the level of assistance from member countries has been increasing (from $858 million in 1970 to $1.2 billion in 1974). However, the 1974 figure represents a drop from the 1973 level of $1.4 billion, largely attributable to the unusually high U.S. figure of $905 million (43 per cent of which was contributed by the United Israel Appeal in response to needs raised by the 1973 Middle East war). In 1974, U.S. private voluntary agencies contributed $735 million, ranking the United States third (after Switzerland and Sweden) in its private aid as a percentage of GNP (Tables E-9, E-10, and E-11).

6. Official development assistance *commitments* from OPEC members totaled $5.3 billion in 1974. Of the $3.8 billion committed bilaterally, over 60 per cent was pledged to Arab countries (Table E-17). *Disbursements* of assistance (both concessional and non-concessional) from OPEC members equaled $4.5 billion in 1974; and concessional assistance alone (that is, official development assistance) amounted to $2.2 billion, or 1.7 per cent of their combined GNP (Table E-16).

7. In 1974, the OPEC countries invested 27 per cent of their $68 billion current account surplus in the United States and the United Kingdom (Table E-18).

8. Commitments of aid from the Soviet Union, the Eastern European countries, and the People's Republic of China dropped from $1.6 billion in 1973 to $1.3 billion in 1974. Argentina, Syria, and Pakistan received over 65 per cent of the 1974 aid commitments (Table E-15).

Explanatory Notes

The members of the Organization for Economic Co-operation and Development (OECD) are Australia, Austria, Belgium, Canada, Denmark, Finland, France, the Federal Republic of Germany, Greece, Iceland, Ireland, Italy, Japan, Luxembourg, the Netherlands, New Zealand, Norway, Portugal, Spain, Sweden, Switzerland, Turkey, the United Kingdom, and the United States. The Development Assistance Committee (DAC) is a specialized committee of the OECD whose members periodically review the amounts and natures of their aid programs and consult each other on their development assistance policies. Except for Greece, Iceland, Ireland, Luxembourg, Portugal, Spain, and Turkey, all members of the OECD are presently members of DAC.

The various agencies that are the sources of the data provided in the Statistical Annexes that follow differ in their classifications of countries. The World Bank, the United Nations, the General Agreement on Tariffs and Trade (GATT), the U.S. Agency for International Development (AID), and DAC (of the OECD) do not agree in all instances on whether to call particular countries "developed" or "developing." Examples of such variations are provided by the cases of Greece, Spain, Turkey, Yugoslavia, Malta, and Israel. The United Nations considers the first four to be "developed" and the latter two "developing." The GATT considers only Israel a developing country. In contrast, the World Bank, AID, and DAC categorize all of them as developing. Differences among these sources also arise from the fact that some of them provide data for more nations than do others; for example, territories and small islands are not always included in the totals. In spite of variations among the data sources, efforts were made to be consistent throughout these Annexes with classifications set out in Table A-7.

Official development assistance (ODA) is defined by DAC as "those flows to developing countries and multilateral institutions provided by official agencies, including state and local governments, or by their executive agencies, each transaction of which meets the following tests: a) it is administered with the promotion of the economic development and welfare of developing countries as its main objective and b) it is concessional in character and contains a grant element of at least 25 per cent." ODA is comprised of 1) soft bilateral loans, 2) bilateral grants, and 3) multilateral flows in the form of grants, capital subscriptions, and concessional loans to multilateral agencies.

Aid commitments are obligations or pledges; disbursements are actual payments. Gross disbursements minus amortization (i.e., repayment of principal) paid on past loans are equal to "net disbursements" or "net flow." Net disbursements minus interest payments on past loans result in "net transfers." Net commitments are equal to gross commitments minus amortization.

As a result of rounding, the "totals" shown may not always be equal to the sum of the other figures. An entry of "n.a." signifies that the information was not available.

The Global Poverty-Affluence Spectrum

A-1. Estimated Population with Insufficient Protein/Energy Supply, 1970 (millions and percentages)

	Total Population (*millions*)	Population with Insufficient Protein/Energy Supply (*millions*)	Population with Insufficient Protein/Energy Supply (*percentages*)
Developed Countries[a]	1,072	28	3
Developing Countries[b]	1,755	434	25
Latin America	284	36	13
Africa	279	67	24
Near East	171	30	18
Far East[b]	1,021	301	30
World[b]	2,827	462	16

[a]Europe, North America, U.S.S.R., and Japan.
[b]Excluding Asian centrally planned economies.

NOTE: The table is based on the daily per capita supply of grams of protein and kilocalories contained in the food locally available.

SOURCE: United Nations World Food Conference, *Assessment of the World Food Situation: Present and Future* (Rome), Doc. No. E/CONF. 65/3, November 5-16, 1974, pp. 66 and 102.

A-2. Gross National Product and Population, 1973 (percentages)

	GNP	Population
North America	30.0	6.1
Europe (excluding U.S.S.R.)	31.8	13.2
U.S.S.R.	10.7	6.5
Asia (including Middle East and excluding Japan)	10.2	52.7
Japan	8.3	2.8
Central and South America[a]	5.2	7.9
Africa	2.4	10.2
Oceania	1.5	0.6
Total	100.0	100.0
Developed Market Economies[b]	65.7	17.9
Centrally Planned Economies[c]	20.2	32.0
Developing Countries	14.2	50.1
Total	100.0	100.0

[a]Includes Mexico.
[b]Australia, Austria, Belgium, Canada, Denmark, Finland, France, Fed. Rep. of Germany, Iceland, Ireland, Italy, Japan, Luxembourg, Netherlands, New Zealand, Norway, Portugal, Puerto Rico, South Africa, Sweden, Switzerland, United Kingdom, United States.
[c]Albania, Bulgaria, People's Rep. of China, Cuba, Czechoslovakia, Dem. Rep. of Germany, Hungary, Dem. Rep. of Korea, Mongolia, Poland, Romania, U.S.S.R., Dem. Rep. of Vietnam.

NOTE: In 1973, world GNP was $4.8 trillion; population was 3.8 billion.

SOURCE: Based on *World Bank Atlas, 1975: Population, Per Capita Product, and Growth Rates* (Washington, D.C.: World Bank Group, 1975).

A-3. Per Capita GNP, 1973
($)

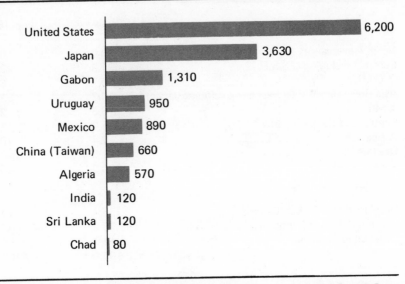

United States	6,200
Japan	3,630
Gabon	1,310
Uruguay	950
Mexico	890
China (Taiwan)	660
Algeria	570
India	120
Sri Lanka	120
Chad	80

SOURCE: *World Bank Atlas, 1975: Population, Per Capita Product, and Growth Rates* (Washington, D.C.: World Bank Group, 1974).

A-4. Deaths of Children under Five as a Percentage of Total Deaths[a]

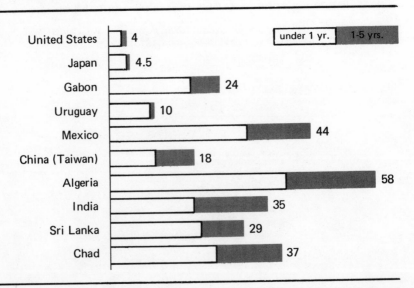

	under 1 yr.	1-5 yrs.
United States		4
Japan		4.5
Gabon		24
Uruguay		10
Mexico		44
China (Taiwan)		18
Algeria		58
India		35
Sri Lanka		29
Chad		37

[a]Data are the most recent available for each country.

SOURCE: United Nations, Department of Economic and Social Affairs, *Demographic Yearbook, 1973*, Table 16, pp. 290-317.

A-5. Death and Birth Rates per 1,000, 1970–1975 Average

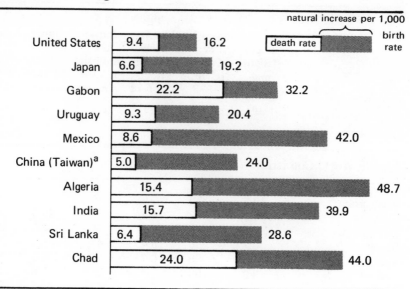

natural increase per 1,000

death rate | birth rate

Country	Death rate	Birth rate
United States	9.4	16.2
Japan	6.6	19.2
Gabon	22.2	32.2
Uruguay	9.3	20.4
Mexico	8.6	42.0
China (Taiwan)[a]	5.0	24.0
Algeria	15.4	48.7
India	15.7	39.9
Sri Lanka	6.4	28.6
Chad	24.0	44.0

[a]Estimate.

SOURCE: Population Reference Bureau, Inc., "1975 World Population Data Sheet" (Washington, D.C.).

A-6. Literacy (percentages)

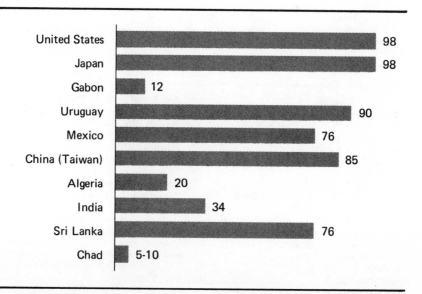

Country	Literacy
United States	98
Japan	98
Gabon	12
Uruguay	90
Mexico	76
China (Taiwan)	85
Algeria	20
India	34
Sri Lanka	76
Chad	5-10

SOURCE: U.S. Agency for International Development, Bureau for Population and Humanitarian Assistance, *Population Program Assistance: Annual Report, FY 1973* (Washington, D.C.: U.S. Government Printing Office, 1973), pp. 162-67.

A-7. Selected Social and Economic Indicators of Development, by Groups of Countries

	Population, mid-1975	Per Capita GNP, 1973	Per Capita GNP Growth Rate, 1965-73	Life Expectancy at Birth, 1970-75 Average	Birth Rate per 1,000, 1970-75 Average	Death Rate per 1,000, 1970-75 Average
	(mil.)	($)	(%)	(yrs.)		

Fourth World Countries

Afghanistan	19.3	90	0.9	40	49.2	23.8
Bangladesh	73.7	80	-1.6	36	49.5	28.1
Bhutan	1.2	60[a]	-0.2[a]	44	43.6	20.5
Botswana	0.7	230[a]	6.4[a]	44	45.6	23.0
Burma	31.2	80	0.7	50	39.5	15.8
Burundi	3.8	80[a]	1.4[a]	39	48.0	24.7
Cameroon	6.4	250	4.9	41	40.4	22.0
Cape Verde Islands	0.3	340[a]	6.0[a]	50	32.8	13.7
Central African Rep.	1.8	160	1.0	41	43.4	22.5
Chad	4.0	80	-3.3	38	44.0	24.0
Dahomey	3.1	110[a]	1.5[a]	41	49.9	23.0
Egypt	37.5	250	0.8	52	37.8	14.0
El Salvador	4.1	350	0.8	58	42.2	11.1
Ethiopia	28.0	90	1.6	38	49.4	25.8
Gambia, The	0.5	130	2.2	40	43.3	24.1
Ghana	9.9	300	0.8	44	48.8	21.9
Guinea	4.4	110	0.1	41	46.6	22.9
Guinea-Bissau	0.5	330	5.9	38	40.1	25.1

[a]Tentative estimate.
[b]Figure for South Africa includes Botswana, Lesotho, Namibia, and Swaziland.
[c]June 1975 figure.
[d]United Nations, *Monthly Bulletin of Statistics,* Vol. 29, No. 12, December 1975.
[e]1973 figure.
[f]March 1974 figure.
[g]U.S. Agency for International Development, Office of Financial Management, Statistics and Reports Division, *Gross National Product: Estimates for Non-Communist Countries for 1973,* No. RC-W-137, July 1975.
[h]1972 figure.
[i]Figure is for 1964-73.
[j]Mid-1974 figure.
[k]United Nations, Department of Economic and Social Affairs, Statistical Office, *Statistical Yearbook, 1974,* U.N. Publication Sales No. E/F. 75. XVIII.1.
[l]1961-66 average.
[m]March 1975 figure.
[n]Figure is for 1971-73.
[o]Figure is for 1962-73.
[p]Average of Sabah, Sarawak, W. Malaysia.
[q]December 1974 figure.
[r]f.o.b.
[s]U.S. Agency for International Development, Bureau for Population and Humanitarian Assistance, *Population Program Assistance: Annual Report, FY 1973* (Washington, D.C.: U.S. Government Printing Office, 1973).
[t]1966 figure.
[u]Figure is for 1961-73.

Infant Mortality per 1,000 Live Births	Literacy (%)	Per Capita Public Education Expend's, 1972 ($)	Per Capita Military Expend's, 1972 ($)	Per Capita Energy Consumption, 1973 (kg. coal equiv.)	Total Exports, f.o.b., 1974 ($ mil.)	Total Imports, c.i.f., 1974 ($ mil.)	International Reserves, Sept. 1975 ($ mil.)
182	8	1	1	71	214[a]	226[a]	65
132	22	1	—	32	347	1,096	n.a.
n.a.	n.a.	n.a.	n.a.	n.a.	n.a.	n.a.	n.a.
97	20	10	—	n.a.[b]	n.a.	n.a.	n.a.
126	60	2	4	62	188	129	144
150	10	2	1	14	30	43	34
137	10-15	9	4	93	478	437	55[c]
91	n.a.	n.a.	n.a.	118	n.a.	n.a.	n.a.
190	5-10	5	4	52	48	46	2[c]
160	5-10	2	4	21	36	92	4[c]
185	20	5	2	32	45[de]	112[de]	24[c]
103	26	11	33	286	1,516	2,349	362
58	60	12	4	244	463	562	107
181	5	2	2	37	267	273	283
165	10	5	—	87	43	47	37
156	25	10	4	175	752	819	192
216	5-10	5	4	92	n.a.	n.a.	n.a.
208	n.a.	n.a.	n.a.	66	n.a.	n.a.	n.a.

[v]Figure is for the first nine months of 1974.
[w]Figure is for Belgium and Luxembourg.
[x]Figure is for 1965-72.
[y]Includes data for Namibia.

SOURCES: Unless otherwise indicated, population, life expectancy, birth rate, death rate, and infant mortality figures are from Population Reference Bureau, Inc., "1975 World Population Data Sheet" (Washington, D.C.); per capita GNP and per capita GNP growth rate figures are from *World Bank Atlas, 1975: Population, Per Capita Product, and Growth Rates* (Washington, D.C.: World Bank Group, 1975); literacy figures are from U.S. Agency for International Development, Bureau for Population and Humanitarian Assistance, *Population Program Assistance: Annual Report, FY 1973* (Washington, D.C.: U.S. Government Printing Office, 1973); per capita public education and military expenditure figures are from Ruth Leger Sivard, *World Military and Social Expenditures, 1974,* published under the auspices of the Institute for World Order (New York); per capita energy consumption figures are from United Nations, Department of Economic and Social Affairs, *World Energy Supplies, 1970-1973,* Statistical Papers Series J, No. 18 (1975); and export, import, and international reserves figures are from International Monetary Fund, *International Financial Statistics,* Vol. 29, No. 1, January 1976.

Fourth World Countries (Continued)

	Population, mid-1975	Per Capita GNP, 1973	Per Capita GNP Growth Rate, 1965-73	Life Expectancy at Birth, 1970-75 Average	Birth Rate per 1,000, 1970-75 Average	Death Rate per 1,000, 1970-75 Average
	(mil.)	($)	(%)	(yrs.)		
Guyana	0.8	410	1.1	68	32.4	5.9
Haiti	4.6	130	0.7	50	35.8	16.5
Honduras	3.0	320	1.1	54	49.3	14.6
India	613.2	120	1.5	50	39.9	15.7
Ivory Coast	4.9	380	3.0	44	45.6	20.6
Kenya	13.3	170	3.3	50	48.7	16.0
Khmer Rep. (Cambodia)	8.1	81[ag]	n.a.	45	46.7	19.0
Laos	3.3	100[ag]	n.a.	40	44.6	22.8
Lesotho	1.1	100[a]	2.6[a]	46	39.0	19.7
Malagasy Rep.	8.0	150	0.9	44	50.2	21.1
Malawi	4.9	110	3.7	41	47.7	23.7
Maldive Islands	0.1	90[a]	0.5[a]	n.a.	46.0[a]	23.0[a]
Mali	5.7	70	0.5	38	50.1	25.9
Mauritania	1.3	200	1.2	38	44.8	24.9
Mozambique	9.2	380[a]	4.1[a]	44	43.1	20.1
Nepal	12.6	90	−0.1	44	42.9	20.3
Niger	4.6	100	−4.6	38	52.2	25.5
Pakistan	70.6	120	2.5	50	47.4	16.5
Rwanda	4.2	70[a]	3.2[a]	41	50.0	23.6
Senegal	4.4	280	−2.8	40	47.6	23.9
Sierra Leone	3.0	160	1.5	44	44.7	20.7
Somalia	3.2	80[a]	1.6[a]	41	47.2	21.7
Sri Lanka	14.0	120	2.0	68	28.6	6.4
Sudan	18.3	130[a]	−0.6[a]	49	47.8	17.5
Tanzania	15.4	130	2.6	44	50.2	20.1
Uganda	11.4	150	1.2	50	45.2	15.9
Upper Volta	6.0	70	−1.1	38	48.5	25.8
Western Samoa	0.2[adj]	250[a]	1.1[a]	63[kl]	36.6[aek]	4.8[aek]
Yemen, Arab Rep.	6.7	100[a]	n.a.	45	49.6	20.6
Yemen, People's Rep.	1.7	110[a]	n.a.	45	49.6	20.6

Third World Countries

	Population, mid-1975	Per Capita GNP, 1973	Per Capita GNP Growth Rate, 1965-73	Life Expectancy at Birth, 1970-75 Average	Birth Rate per 1,000, 1970-75 Average	Death Rate per 1,000, 1970-75 Average
Angola	6.4	490	3.2	38	47.3	24.5
Argentina	25.4	1,640	2.9	68	21.8	8.8
Bahamas	0.2	2,320[a]	−1.1[a]	n.a.	23.8	5.7
Bahrain	0.3	900	−7.7[n]	47	49.6	18.7

Infant Mortality per 1,000 Live Births	Literacy	Per Capita Public Education Expend's, 1972	Per Capita Military Expend's, 1972	Per Capita Energy Consumption, 1973	Total Exports, f.o.b., 1974	Total Imports, c.i.f., 1974	International Reserves, Sept. 1975
	(%)	($)	($)	(kg. coal equiv.)	($ mil.)	($ mil.)	($ mil.)
40	80	17	5	1,149	267	253	24[f]
150	10	1	2	25	71	109	11[c]
115	45	10	5	234	258	382	81
139	34	3	4	192	3,927	5,043	1,449
164	20	28	5	368	1,214	969	34[c]
135	20-25	7	2	167	603	1,026	166
127	41	7	14	30	15[dh]	98[dh]	n.a.
123	20-25	1	6	83	5[de]	57[de]	n.a.
181	n.a.	4	—	n.a.[b]	n.a.	n.a.	n.a.
170	39	5	2	69	203[de]	203[de]	35
148	22	3	—	55	121	188	76
n.a.	n.a.	n.a.	n.a.	n.a.	n.a.	n.a.	n.a.
188	5	3	2	25	35	100	5
189	1-5	6	8	115	166	160	95[c]
165	7	n.a.	n.a.	158	224[de]	464[de]	n.a.
169	9	1	1	13	n.a.	n.a.	113[c]
200	5	2	1	30	53	97	48[c]
132	16	2	9	184	1,113	1,732	540
133	10	2	1	13	37	58	16
159	5-10	1	5	158	368	458	6[c]
136	10	6	1	153	144	223	29
177	5	1	4	37	47[de]	92[de]	70
45	76	7	2	147	521	691	69
141	10-15	6	7	123	350	642	34
162	15-20	4	3	81	427	811	42
160	20	9	3	56	315	213	n.a.
182	5-10	2	1	13	36	144	76[c]
41[aek]	97	n.a.	n.a.	119	13	29	4
152	10	n.a.	3	15	13	190	n.a.
152	10	4	8	485	203[d]	187[d]	62[m]
203	10-15	n.a.	n.a.	197	1,202	614	n.a.
60	91	25	17	1,913	3,932	3,570	342
33	85	n.a.	n.a.	7,883	1,444	1,906	58
138	29	n.a.	n.a.	2,075	1,057	1,126	300

	Popu-lation, mid-1975	Per Capita GNP, 1973	Per Capita GNP Growth Rate, 1965-73	Life Expec-tancy at Birth, 1970-75 Average	Birth Rate per 1,000, 1970-75 Average	Death Rate per 1,000, 1970-75 Average
	(*mil.*)	(*$*)	(%)	(*yrs.*)		
Barbados	0.2	1,000	5.8	69	21.6	8.9
Bolivia	5.4	230	2.2	47	43.7	18.0
Brazil	109.7	760	6.0	61	37.1	8.8
Chile	10.3	720	1.4	63	27.9	9.2
China, People's Rep.	822.8	270[a]	4.6[a]	62	26.9	10.3
China (Taiwan)	16.0	660	7.3	69	24.0[a]	5.0[a]
Colombia	25.9	440	3.1	61	40.6	8.8
Congo, People's Rep.	1.3	340	1.9	44	45.1	20.8
Costa Rica	2.0	710	3.5	68	33.4	5.9
Cuba	9.5	540[a]	−0.7[a]	70	29.1	6.6
Cyprus	0.7	1,400	6.5	71	22.2	6.8
Dominican Rep.	5.1	520	5.1	58	45.8	11.0
Equatorial Guinea	0.3	260	−3.1[o]	44	36.8	19.7
Grenada	0.1	330	3.7	69	27.9	7.8
Guadeloupe	0.4	1,050[a]	4.9[a]	69	29.3	6.4
Guatemala	6.1	500	3.8	53	42.8	13.7
Hong Kong	4.2	1,430	5.8	70	19.4	5.5
Jamaica	2.0	990	4.8	70	33.2	7.1
Jordan	2.7	340	−2.6	53	47.6	14.7
Korea, Dem. Rep.	15.9	340	2.7	61	35.7	9.4
Korea, Republic of	33.9	400	8.7	61	28.7	8.8
Lebanon	2.9	940	3.5	63	39.8	9.9
Liberia	1.7	310	4.7	44	43.6	20.7
Malaysia	12.1	570	3.7	59	38.7	9.9
Martinique	0.4	1,330[a]	4.8[a]	69	29.7	6.7
Mauritius	0.9	410	1.4	66	24.4	6.8
Mexico	59.2	890	2.8	63	42.0	8.6
Mongolia	1.4	550[a]	1.6[a]	61	38.8	9.4
Morocco	17.5	320	2.5	53	46.2	15.7
Netherlands Antilles	0.2	1,530[a]	0.7[a]	74	19.7	4.7
Nicaragua	2.3	540	1.6	53	48.3	13.9
Oman	0.8	840	19.4	47	49.6	18.7
Panama	1.7	920	4.3	66	36.2	7.2
Papua New Guinea	2.7	410	5.0	48	40.6	17.1
Paraguay	2.6	410	2.2	62	39.8	8.9
Peru	15.3	620	1.8	56	41.0	11.9
Philippines	44.4	280	2.6	58	43.8	10.5
Réunion	0.5	1,210[a]	4.6[a]	63	31.2	8.5

Infant Mortality per 1,000 Live Births	Literacy	Per Capita Public Education Expend's, 1972	Per Capita Military Expend's, 1972	Per Capita Energy Consumption, 1973	Total Exports, f.o.b. 1974	Total Imports, c.i.f., 1974	International Reserves, Sept. 1975
	(%)	($)	($)	(kg. coal equiv.)	($ mil.)	($ mil.)	($ mil.)
31	91	n.a.	n.a.	1,212	85	204	49
108	40	8	5	269	280[de]	196[de]	124
94	67	16	13	625	7,951	14,162	4,496[m]
71	87	33	33	1,363	2,481	1,911	162
55	25	7	11	583	n.a.	n.a.	n.a.
28	85	18	46	n.a.	5,533	6,964	1,258
76	73	11	5	644	1,403	1,325	378
180	20	22	10	202	62[de]	84[de]	15[c]
54	89	34	2	549	433	716	48
25	78	31	33	1,188	835[dh]	1,292[dh]	n.a.
33	76	28	15	1,892	152	407	226
98	64	13	7	407	637	774	154
165	20	3	3	170	n.a.	n.a.	n.a.
34	76	n.a.	n.a.	185	n.a.	n.a.	n.a.
46	83	n.a.	n.a.	550	58	230	n.a.
79	38	9	4	277	586	700	299
17	71	n.a.	n.a.	1,040	5,959	6,768	n.a.
26	82	40	4	1,706	649	936	133
99	32	9	50	349	155	488	464
n.a.	n.a.	10	32	2,279	n.a.	n.a.	n.a.
60	71	12	14	910	4,461	6,844	1,271
59	86	19	17	1,075	588[de]	1,331[de]	1,577
159	9	6	2	463	400	288	17
75	43	23	21	498[p]	4,233	4,155	1,362
32	85	n.a.	n.a.	797	72	293	n.a.
65	61	10	1	243	310	309	96
61	76	20	6	1,173	3,540	6,504	1,399[c]
n.a.	95	30	32	974	n.a.	n.a.	n.a.
149	14	14	9	250	1,706	1,914	483
25	n.a.	n.a.	n.a.	n.a.	1,376[de]	1,600[de]	82
123	58	12	8	452	381	562	129
138	n.a.	n.a.	n.a.	346	1,294	711	n.a.
47	79	39	1	909	205	800	39[d]
159	n.a.	n.a.	n.a.	237	702	490	n.a.
84	74	6	5	172	170	174	111
110	61	20	18	644	1,511	1,531	640[c]
78	72	6	4	304	2,671	3,436	1,493
n.a.	63	n.a.	n.a.	467	72	352	n.a.

Third World Countries (Continued)

	Popu-lation, mid-1975	Per Capita GNP, 1973	Per Capita GNP Growth Rate, 1965-73	Life Expec-tancy at Birth, 1970-75 Average	Birth Rate per 1,000, 1970-75 Average	Death Rate per 1,000, 1970-75 Average
	(*mil.*)	($)	(%)	(*yrs.*)		
Rhodesia	6.3	430	3.5	52	47.9	14.4
Singapore	2.2	1,830	9.4	70	21.2	5.2
Surinam	0.4	870	2.4	66	41.6	7.5
Swaziland	0.5	330[a]	6.3[a]	44	49.0	21.8
Syrian Arab Rep.	7.3	400	3.6	54	45.4	15.4
Thailand	42.1	270	4.5	58	43.4	10.8
Togo	2.2	180	2.5	41	50.6	23.5
Tonga	0.1[aej]	210[a]	−0.9[a]	56[hs]	39.0[hs]	10.0[hs]
Trinidad and Tobago	1.0	1,310	2.2	70	25.3	5.9
Tunisia	5.7	460	4.9[u]	54	40.0	13.8
Uruguay	3.1	950	0.0	70	20.4	9.3
Vietnam, Dem. Rep.	23.8	110	−0.5	48	41.4	17.9
Vietnam, Republic of	19.7	160	−0.7	40	41.7	23.6
Zaire	24.5	140	2.9	44	45.2	20.5
Zambia	5.0	430	−0.2	44	51.5	20.5

OPEC Countries

Algeria	16.8	570	4.3	53	48.7	15.4
Ecuador	7.1	380	2.8	60	41.8	9.5
Gabon	0.5	1,310	6.1	41	32.2	22.2
Indonesia	136.0	130	4.5	48	42.9	16.9
Iran	32.9	870	7.4	51	45.3	15.6
Iraq	11.1	850	2.9	53	48.1	14.6
Kuwait	1.1	12,050	−2.9	67	47.1	5.3
Libyan Arab Rep.	2.3	3,530	5.7[o]	53	45.0	14.8
Nigeria	62.9	210	8.3	41	49.3	22.7
Qatar	0.1	6,040	7.9	47	49.6	18.7
Saudi Arabia	9.0	1,610	10.1	45	49.5	20.2
United Arab Emirates	0.2	11,630	16.1	47	49.6	18.7
Venezuela	12.2	1,630	1.3	65	36.1	7.1

Developed Countries

Albania	2.5	460[a]	5.1[a]	69	33.4	6.5
Australia	13.8	4,350	3.0	72	21.0	8.1
Austria	7.5	3,510	5.1	71	14.7	12.2
Belgium	9.8	4,560	4.6	73	14.8	11.2
Bulgaria	8.8	1,590[a]	3.6[a]	72	16.2	9.2

Infant Mortality per 1,000 Live Births	Literacy	Per Capita Public Education Expend's, 1972	Per Capita Military Expend's, 1972	Per Capita Energy Consumption, 1973	Total Exports, f.o.b., 1974	Total Imports, c.i.f., 1974	International Reserves, Sept. 1975
	(%)	($)	($)	(kg. coal equiv.)	(S mil.)	($ mil.)	($ mil.)
122	25-30	8	5	716	652[de]	541[der]	n.a.
20	75	38	84	2,834	5,811	8,380	3,153[c]
30	84	n.a.	n.a.	2,912	169[dh]	144[dh]	n.a.
149	36	12	n.a.	n.a.[b]	n.a.	n.a.	n.a.
93	31	12	37	435	784	1,230	1,205[m]
65	68	7	7	319	2,466	3,144	1,895
179	5-10	5	2	72	189	120	65[c]
107st	90-95	n.a.	n.a.	n.a.	7	17	n.a.
35	89	44	3	4,304	2,014	1,865	520
128	30	30	6	364	921	1,128	428
40	90	28	19	1,016	382	487	189
n.a.	n.a.	2	14	138	n.a.	n.a.	n.a.
n.a.	65	2	32	407	59[de]	618[de]	201[f]
160	15-20	6	4	92	1,303	1,389	38
157	15-20	21	17	506	1,406	912	50
128	20	38	7	489	4,336	4,058	1,284
78	67	10	7	359	1,067	948	242
229	n.a.	19	10	984	979	360	9[ac]
125	43	2	3	155	7,426	3,842	437
139	23	14	54	1,050	24,002	5,672	8,668
99	24	23	47	701	8,177	2,273	2,403
44	55	180	107	12,314	10,957	1,552	1,544
130	27	101	48	5,057	8,259	2,763	2,129
180	25	3	8	63	9,567	2,737	5,652
138	10-15	n.a.	n.a.	26,817	2,303	271	n.a.
152	15	46	86	1,218	35,657	3,473	21,098
138	20	n.a.	n.a.	14,325	7,371	1,145[v]	n.a.
50	77	60	25	2,705	10,732	4,200	8,662
87	70	25	55	674	n.a.	n.a.	n.a.
17	98	169	109	6,064	11,030	12,399	4,169
24	98	132	28	3,968	7,161	9,023	4,127
17	97	197	104	7,035[w]	28,260[w]	29,703[w]	5,761
26	95	58	180	4,250	3,836[d]	4,326[dr]	n.a.

Developed Countries (Continued)

	Popu-lation, mid-1975	Per Capita GNP, 1973	Per Capita GNP Growth Rate, 1965-73	Life Expec-tancy at Birth, 1970-75 Average	Birth Rate per 1,000, 1970-75 Average	Death Rate per 1,000, 1970-75 Average
	(mil.)	($)	(%)	(yrs.)		
Canada	22.8	5,450	3.5	72	18.6	7.7
Czechoslovakia	14.8	2,870[a]	2.6[a]	69	17.0	11.2
Denmark	5.0	5,210	3.8	74	14.0	10.1
Finland	4.7	3,600	5.2	70	13.2	9.3
France	52.9	4,540	5.0	73	17.0	10.6
Germany, Dem. Rep.	17.2	3,000	2.9	73	13.9	12.4
Germany, Fed. Rep.	61.9	5,320	4.0	71	12.0	12.1
Greece	8.9	1,870	7.6	72	15.4	9.4
Hungary	10.5	1,850[a]	2.7[a]	70	15.3	11.5
Iceland	0.2	5,030	2.6	74	19.3	7.7
Ireland	3.1	2,150	3.9	72	22.1	10.4
Israel	3.4	3,010	6.7	71	26.5	6.7
Italy	55.0	2,450	4.2	72	16.0	9.8
Japan	111.1	3,630	9.6	73	19.2	6.6
Luxembourg	0.3	4,940	3.1	71	13.5	11.7
Malta	0.3	1,060	7.0	71	17.5	9.0
Netherlands	13.6	4,330	4.3	74	16.8	8.7
New Zealand	3.0	3,680	2.0	72	22.3	8.3
Norway	4.0	4,660	3.8	74	16.7	10.1
Poland	33.8	2,090[a]	4.2[a]	70	16.8	8.6
Portugal	8.8	1,410	8.0	68	18.4	10.1
Romania	21.2	810[h]	6.7[x]	67	19.3	10.3
South Africa	24.7	1,050[y]	2.0[y]	52	42.9	15.5
Spain	35.4	1,710	5.3	72	19.5	8.3
Sweden	8.3	5,910	2.4	73	14.2	10.5
Switzerland	6.5	6,100	3.0	72	14.7	10.0
Turkey	39.9	600	4.4	57	39.4	12.5
U.S.S.R.	255.0	2,030[a]	3.5[a]	70	17.8	7.9
United Kingdom	56.4	3,060	2.3	72	16.1	11.7
United States	213.9	6,200	2.5	71	16.2	9.4
Yugoslavia	21.3	1,060	6.0	68	18.2	9.2

Infant Mortality per 1,000 Live Births	Literacy	Per Capita Public Education Expend's, 1972	Per Capita Military Expend's, 1972	Per Capita Energy Consumption, 1973	Total Exports, f.o.b., 1974	Total Imports, c.i.f., 1974	International Reserves, Sept. 1975
	(%)	($)	($)	(kg. coal equiv.)	($ mil.)	($ mil.)	($ mil.)
17	98	404	103	9,921	34,228	34,573	5,218
21	100	103	107	6,817	7,053[d]	7,532[dr]	n.a.
14	99	317	97	5,642	7,719	9,902	856
10	99	176	50	5,007	5,512	6,839	542
16	97	135	141	4,491	46,473	52,914	10,647
18	99	114	112	6,375	8,748[d]	9,646[dr]	n.a.
20	99	189	146	5,993	89,055	68,897	31,132
27	80	26	64	2,066	2,030	4,385	971
34	97	68	44	3,502	5,130[d]	5,576[d]	n.a.
12	99	160	—	5,208	332	518	40
18	98	89	27	3,472	2,628	3,799	1,334
21	84	133	484	2,976	1,825	5,389	1,235
26	93-95	103	68	3,103	30,240	40,927	5,802
12	98	119	31	3,932	55,596	62,075	13,269
16	98	197	34	7,035[w]	28,260[w]	29,703[w]	n.a.
24	83	56	—	1,199	134	361	460
12	98	274	116	6,260	33,016	32,204	6,818
16	98	154	52	3,345	2,434	3,651	457
13	99	238	124	5,028	6,282	8,420	2,132
28	98	67	59	4,596	8,315[d]	10,482[dr]	n.a.
44	65	14	67	1,176	2,277	4,496	1,775
40	98-99	48	30	3,493	4,872	5,553	n.a.
117	35	2	19	2,715[b]	4,979	7,873	1,206
15	86	31	44	2,021	7,093	15,367	6,371
10	99	410	179	5,973	15,912	15,813	2,781
13	98	203	94	3,951	11,866	14,432	8,281
119	51	17	19	619	1,574	3,775	1,150
26	99	64	263	5,058	27,405[d]	24,890[dr]	n.a.
18	98-99	161	147	5,588	38,638	54,141	5,857
18	98	314	372	11,897	98,507	107,996	15,887
43	80	38	32	1,744	3,805	7,542	965

A-8. Daily Per Capita Grain, Meat, and Milk Consumption in Selected Developed and Developing Countries, 1970

	Total Calories[a]	Grain			Meat			Milk		
		grams/ day	cal./ day	% of total cal.	grams/ day	cal./ day	% of total cal.	grams/ day	cal./ day	% of total cal.
Developed Countries[b]	3,079	288	1,014	33	167	352	11	508	325	11
Australia	3,160	216	760	24	294	620	20	646	420	13
Denmark	3,250	192	676	21	170	359	11	731	475	15
Germany, Fed. Rep.	3,180	189	665	21	220	464	15	567	369	12
Japan	2,470	352	1,239	50	48	101	4	137	89	4
United Kingdom	3,170	200	704	22	209	441	14	592	385	12
United States	3,300	176	620	19	310	654	20	689	448	14
Developing Countries[c]	2,239	333	1,172	52	57	120	5	127	81	4
El Salvador	1,850	301	1,060	57	29	61	3	158	103	6
Ethiopia	1,980	403	1,419	72	55	116	6	66	43	2
India	1,990	384	1,352	68	4	8	4	116	75	4
Sri Lanka	2,340	385	1,348	58	5	11	1	54	35	2
Tanzania	1,700	145	510	30	40	84	5	159	103	6
Uruguay	2,740	217	764	28	286	603	22	557	362	13
World Average[d]	2,659	310	1,091	41	112	236	9	318	203	8

[a]Calories not derived from grain, meat, and milk are derived from potatoes, sugar and sweets, pulses, nuts and seeds, and fats and oils.
[b]Average for 32 developed countries, based on the most recent data available.
[c]Average for 101 developing countries, based on the most recent data available.
[d]Average for 133 countries, based on the most recent data available.

SOURCE: Based on United Nations, Department of Economic and Social Affairs, Statistical Office, *Statistical Yearbook, 1972*, U.N. Publication Sales No. E/F.73.XVII.1, Table 162, pp. 524-30.

A-9. Relative Shares of Selected Resources and Expenditures of Developed and Developing Countries, 1960 and 1972 (percentages)

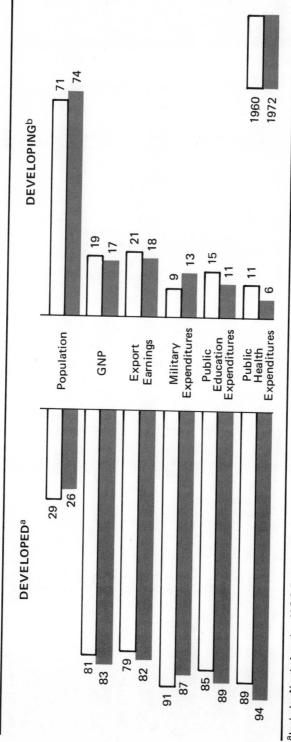

SOURCES: Based on Ruth Leger Sivard, *World Military and Social Expenditures, 1974,* published under the auspices of the Institute for World Order (New York), pp. 6 and 17; export figures from *International Trade, 1973-74* (Geneva: General Agreement on Tariffs and Trade, 1974), Publication Sales No. GATT/1974-4, Table E.

[a]Includes North America, U.S.S.R., most European countries, Oceania, Israel, Japan, and South Africa.
[b]Includes Latin America, a few southern European countries, Asia (except Israel and Japan), and Africa (except South Africa).

A-10. Population Below $75 Per Capita GNP in Selected Developing Countries, 1969

	Per Capita GNP, 1969 ($)	Population, 1969 (millions)	Population Below $75 Per Capita GNP (millions)	Population Below $75 Per Capita GNP (percentage)	Population Below $50 Per Capita GNP (millions)	Population Below $50 Per Capita GNP (percentage)
Latin America[a]	**545**	**244.5**	**42.5**	**17.4**	**26.6**	**10.8**
Ecuador	264	5.9	3.5	58.5	2.2	37.0
Honduras	265	2.5	1.0	38.0	0.7	28.0
El Salvador	295	3.4	0.6	18.4	0.5	13.5
Dominican Republic	323	4.2	0.7	15.9	0.5	11.0
Colombia	347	20.6	5.6	27.0	3.2	15.4
Brazil	347	90.8	18.2	20.0	12.7	14.0
Guyana	390	0.7	0.1	15.1	0.1	9.0
Peru	480	13.1	3.3	25.5	2.5	18.9
Costa Rica	512	1.7	0.1	8.5	—	2.3
Jamaica	640	2.0	0.3	15.4	0.2	10.0
Mexico	645	48.9	8.7	17.8	3.8	7.8
Uruguay	649	2.9	0.2	5.5	0.1	2.5
Panama	692	1.4	0.2	11.0	0.1	3.5
Chile	751	9.6	—	—	—	—
Venezuela	974	10.0	—	—	—	—
Argentina	1,054	24.0	—	—	—	—
Puerto Rico	1,600	2.8	—	—	—	—
Asia[a]	**132**	**872.0**	**499.1**	**57.2**	**320.0**	**36.7**
Burma	72	27.0	19.2	71.0	14.5	53.6
Sri Lanka	95	12.2	7.8	63.5	4.0	33.0
India	100	537.0	359.3	66.9	239.0	44.5
Pakistan[b]	100	111.8	64.7	57.9	36.3	32.5
Thailand	173	34.7	15.4	44.3	9.3	26.8

Korea, Republic of	224	31.0	5.3	17.0	1.7	5.5
Philippines	233	37.2	11.2	30.0	4.8	13.0
Turkey	290	34.5	8.2	23.7	4.1	12.0
Iraq	316	9.4	3.1	33.3	2.3	24.0
Taiwan	317	13.8	2.0	14.3	1.5	10.7
Malaysia	323	10.6	1.6	15.5	1.2	11.0
Iran	350	27.9	4.2	15.0	2.3	8.5
Lebanon	570	2.6	0.1	5.0	—	1.0
Africa[a]	303	83.8	36.6	43.6	23.8	28.4
Chad	75	3.5	2.7	77.5	1.5	43.1
Dahomey	90	2.6	2.3	90.1	1.1	41.6
Tanzania	92	12.8	9.3	72.9	7.4	57.9
Niger	94	3.9	2.3	59.9	1.3	33.0
Malagasy Republic	119	6.7	4.7	69.6	3.6	53.8
Uganda	128	8.3	4.1	49.8	1.8	21.3
Sierra Leone	165	2.5	1.5	61.5	1.1	43.5
Senegal	229	3.8	1.3	35.3	0.9	22.3
Ivory Coast	237	4.8	1.4	28.5	0.3	7.0
Tunisia	241	4.9	1.6	32.1	1.1	22.5
Rhodesia	274	5.1	1.9	37.4	0.9	17.4
Zambia	340	4.2	0.3	7.5	0.3	6.3
Gabon	547	0.5	0.1	23.0	0.1	15.7
South Africa	729	20.2	3.1	15.5	2.4	12.0
Total[a]	228	1,200.3	578.2	48.2	370.4	30.9

[a]Covers only listed countries.
[b]Includes Bangladesh.

SOURCE: Hollis Chenery et al., *Redistribution with Growth* (Oxford: Oxford University Press for World Bank and Institute of Development Studies, University of Sussex, 1974), p. 12.

A-11. Regional Distribution of World Population by Per Capita Income Groups, 1973

	Per Capita GNP under $200	Per Capita GNP $200–$499	Per Capita GNP $500–$999	Per Capita GNP $1,000–$2,999	Per Capita GNP $3,000 and over	Total
			(millions)			
Latin America and Caribbean	6	46	204	38	—	294
Africa	223	123	a	2	—	348
Asia, Middle East, and Pacific	1,818	153	69	10	108	2,158
Europe, North America, and Oceania	—	44	32	102	477	655
U.S.S.R. and Eastern Europe	—	—	30	326	—	356
Total	2,047	366	335	478	585	3,811
(percentage of world population)	54%	10%	9%	12%	15%	100%

aUnder one million.

NOTE: Population figures are based on *national* per capita GNP and thus do not reflect higher or lower individual incomes within nations.

SOURCES: Based on GNP data from Report by the Chairman of the Development Assistance Committee, *Development Co-operation, 1975 Review* (Paris: OECD, 1975), Table 48, pp. 260-61, and on population data from Population Reference Bureau, Inc., "1973 World Population Data Sheet" (Washington, D.C.).

A-12. Population and Per Capita GNP Levels and GNP Growth Rates for Developing and Developed Countries,[a] 1970-1980

	Population[b]	Per Capita GNP 1970	Per Capita GNP 1980	Per Capita GNP Growth Rate, 1970-1980
	(millions)	(1970 $)		(percentages)
Low Income Developing Countries (under $200 per capita GNP)	1,000	105	108	0.2
Middle Income Developing Countries (over $200 per capita GNP)	725	410	540	2.8
Developed Countries	675	3,100	4,000	2.6

[a]Excludes centrally planned economies and OPEC countries.
[b]Estimates for the latter half of the 1970s.

NOTE: These figures assume that capital flows to developing countries will increase in nominal terms but not in real terms between 1975 and 1980; that industrialized countries will make a rather rapid recovery from the current recession; and that per capita growth rates for the remainder of the decade will be 1.2 per cent for the low income countries and 2.8 per cent for the middle-income countries.

SOURCE: Robert S. McNamara, "Address to the Board of Governors," Washington, D.C., September 1, 1975 (Washington, D.C.: World Bank, 1975), p. 7.

A-13. Cross-Classification of Selected Countries by Per Capita Income Level and Inequality

Per Capita GNP up to $300

	High Inequality[a]				Moderate Inequality[b]				Low Inequality[c]			
	Per Capita GNP ($)	Lowest 40%	Middle 40%	Top 20%	Per Capita GNP ($)	Lowest 40%	Middle 40%	Top 20%	Per Capita GNP ($)	Lowest 40%	Middle 40%	Top 20%
		(percentages)				*(percentages)*				*(percentages)*		
Kenya (1969)	136	10.0	22.0	68.0								
Sierra Leone (1968)	159	9.6	22.4	68.0								
Iraq (1956)	200	6.8	25.2	68.0								
Philippines (1971)	239	11.6	34.6	53.8								
Senegal (1960)	245	10.0	26.0	64.0								
Ivory Coast (1970)	247	10.8	32.1	57.1								
Rhodesia (1968)	252	8.2	22.8	69.0								
Tunisia (1970)	255	11.4	53.6	55.0								
Honduras (1968)	265	6.5	28.5	65.0								
Ecuador (1970)	277	6.5	20.0	73.5								
Burma (1958)					82	16.5	38.7	44.8				
Dahomey (1959)					87	15.5	34.5	50.0				
Tanzania (1967)					89	13.0	26.0	61.0				
India (1964)					99	16.0	32.0	52.0				
Malagasy Republic (1960)					120	13.5	25.5	61.0				
Zambia (1959)					230	14.5	28.5	57.0				
Turkey (1968)					282	9.3	29.9	60.8				
El Salvador (1969)					295	11.2	36.4	52.4				
Chad (1958)									78	18.0	39.0	43.0
Sri Lanka (1969)									95	17.0	37.0	46.0
Niger (1960)									97	18.0	40.0	42.0
Pakistan (1964)									100	17.5	37.5	30.0
Uganda (1970)									126	17.1	35.8	47.1
Thailand (1970)									180	17.0	37.5	45.5
Korea (1970)									235	18.0	37.0	45.0
Taiwan (1964)									241	20.4	39.5	40.1

Country (year)	Per Capita GNP	Lowest 40%	Middle 40%	Top 20%
Per Capita GNP $300–$750				
Malaysia (1970)	330	11.6	32.4	56.0
Colombia (1970)	358	9.0	30.0	61.0
Brazil (1970)	390	10.0	28.4	61.5
Peru (1971)	480	6.5	33.5	60.0
Gabon (1968)	497	8.8	23.7	67.5
Jamaica (1958)	510	8.2	30.3	61.5
Costa Rica (1971)	521	11.5	30.0	58.5
Mexico (1969)	645	10.5	25.5	64.0
South Africa (1965)	669	6.2	35.8	58.0
Panama (1969)	692	9.4	31.2	59.4
Dominican Republic (1969)	323	12.2	30.3	57.5
Iran (1968)	332	12.5	33.0	54.5
Lebanon (1960)	508	13.0	26.0	61.0
Guyana (1956)	550	14.0	40.3	45.7
Uruguay (1968)	618	16.5	35.5	48.0
Chile (1968)	744	13.0	30.2	56.8
Surinam (1962)	394	21.7	35.7	42.6
Greece (1957)	500	21.0	29.5	49.5
Yugoslavia (1968)	529	18.5	40.0	41.5
Bulgaria (1962)	530	26.8	40.0	33.2
Spain (1965)	750	17.6	36.7	45.7
Per Capita GNP above $750				
Venezuela (1970)	1,004	7.9	27.1	65.0
Finland (1962)	1,599	11.1	39.6	49.3
France (1962)	1,913	9.5	36.8	53.7
Argentina (1970)	1,079	16.5	36.1	47.4
Puerto Rico (1968)	1,100	13.7	35.7	50.6
Netherlands (1967)	1,990	13.6	37.9	48.5
Norway (1968)	2,010	16.6	42.9	40.5
Germany, Fed. Rep. (1964)	2,144	15.4	31.7	52.9
Denmark (1968)	2,563	13.6	38.8	47.6
New Zealand (1969)	2,859	15.5	42.5	42.0
Sweden (1963)	2,949	14.0	42.0	44.0
Poland (1964)	850	23.4	40.6	36.0
Japan (1963)	950	20.7	39.3	40.0
Hungary (1969)	1,140	24.0	42.5	33.5
Czechoslovakia (1964)	1,150	27.6	41.4	31.0
United Kingdom (1968)	2,015	18.8	42.2	39.0
Australia (1968)	2,509	20.0	41.2	38.8
Canada (1965)	2,920	20.0	39.8	40.2
United States (1970)	4,850	19.7	41.5	38.8

[a] The share of the lowest 40 per cent is less than 12 per cent.

[b] The share of the lowest 40 per cent is between 12 per cent and 17 per cent.

[c] The share of the lowest 40 per cent is 17 per cent and above.

NOTE: The income shares of each percentile group were read off a free-hand Lorenz curve fitted to observed points in the cumulative distribution of pre-tax income. This table uses GNP figures at factor cost for the year indicated in constant 1971 U.S. dollars.

SOURCE: Hollis Chenery et al., *Redistribution with Growth* (Oxford: Oxford University Press for the World Bank and the Institute of Development Studies, University of Sussex, 1974), pp. 8-9.

Food, Fertilizer, Energy, and Minerals

B-1. Indicators of World Food Security, 1961-1976 (million metric tons and days)

	Reserve Stocks of Grain[a]	Grain Equivalent of Idled U.S. Cropland	Total Reserves	Reserves as Days of Annual Grain Consumption
		(million metric tons)		
1961	163	68	231	105
1962	176	81	257	105
1963	149	70	219	95
1964	153	70	223	87
1965	147	71	218	91
1966	151	78	229	84
1967	115	51	166	59
1968	144	61	205	71
1969	159	73	232	85
1970	188	71	259	89
1971	168	41	209	71
1972	130	78	208	69
1973	148	24	172	55
1974	108	0	108	33
1975	111	0	111	35
1976[b]	100	0	100	31

[a]Based on carry-over stocks of grain at beginning of crop year in individual countries for year shown. Stock levels now include reserve stocks of importing as well as of exporting countries, and thus are slightly higher than previous published estimates.
[b]Preliminary estimates.

SOURCE: Lester R. Brown, *The Politics and Responsibility of the North American Breadbasket,* Worldwatch Paper 2, October 1975, p. 8.

B-2. World Net Grain Trade, 1960-1963 and 1969-1976 (million metric tons)

	1960/61- 1962/63 Average	1969/70- 1971/72 Average	1973/74	1974/75	1975/76[b]
Developed Market Economies	**19.9**	**30.3**	**57.5**	**54.5**	**68.1**
North America	42.5	54.6	85.8	75.8	93.0
Western Europe	−26.0	−21.9	−22.5	−18.7	−17.7
Australia and New Zealand	6.6	10.7	9.5	12.1	9.0
Other developed[a]	−3.2	−13.1	−15.2	−14.7	−16.0
Centrally Planned Economies	**−3.1**	**−6.7**	**−16.3**	**−12.8**	**−30.5**
People's Republic of China	−3.6	−3.1	−5.8	−4.4	−2.2
U.S.S.R. and Eastern Europe	0.6	−3.6	−10.5	−8.4	−28.3
Developing Countries	**−12.0**	**−22.2**	**−33.2**	**−37.5**	**−33.9**
Africa and Middle East	−6.3	−11.1	−15.4	−19.0	−18.5
Latin America	0.8	0.1	−2.5	−1.5	1.6
Asia	−6.6	−11.2	−15.3	−17.1	−17.0
Other	**−0.9**	**−0.4**	**−0.6**	**−0.6**	**−2.1**
Total Interregional Exports	**50.5**	**65.4**	**95.3**	**87.9**	**103.6**
Total World Exports	**n.a.**	**n.a.**	**153.7**	**144.9**	**160.8**

[a]Japan and South Africa.
[b]Preliminary estimate.

NOTE: The twelve-month period signified by a given year varies somewhat among crops, although many crop years run concurrently with the U.S. fiscal year.

SOURCES: U.S. Department of Agriculture, Economic Research Service, *World Agricultural Situation,* Publication No. WAS-8, October 1975, p. 27, and U.S. Department of Agriculture, Foreign Agricultural Service, "World Grain Situation: Outlook for 1975/76," *Foreign Agriculture Circular: Grains,* No. FG 16-75, December 22, 1975, pp. 2 and 8.

B-3. U.S. Agricultural Exports, FYs 1960, 1965, and 1970-1975 ($ millions)

| | Public Law 480 | | | | | Other Agricultural Exports | | Total Agricultural Exports[e] | Public Law 480 as Percentage of Total |
| | Title I | | | | | | | | |
	Sales for foreign currency	Long-term dollar credit sales	Title II[a]	Title II[b]	Total	Mutual Security (AID) Programs[c]	Commercial Sales[d]		
1960	824	–	143	149	1,116	167	3,236	4,519	25
1965	1,142	158	238	32	1,570	26	4,501	6,097	26
1970	309	506	241	–	1,056	12	5,650	6,718	16
1971	204	539	280	–	1,023	56	6,674	7,753	13
1972	143	535	380	–	1,058	66	6,922	8,046	13
1973	6	661	287	–	954	84	11,864	12,902	7
1974	–	575	292	–	867	76	20,350	21,293	4
1975[f]	–	762	331	–	1,093	123	20,368	21,584	5
Total[fg]	12,292	4,946	5,278	1,732	24,248	2,652	128,113	155,013	

[a]Transfers of commodities for emergency relief or to promote economic development, and donations to the World Food Program and voluntary relief agencies.

[b]Barter and, for 1960, some shipments in exchange for goods and services for U.S. agencies.

[c]Sales for foreign currency, economic aid, and expenditures under development loans.

[d]Commercial sales for dollars include, in addition to unassisted commercial transactions, shipments of some commodities with government assistance in the form of barter shipments for overseas procurement for U.S. agencies, short-term credit and credit guarantees, sales of government-owned commodities at less than domestic market prices, and export payments in cash or in kind.

[e]Figures do not include furskins or bulk tobacco and, for 1970 and 1971, also exclude citric acid, fatty acids, glues, and adhesives.

[f]Preliminary.

[g]1955-1975.

SOURCE: U.S. Department of Agriculture, Economic Research Service, *Foreign Agricultural Trade of the United States*, December 1975, p. 16.

B-4. Ten Major Recipients of P.L. 480, Titles I and II, FYs 1970 and 1975 ($ millions)

	Title I[a]			Title II[b]		
	FY 1970		**FY 1975[c]**	**FY 1970**		**FY 1975[c]**
India	181	Bangladesh	237	Brazil	43	India	106
Indonesia	122	India	122	India	42	Tanzania	16
Pakistan[d]	81	Egypt	105	Colombia	41	Morocco	13
Rep. of Korea	76	Cambodia	98	Rep. of Vietnam	35	Indonesia	12
Rep. of Vietnam	76	Pakistan	80	Rep. of Korea	28	Philippines	11
Israel	41	Chile	58	Indonesia	25	Tunisia	10
Turkey	34	Rep. of Vietnam	46	Morocco	17	Mali	9
Brazil	20	Indonesia	35	Tunisia	13	Sudan	8
Tunisia	15	Rep. of Korea	26	Turkey	12	Niger	8
Colombia	12	Sri Lanka	25	Nigeria	8	Peru	6
Total, 10 Major Recipients	657		832		264		199
Total, All Recipients	711		892		426		461
5 Major Recipients, as Percentage of Total	75.4%		72.0%		44.4%		34.3%
10 Major Recipients, as Percentage of Total	92.4%		93.3%		62.0%		43.2%

[a]Figures represent commitments, which may increase or decrease by time of actual shipment or delivery.
[b]Figures represent actual shipments, including ocean freight costs.
[c]Preliminary.
[d]Includes Bangladesh.

SOURCE: FY 1970 figures are based on U.S. Agency for International Development, Office of Financial Management, Statistics and Reports Division, *U.S. Overseas Loans and Grants and Assistance from International Organizations: Obligations and Loan Authorizations, July 1, 1945–June 30, 1973*; those for FY 1975 are based on *U.S. Overseas Loans and Grants, Preliminary FY 1975 Data: Obligations and Loan Authorizations, July 1, 1974–June 30, 1975*.

B-5. Developing-Country Imports of Grains, 1971-1974
(million metric tons and $ millions)

	1971	1972	1973	1974
	(million metric tons)			
Wheat and wheat flour	30.2	29.0	38.5	39.5
Rice[a]	7.6	7.7	8.2	7.2
Other[b]	5.9	7.7	12.2	12.9
Total	**43.7**	**44.4**	**58.9**	**59.6**
	($ millions)			
Wheat and wheat flour	2,235	2,198	4,174	7,581
Rice[a]	1,025	1,102	1,946	2,874
Other[b]	430	526	1,271	1,934
Total	**3,690**	**3,826**	**7,391**	**12,389**

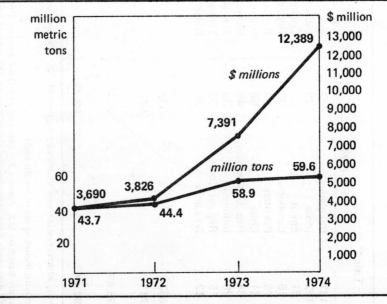

[a]Data for trade in paddy rice are shown in terms of milled rice.
[b]Includes barley, maize, rye, and oats, but excludes the flour of these cereals.

NOTES: In 1971, ten million tons of imported grain cost the developing countries $850 million. By 1974, the cost per ten million tons was $2,080 million. Data include oil-exporting developing countries as well as the People's Rep. of China.

SOURCE: Food and Agriculture Organization, Statistics Division of the Economic and Social Policy Dept., *Trade Yearbook,* 1974, Vol. 28 (Rome: 1975).

B-6. Developing-Country Imports of Manufactured Fertilizers, 1971-1974
(million metric tons and $ millions)

	1971	1972[a]	1973[a]	1974[a]
	(million metric tons)			
Nitrogenous	2.3	2.5	2.6	2.0
Phosphate	1.0	1.2	1.4	1.1
Potash	1.3	1.5	1.8	1.8
Total	**4.6**	**5.2**	**5.8**	**4.9**
	($ millions)			
Nitrogenous	311	341	462	900
Phosphate	126	183	275	380
Potash	96	101	138	170
Total	**533**	**625**	**875**	**1,450**

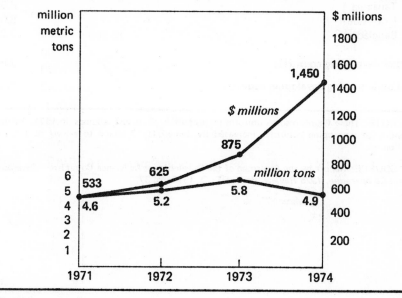

[a]Estimate.

NOTES: In 1971, one million tons of imported manufactured fertilizer cost the developing countries $116 million. By 1974, the cost per million tons was $296 million. Data do not include the oil-exporting developing countries or the People's Rep. of China.

SOURCE: *CERES: FAO Review on Development*, March-April 1975, p. 7.

B-7. Estimated Additional Oil-Import Bill of Non-OPEC Developing Countries, 1974
(as percentages of total 1973 imports)

Major developing-country oil importers	**17.8**
of which:	
Philippines	24.4
Chile	22.2
Thailand	20.7
Brazil	17.9
Korea, Republic of	15.6
Fourth World countries	**15.1**
of which:	
India	27.1
Sri Lanka	18.6
Sudan	17.4
Ghana	14.4
Pakistan	11.3
Kenya	11.1
Tanzania	8.9
Ivory Coast	8.0
Bangladesh	7.2
Other developing countries	**2.5**
All oil-importing developing countries	**9.0**

NOTE: These figures assume uniform prices and 1973 import volumes. In 1974, the oil imports of developing countries increased by some $10-12 billion to a level of $15-17 billion.

SOURCE: Report by the Chairman of the Development Assistance Committee, *Development Co-operation, 1975 Review* (Paris: OECD, 1975), p. 37.

B-8. Incremental Costs of Oil Imports, 1974-1977 ($ billions)[a]

	1974	1975	1976	1977
United States	15.0	13.0	15.5	18.7
Western Europe	34.3	30.5	28.0	25.2
Japan	12.5	11.3	10.3	10.4
Other Industrial Countries	1.2	1.5	1.5	1.8
Developing Countries	10.1	9.4	9.7	10.3
Total	73.1	65.7	65.0	66.4

[a]1974 constant dollars.

NOTE: Incremental costs represent the difference between pre-1973 projections of import requirements at $2.75 a barrel and present projections of import requirements at $10 a barrel. Production costs and company profits are assumed to be constant. In these figures, changes in stocks are disregarded; specifically, no allowance is made for the substantial stock increases in 1974 or for the stock decreases in 1975.

SOURCE: "Overview," in Edward R. Fried and Charles L. Schultze (eds.), *Higher Oil Prices and the World Economy* (Washington, D.C.: Brookings Institution, 1975), p. 11.

B-9. OPEC Countries: Oil Revenues, Trade, Per Capita GNP, Population, International Reserves, Crude Production, and Petroleum Reserves

	Estimated Oil Revenues		Non-Oil Exports, 1974	Imports, 1974b	Estimated Per Capita GNPc		Population, mid-1975	International Reserves, September 1975	Crude Production, 1974	Estimated Petroleum Reservesd	Petroleum Reserves at 1974 Production Rate
	1973	1974a			1973	1974					
	($ millions)		($ millions)	($ millions)	($)		(millions)	($ millions)	(million barrels/day)	(billion barrels)	(years)
High-Income											
Saudi Arabia	5,100	20,000	15,657	3,473	1,610	2,080	9.0	21,098	8.8	164.5	51
Kuwait	1,900	7,000	3,957	1,552	12,050	11,640	1.1	1,544	2.2	72.8	91
United Arab Emirates	900e	4,100e	3,271	1,145f	11,630	13,500	0.2	n.a.	1.5g	33.9	62
Qatar	400	1,600	703	271	6,040	5,830	0.1	n.a.	0.5g	6.0	33
Libya	2,300	7,600	659	2,763	3,530	3,360	2.3	2,129	1.3	26.6	56
Middle-Income											
Iran	4,100	17,400	6,602	5,672	870	1,060	32.9	8,668	6.0	66.0	30
Venezuela	2,800	10,600	132	4,200	1,630	1,710	12.2	8,662	3.0	15.0	14
Iraq	1,500	6,800	1,377	2,273	850	970	11.1	2,403	1.9	35.0	51
Algeria	900	3,700	636	4,058	570	650	16.8	1,284	0.9	7.7	23
Ecuador	100	800	267	948	380	460	7.1	242	0.29g	2.5	34
Gabong	100	400	579	360	1,310	1,560	0.5	24h	0.29g	1.8	25

Low-Income											
Nigeria	2,000	7,000	2,567	2,737	210	240	62.9	5,652	2.3	20.9	25
Indonesia	900	3,000	4,426	3,842	130	150	136.0	437	1.4	15.0	29
Total OPEC	**23,000**	**90,000**	**40,833**	**33,294**			**292.2**	**52,143**	**30.2**	**467.7**	

a These are tentative estimates.

b The International Monetary Fund estimates the 1974 import bill for the 13 OPEC members plus Bahrain, Brunei, Oman, and Trinidad and Tobago to be $37.4 billion, a sharp rise from their $22 billion import bill for 1973.

c The estimates for per capita GNP of some OPEC countries vary widely among sources, sometimes by 50 per cent or more. Because of a new method of calculating GNP, the World Bank's current estimates for 1973 GNP are considerably higher than its previous estimates for the same year. 1974 GNP figures are also calculated by the new method.

d As of January 1, 1975.

e Figure is for Abu Dhabi, one member of the United Arab Emirates.

f As of September 1974.

g 1973 figure.

h August 1975 figure.

SOURCES: Estimates of oil revenues are from Report by the Chairman of the Development Assistance Committee, *Development Co-operation, 1974 Review* (Paris: OECD, 1974), p. 44; figures for non-oil exports, imports, and international reserves are from International Monetary Fund, *International Financial Statistics*, Vol. 29, No. 1, January 1976; per capita GNP figures are from *World Bank Atlas, 1975: Population, Per Capita Product and Growth Rates* (Washington, D.C.: World Bank Group, 1975); population figures are from Population Reference Bureau, Inc., "1975 World Population Data Sheet" (Washington, D.C.); figures for crude production are from Joseph A. Yager and Eleanor B. Steinberg, "Trends in the International Oil Market," in Edward R. Fried and Charles L. Schultze (eds.), *Higher Oil Prices and the World Economy* (Washington, D.C.: Brookings Institution, 1975), p. 237; petroleum reserve figures are from U.S. Department of the Interior, Bureau of Mines, *International Petroleum Annual, 1973*, March 1975, Table 9, pp. 24-25; years of petroleum reserves at 1974 production rates are calculated on the basis of crude production rates and petroleum reserves.

B-10. World Petroleum Production and Consumption, 1973 (million barrels per day)

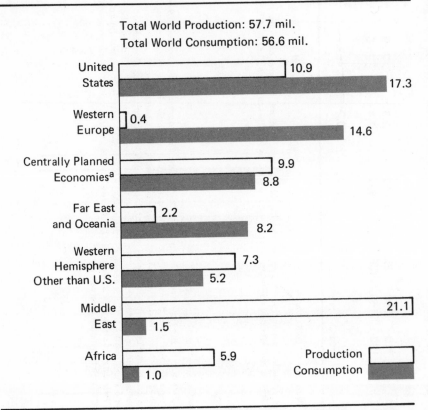

Total World Production: 57.7 mil.
Total World Consumption: 56.6 mil.

United States — Production: 10.9, Consumption: 17.3
Western Europe — Production: 0.4, Consumption: 14.6
Centrally Planned Economies[a] — Production: 9.9, Consumption: 8.8
Far East and Oceania — Production: 2.2, Consumption: 8.2
Western Hemisphere Other than U.S. — Production: 7.3, Consumption: 5.2
Middle East — Production: 21.1, Consumption: 1.5
Africa — Production: 5.9, Consumption: 1.0

Production / Consumption

[a]U.S.S.R., Eastern Europe, People's Rep. of China, Cuba.

SOURCE: Based on U.S. Department of the Interior, *Energy Perspectives: A Presentation of Major Energy and Energy Related Data* (Washington, D.C.: U.S. Government Printing Office, February 1975), p. 13.

B-11. Dependence of Selected Developed Countries on Imported Energy, 1973 (percentages)

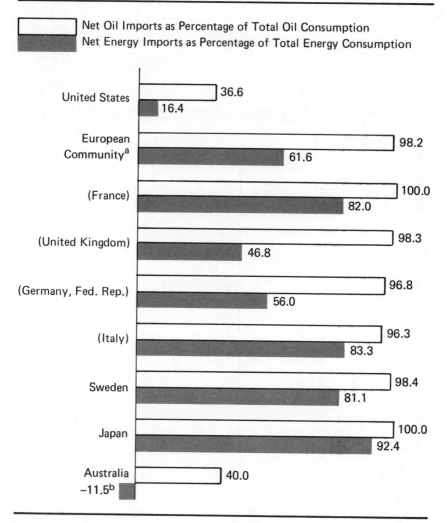

Net Oil Imports as Percentage of Total Oil Consumption
Net Energy Imports as Percentage of Total Energy Consumption

Country	Net Oil Imports	Net Energy Imports
United States	36.6	16.4
European Community[a]	98.2	61.6
(France)	100.0	82.0
(United Kingdom)	98.3	46.8
(Germany, Fed. Rep.)	96.8	56.0
(Italy)	96.3	83.3
Sweden	98.4	81.1
Japan	100.0	92.4
Australia	40.0	−11.5[b]

[a]Belgium, Denmark, France, Fed. Rep. of Germany, Ireland, Italy, Luxembourg, Netherlands, and United Kingdom.
[b]Net energy exporter.

SOURCE: Committee for Economic Development, Research and Policy Committee, *International Economic Consequences of High-Priced Energy: A Statement on National Policy*, September 1975 (New York), p. 77.

B-12. Known Nonrenewable Energy Reserves, by Region and Types of Energy (percentages and quadrillion Btus[a])

| | Fossil Fuels | | | | | Uranium (nonbreeders) | Total | |
	Solid Fuels	Crude Oil	Natural Gas	Oil Shale and Tar Sands	Total	(percentages)	(percentages)	(quad. Btus)
			(percentages)					
Africa	2.5	14.0	11.0	0.8	3.9	25.4	4.4	1,369.5
Asia	18.0	59.0	23.6	8.4	20.2	0.4	19.7	6,126.0
Europe	17.9	1.5	8.4	1.1	9.6	5.9	9.5	2,955.6
U.S.S.R.	23.0	8.9	31.6	1.3	14.4	n.a.[b]	14.0	4,376.0
North America	35.1	8.0	20.8	88.0[c]	48.9	54.1	49.0	15,286.2
Latin America	0.3	8.3	3.3	0.2	1.5	1.5	1.5	457.5
Oceania	3.2	0.3	1.4	0.1	1.7	12.7	1.9	602.4
Total	100.0	100.0	100.0	100.0	100.0	100.0	100.0	31,173.2
Amount of Source Available in quad. Btus[a]	14,457.9	3,750.6	1,831.9	10,351.5	30,391.9	781.3		31,173.2
Source as Percentage of Total Energy Reserves	46.4	12.0	5.9	33.2	97.5	2.5		100.0

[a]British thermal unit. One quadrillion Btus is equivalent to 500,000 barrels of petroleum per day for a year; 40 million tons of bituminous coal; 1 trillion cubic feet of natural gas; or 100 billion kilowatt hours.

[b]Unknown.

[c]According to the U.S. Bureau of Mines, North American oil shale and tar sands reserves may be severely overstated, since development of most of these reserves is not economic at the present time.

SOURCE: Based on U.S. Department of the Interior, *Energy Perspectives: A Presentation of Major Energy and Energy Related Data* (Washington, D.C.: U.S. Government Printing Office, February 1975), p. 2.

B-13. World Energy Production, by Groups of Countries and Types of Energy, 1960, 1970, 1972, 1973 (as percentage of world production of energy type)

		Developed Market Economies					Centrally Planned Economies	Developing Countries		
		North America	Western Europe[a]	Japan	Other[b]	Total		OPEC	Non-OPEC	Total
Coal and Lignite	1960	18.2	22.6	2.3	3.0	46.1	50.0	0.1	3.5	3.6
	1970	23.5	15.8	1.6	4.6	45.7	49.5	—	4.8	4.8
	1972	22.9	13.9	1.1	5.0	43.0	52.1	—	4.6	4.8
	1973	22.2	13.9	0.9	5.2	42.3	52.6	—	4.9	5.0
Crude Petroleum	1960	36.3	1.4	0.1	0.0	37.7	15.6	40.3	6.2	46.6
	1970	25.8	1.0	—	0.3	27.5	16.6	48.6	7.4	56.0
	1972	23.5	0.9	—	0.6	25.4	17.0	50.8	6.8	57.7
	1973	21.6	0.8	—	0.7	23.4	17.3	53.0	6.3	59.4
Natural Gas	1960	80.4	2.6	0.2	0.0	82.9	12.0	1.7	3.2	5.0
	1970	62.8	7.5	0.2	0.1	70.8	22.5	3.5	3.0	6.6
	1972	55.4	10.8	0.3	0.3	69.5	22.4	4.6	3.2	7.9
	1973	56.1	11.8	0.2	0.3	68.5	22.8	5.1	3.4	8.5
Hydro and Nuclear Electricity	1960	37.2	33.7	8.1	1.1	80.2	10.4	1.0	19.8	21.0
	1970	34.3	29.9	7.0	1.9	73.2	14.0	0.6	11.5	12.1
	1972	36.3	29.6	6.7	1.6	74.3	13.4	1.1	11.2	12.3
	1973	37.5	29.1	5.8	2.1	74.6	12.6	1.1	11.6	12.7

[a]Includes Israel.
[b]Australia, New Zealand, South Africa.

SOURCE: United Nations, Dept. of Economic and Social Affairs, *World Energy Supplies, 1970-1973,* Statistical Papers Series J, Nos. 7 (1965) and 18 (1975).

B-14. World Energy Consumption, by Region, 1960, 1970, 1980, and 1990 (quadrillion Btus[a] and percentages)

	1960		1970		1980		1990	
	quad. Btus	percen- tages	quad. Btus	percen- tages	quad. Btus	percen- tages	quad. Btus	percen- tages
United States	44.6	33.9	67.0	30.9	86.3	29.1	121.9	29.6
Western Europe	26.4	20.1	46.0	21.2	62.6	21.1	87.2	21.1
Japan	3.7	2.8	12.0	5.5	20.4	6.9	34.0	8.2
Centrally Planned Economies[b]	39.0	29.6	58.3	26.9	82.0	27.7	109.0	26.4
Rest of world	18.0	13.7	33.6	15.5	45.0	15.2	60.4	14.6
Total	131.7	100.0	216.9	100.0	296.3	100.0	412.5	100.0

[a]British thermal unit. One quadrillion Btu is equivalent to 500,000 barrels of petroleum per day for a year; 40 million tons of bituminous coal; 1 trillion cubic feet of natural gas; or 100 billion kilowatt hours.

[b]U.S.S.R., Eastern Europe, People's Rep. of China, Cuba.

SOURCE: Based on U.S. Department of the Interior, *Energy Perspectives: A Presentation of Major Energy and Energy Related Data* (Washington, D.C.: U.S. Government Printing Office, February 1975), p. 6.

B-15. World Energy Consumption, by Types of Energy, 1960, 1970, 1980, and 1990 (quadrillion Btus[a] and percentages)

	1960		1970		1980		1990	
	quad. Btus	percen- tages	quad. Btus	percen- tages	quad. Btus	percen- tages	quad. Btus	percen- tages
Coal	61.5	46.7	66.8	30.8	79.2	26.7	92.0	22.1
Petroleum	45.3	34.4	96.9	44.7	132.3	44.7	165.0	39.6
Natural Gas	18.0	13.7	40.6	18.7	56.8	19.2	77.1	18.5
Hydropower and Geothermal	6.9	5.2	11.8	5.4	15.4	5.2	18.8	4.5
Nuclear	—	—	0.8	0.4	12.6	4.3	63.6	15.3
Total	131.7	100.0	216.9	100.0	296.3	100.0	416.5	100.0

[a]British thermal unit. One quadrillion Btus is equivalent to 500,000 barrels of petroleum per day for a year; 40 million tons of bituminous coal; 1 trillion cubic feet of natural gas; or 100 billion kilowatt hours.

SOURCE: Based on U.S. Department of the Interior, *Energy Perspectives: A Presentation of Major Energy and Energy Related Data* (Washington, D.C.: U.S. Government Printing Office, February 1975), p. 8.

B-16. Developing-Country Exports of Selected Commodities, 1974 and 1970-1972 Average ($ millions and percentages)

	Developing Country Exports, 1974	Developing Country Exports, 1970-1972 Average		Major Developing Country Suppliers, 1970-1972, with Percentage of Total Exports Supplied by Each
	($ millions)	($ millions)	(as percentage of world exports of commodity)	
Cocoa	1,545	770	99	Ghana, 31% Nigeria, 23%	Ivory Coast, 12% Brazil, 9%
Coffee	4,149	2,894	97	Brazil, 30%	Colombia, 14%
Tea	670	581	83	India, 29%	Sri Lanka, 27%
Wheat	284	128	4	Argentina, 3%	
Rice	1,057	440	36	Thailand, 13%	
Maize	1,086	466	23	Argentina, 13%	
Cotton	2,464	1,610	58	Egypt, 13%	Sudan, 7%
Jute	222	217	96	Bangladesh, 69%	Thailand, 19%
Sisal	313	71	98	Tanzania, 29% Brazil, 25%	Mexico, 14% Angola, 13%
Copra	261	169	99	Philippines, 61% Indonesia, 8%	Papua-New Guinea, 8%
Coconut oil	497	150	83	Philippines, 52%	Sri Lanka, 12%
Palm oil	735	198	92	Malaysia, 53% Indonesia, 19%	Zaire, 11%

Commodity				
Groundnuts	219	157	Nigeria, 19%	Sudan, 10%
Groundnut oil	214	124	Senegal, 32% Nigeria, 15%	Brazil, 12% Argentina, 9%
Fish meal	n.a.	318	Peru, 54%	Philippines, 7%
Sugar	6,724	1,995	Cuba, 23%	
Bananas	594	518	Ecuador, 18% Honduras, 15%	Costa Rica, 13% Panama, 11%
Natural rubber	2,262	976	Malaysia, 50% Indonesia, 22%	Thailand, 10%
Copper	3,259[a]	2,477	Zambia, 17% Chile, 16%	Zaire, 10%
Tin	1,274[b]	646	Malaysia, 42% Bolivia, 14%	Thailand, 10% Indonesia, 8%
Iron ore	1,672[b]	1,009	Brazil, 9%	Liberia, 6%
Petroleum	36,812[a]	20,047	Venezuela, 10% Saudi Arabia, 10%	Iran, 9% Libya, 9%

[a]1973 figure.
[b]Preliminary estimate.

NOTE: The data do not include the exports of centrally planned developing countries; except for petroleum products, the exports of Hong Kong and Singapore are also excluded, because of their substantial re-exports.

SOURCE: World Bank/International Development Association, *Commodity Trade and Price Trends (1975 Edition)*, Report No. EC-166/75, August 1975; export figures for 1974 agricultural commodities are from Food and Agriculture Organization, Statistics Division of the Economics and Social Policy Dept., *Trade Yearbook, 1974*, Vol. 28 (Rome: 1975); minerals and petroleum export figures are informal preliminary estimates from World Bank, Economic Analysis and Projections Dept.

B-17. Prices of Selected Commodities, 1971-1975 (Annual and Quarterly)

	1971	1972	1973	1974	1975	1974 (iv)	1975 (i)	(ii)	(iii)	(iv)
Cocoa[a] (cents/lb.)	27	32	65	98	75	101	85	66	75	69
Coffee[b] (cents/lb.)	46	51	63	68	71	64	63	60	84	86
Tea[c] (cents/kg.)	94	96	106	141	139	149	154	139	133	129
Wheat[d] ($/metric ton)	64	71	147	209	160	223	173	148	163	156
Rice[e] ($/metric ton)	107	116	237	435	363	397	400	378	344	331
Maize[f] ($/metric ton)	68	70	119	157	120	169	124	118	125	112
Cotton[g] (cents/lb.)	48	50	79	107	54	94	46	52	58	60
Jute[h] ($/metric ton)	346	359	354	416	384[i]	524	470	416	336	316
Sisal[j] ($/metric ton)	170	240	527	1,056[i]	617[i]	1,070	941	688	440	400
Copra[k] ($/metric ton)	189	141	353	662	256	513	329	252	237	207
Coconut Oil[l] ($/metric ton)	371	234	513	998	394	763	488	372	376	338
Palm Oil[m] ($/metric ton)	261	217	378	669	433	766	522	402	422	384[i]
Groundnuts[n] ($/metric ton)	249	261	393	595	452	n.a.	n.a.	452	n.a.	n.a.
Groundnut oil[n] ($/metric ton)	441	426	546	1,077	n.a.	1,102	n.a.	n.a.	n.a.	n.a.
Fish meal[o] ($/metric ton)	167	239	542	372[i]	245	301[i]	242	223	230	287
Sugar[o] (cents/lb.)	4.5	7.3	9.5	29.7	20.4[i]	46.8	32.9	18.3	16.9	13.6[i]
Bananas[p] (cents/lb.)	6.4	7.3	7.5	8.3	22.5	8.1	23.7	24.4	19.4	n.a.
Natural rubber[q] (cents/kg.)	39	39	79	82[i]	28	62	28	27	28	28
Copper[r] ($/metric ton)	1,108	1,094	1,541	1,875	56	1,517	58	57	56	53

Tin^s ($/metric ton)	3,595	3,839	4,921	8,468	318	7,676	345	325	309	293
Iron ore^t ($/metric ton)	10.5	10.8	10.1	12.8^i	18.8	13.4^i	18.9	18.8	18.7	n.a.
Petroleum^u ($/barrel)	1.7	1.9	2.7	9.8	10.7	10.4	10.5	10.5	10.5	11.5

[a] Ghana.
[b] Average of Colombia, Guatemala, Brazil, Angola.
[c] Average of northern India, Kenya, Malawi through 1974; London for 1975.
[d] Canada through 1974; Canada and United States average for 1975.
[e] Average of Thailand, Burma through 1974; Thailand for 1975.
[f] Average of Argentina, United States through 1974; United States for 1975.
[g] Average of United States, Mexico.
[h] Bangladesh.
[i] Estimate.
[j] East Africa.
[k] Philippines.
[l] Average of Philippines, Indonesia.

[m] Malaysia.
[n] Nigeria.
[o] World.
[p] World through 1974; Ecuador for 1975.
[q] Average of London and New York markets.
[r] Average of London Metal Exchange and New York market through 1974; London Metal Exchange for 1975.
[s] Average of London Metal Exchange and New York market through 1974; average of Malaysia, United Kingdom, United States for 1975.
[t] Sweden through 1974; average of Europe, United States for 1975.
[u] Saudi Arabia.

SOURCES: Annual figures for 1971-1974 are based on World Bank/International Development Association, *Commodity Trade and Price Trends (1974 Edition)*, Report No. EC-166/74, August 1974; 1975 and quarterly figures are based on World Bank, Economic Analysis and Projections Dept., "Commodity Price Data," January 15, 1976.

B-18. U.S., European Community, and Japanese Dependence on Selected Imported Industrial Raw Materials, 1973 (percentages)

	United States	European Community	Japan
	(imports as percentage of consumption)		
Bauxite[a]	86	60	100
Chromium	91	100	100
Cobalt	96	100	100
Copper	6	96	83
Iron ore	20	59	99
Lead	26	70	70
Manganese	98	99	86
Natural rubber	100	100	100
Nickel	72	100	100
Phosphates	b	100	100
Tin	87	99	93
Tungsten	68	100	100
Zinc	63	60	68

[a]Raw material for the production of aluminum.
[b]Net exporter.

SOURCE: *International Economic Report of the President,* transmitted to Congress March 1975 (Washington, D.C.: U.S. Government Printing Office, 1975), p. 161.

B-19. Costs Implicit in Fulfilling Natural Resource Requirements of Annual Population Increments in Developed and Developing Countries, 1970 ($ and $ millions)

	Per Capita ($)		Total ($ millions)	
	Developed Market Economies	Developing Countries	Developed Market Economies	Developing Countries
Food stuffs	71.4	28.6	550	1,240
Fibers	13.2	2.0	102	87
Fossil fuels	65.0	3.6	500	156
Metals	87.8	7.7	675	333
Total	237.4	41.9	1,827	1,816

NOTE: These calculations are based on estimated average annual consumption of major commodities in 1965–1970; approximate 1970 prices in international trade for the individual commodities included in each commodity grouping; a developed-market-economy population of 702 million growing at a rate of 1.1% annually; and a developing-country population of 1,730 million growing at a rate of 2.5% annually. Thus the annual increment in population in 1970 was 7.7 million in developed market economies and 43.2 million in developing countries.

SOURCE: United Nations, Department of Economic and Social Affairs, *World Economic Survey, 1973. Part One: Population and Development,* Publication Sales No. E. 74.II.C.1, Table 8, p. 31.

World Trade

C-1. Exports, by Groups of Countries, 1960, 1970, and 1972–1974
($ billions and percentages)

To: From:	Industrial Areas[a]		Developing Areas		Eastern Trading Areas[b]		World[c]	
	$ billions, f.o.b.	percentage of total world exports	$ billions, f.o.b	percentage of total world exports	$ billions, f.o.b.	percentage of total world exports	$ billions, f.o.b.	percentage of total world exports
Industrial Areas[a]								
1960	54.5	42.3	21.0	16.3	3.1	2.4	82.1	63.8
1970	160.6	51.3	40.0	12.8	8.8	2.8	216.5	69.1
1972	217.7	52.2	50.3	12.1	12.7	3.0	287.8	69.0
1973	293.1	51.0	69.5	12.1	19.2	3.3	392.3	68.2
1974	375.0	44.2	107.1	12.6	27.6	3.3	526.1	62.0
Developing Areas								
1960	19.2	14.9	6.3	4.9	1.2	1.0	27.5	21.3
1970	40.0	12.8	11.1	3.5	3.2	1.0	55.5	17.7
1972	55.3	13.2	15.7	3.7	3.4	0.8	75.6	18.1
1973	80.9	14.1	21.7	3.8	4.7	0.8	109.4	19.0
1974	171.9	20.3	47.4	5.6	8.5	1.0	232.8	27.4

Eastern Trading Areas[b]

1960	3.0	2.4	1.4	1.0	10.9	8.4	15.3	11.9
1970	8.2	2.6	5.2	1.6	20.0	6.4	33.4	10.6
1972	10.8	2.6	6.0	1.4	26.3	6.3	43.2	10.4
1973	16.2	2.8	8.8	1.5	32.8	5.7	57.9	10.1
1974	23.5	2.8	11.1	1.3	36.4	4.3	71.1	8.4

World[c]

1960	79.6	61.8	29.2	22.7	15.4	12.0	128.7	100.0
1970	214.3	68.4	57.6	18.4	32.3	10.3	313.1	100.0
1972	291.3	69.8	74.0	17.7	42.6	10.2	417.1	100.0
1973	401.2	69.8	102.8	17.9	57.2	9.9	575.0	100.0
1974	582.4	68.7	169.6	20.0	73.2	8.6	848.2	100.0

[a]Austria, Belgium-Luxembourg, Canada, Denmark, Fed. Rep. of Germany, Finland, France, Gibraltar, Greece, Iceland, Ireland, Italy, Japan, Malta, Netherlands, Norway, Portugal, Spain, Sweden, Switzerland, Turkey, United Kingdom, United States, Yugoslavia.
[b]Albania, Bulgaria, China, Czechoslovakia, Dem. Rep. of Korea, Dem. Rep. of Vietnam, Dem. Rep. of Germany, Hungary, Mongolia, Poland, Romania, U.S.S.R.
[c]Including Australia, New Zealand, and South Africa, which are excluded elsewhere.

SOURCE: *International Trade, 1974-1975* (Geneva: General Agreement on Tariffs and Trade, 1975), Publication Sales No. GATT/1975-3, Table 2, p. 4.

C-2. Terms of Trade of Primary Commodities, 1954-1975 (World Bank Index)

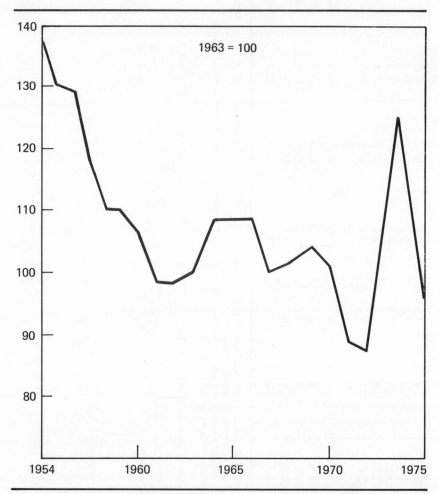

1963 = 100

NOTE: The World Bank primary commodity terms of trade index is based on unit values of developing countries' exports of 34 primary commodities, excluding petroleum. The index is weighted by 1967-69 values of these exports and is deflated by the World Bank's index of prices of manufactured goods in world trade. In 1967-69, the total export value of these 34 commodities from developing countries represented approximately 60% of their total exports, excluding petroleum.

SOURCE: United Nations Conference on Trade and Development, "Commodity Trade: Indexation," Publication No. TD/B/563, July 7, 1975, pp. 1-6, and informal estimates from World Bank, Commodities and Export Projections Division.

C-3. Composition of World Exports and Imports, by Groups of Countries, 1973 (percentages)

	Developed Market Economies	Developing Market Economies	Centrally Planned Economies	World
EXPORTS				
Primary Products	**24.4**	**74.3**	**31.3**	**34.6**
Food, beverages, and tobacco	12.3	19.0	11.1	13.4
Crude materials excluding fuels; oils and fats	8.6	15.7	10.3	10.1
Mineral fuels and related materials	3.5	39.6	9.9	11.1
Manufactured products	**74.3**	**24.8**	**60.3**	**63.5**
Chemicals	8.8	1.6	4.8	7.0
Machinery and transport equipment	35.0	4.2	30.4	28.7
Other manufactured goods	30.5	19.0	25.1	27.8
Miscellaneous transactions and commodities, and residual	**1.3**	**1.0**	**8.4**	**1.9**
Total	100.0	100.0	100.0	100.0
IMPORTS				
Primary products	**36.5**	**28.5**	**29.6**	**34.6**
Food, beverages, and tobacco	13.4	13.4	13.7	13.4
Crude materials excluding fuels; oils and fats	10.9	6.7	10.4	10.1
Mineral fuels and related materials	12.3	8.4	5.5	11.0
Manufactured products	**62.3**	**67.1**	**67.6**	**63.5**
Chemicals	6.6	8.9	6.4	7.0
Machinery and transport equipment	26.6	33.7	34.5	28.7
Other manufactured goods	29.0	24.5	26.7	27.8
Miscellaneous transactions and commodities, and residual	**1.2**	**4.4**	**2.8**	**1.9**
Total	100.0	100.0	100.0	100.0

NOTE: Slight discrepancies in subtotals or totals are due to rounding.

SOURCE: United Nations, *Monthly Bulletin of Statistics,* Vol. 29, No. 7, July 1975, Special Table D, pp. XXIV-XLI.

C-4. Developing-Country Exports and Imports, by Groups of Countries and Commodity Groups, 1973–1975 ($ billions)

	1973 Exports	1973 Imports	1974[a] Exports	1974[a] Imports	1975[b] Exports	1975[b] Imports
By Country Group						
Oil exporters	41.5	21.9	118.8	25.7	126.5	28.0
Other minerals exporters	8.3	5.2	10.6	7.0	9.9	7.5
Other developing countries						
Over $375 per capita GNP	39.6	46.3	52.9	66.5	52.6	71.1
$200-$375 per capita GNP	13.6	16.4	17.8	23.2	18.1	24.7
Under $200 per capita GNP	9.2	9.9	11.4	14.2	11.7	14.9
Total	**112.2**	**99.7**	**211.5**	**136.6**	**218.8**	**146.2**
By Commodity Group						
Oil and products	42.7	7.1	122.0	24.0	129.5	25.2
Food grains	2.6	8.3	3.7	11.0	3.3	10.5
Other foods, raw materials	43.1	24.3	56.9	25.8	54.3	27.0
Manufactures	23.8	60.0	28.9	75.8	31.7	83.5
Total	**112.2**	**99.7**	**211.5**	**136.6**	**218.8**	**146.2**
Total excluding oil exporters	**70.7**	**77.8**	**92.7**	**110.9**	**92.3**	**118.2**

[a]1973 volumes at 1974 prices.
[b]1973 volumes at 1975 prices.

SOURCE: Wouker Tims, "The Developing Countries," in Edward R. Fried and Charles L. Schultze (eds.), *Higher Oil Prices and the World Economy* (Washington, D.C.: Brookings Institution, 1975), p. 179.

C-5. Export Earnings of Developing Countries from Nine Selected Commodities, 1967–1969 Average and 1980 ($ millions)

| | Average Value, 1967-1969 | Projected Value in 1980 | |
		Without Trade Liberalization	With Trade Liberalization
	(current terms)	*(1974 constant terms)*	
Beef (fresh, chilled, and frozen)	388	2,120	2,950
Bananas (fresh)	474	1,606	1,962
Cocoa (beans and products)	782	1,334	1,342
Coffee (all)	2,324	4,768	5,095
Tea	523	563	564
Sugar (raw value)	1,492	3,151	4,995
Cotton (lint)	1,293	2,906	3,902
Wood products	418	2,752	4,119[a]
Citrus (all)	311	522	1,900[b]
Total	8,005	19,722	26,829

[a]The gains from trade liberalization would come from effects on processed timber exports of developing countries. The figure given is net of probable reduction in export of logs.
[b]Estimate based on assumption that trade liberalization takes place immediately. In view of production lead times (5 to 7 years), the effects would only appear fully by the middle of the next decade if the process of liberalization is gradual from now to 1980.

NOTE: These figures are based on a World Bank study of the hypothetical removal of tariff and non-tariff barriers to agricultural imports of OECD countries, with the exception of Australia and New Zealand, because these were not included in the data for the base period, 1967-69, since they only joined the OECD in 1971 and 1973, respectively.

These nine commodities represented about 20 per cent of total export earnings among the developing countries for the 1967-69 period and almost 50 per cent of their earnings from agricultural commodities.

SOURCE: Based on Economic Analysis and Projections Department, Development Policy Staff, International Bank for Reconstruction and Development, "Possible Effects of Trade Liberalization on Trade in Primary Commodities," Bank Staff Working Paper No. 193, January 1975, p. 6.

C-6. Export Credits from DAC Countries to Developing Countries, 1971–1974 ($ millions)

	Net Export Credits Extended				Stock of Export Credits Outstanding
	1971	1972	1973	1974	1974 (end)
Australia	182	38	−65	−38	164
Austria	72	15	44	74	448
Belgium	77	81	160	222	1,089
Canada	144	101	48	253	1,028
Denmark	48	6	48	5	305
Finland	14[a]	14	7	21	60[a]
France	222	271	354	268	6,099
Germany	508	−31	−223	573	4,681
Italy	447	134	72	43	3,315
Japan	766	457	694	157	6,134
Netherlands	5	68	44	52	584
New Zealand	1[a]	3	n.a.	n.a.	5
Norway	6	−24	−13	9	41
Sweden	19	−4	3	142	338
Switzerland	88	−20	115	107	1,561
United Kingdom	583	535	281	354	7,223
United States	238	529	745	929	8,223
DAC Total	3,420	2,173	2,314	3,171	41,298

[a]Estimate.

NOTE: The figures include official export credits. Negative figures result from repayments on old credits exceeding new credit extensions.

SOURCE: Report by the Chairman of the Development Assistance Committee, *Development Co-operation, 1975 Review* (Paris: OECD, 1975), p. 244.

C-7. U.S. Trade, 1972–1975
($ millions)

	1972	1973	1974	1975
U.S. Trade with All Countries				
Exports	49,778	71,339	98,506	107,652
Imports	55,583	69,475	100,973	96,903
Trade Balance	−5,805	+1,864	−2,466	+10,749
U.S. Trade with Developing Countries				
Exports	14,015	19,994	31,485	38,319
Imports	14,114	20,007	39,163	39,149
Trade Balance	−99	−13	−7,678	−830
U.S. Trade with Fourth World Countries[a]				
Exports	1,302	1,806	2,727	4,138
Imports	1,271	1,572	1,914	2,005
Trade Balance	+32	+234	+813	+2,133
U.S. Trade with Third World Countries				
Exports	9,947	14,568	22,036	23,414
Imports	10,156	13,845	21,606	20,062
Trade Balance	−209	+723	+430	+3,352
U.S. Trade with OPEC Countries				
Exports	2,766	3,620	6,723	10,767
Imports	2,687	4,590	15,644	17,082
Trade Balance	+78	−970	−8,921	−6,315
U.S. Trade Balance with Developing Countries, by Region				
Africa	−286	−621	−3,490	−3,812
Africa excl. OPEC[b]	−94	+30	+277	+611
East and South Asia	−891	−443	−1,067	−171
East and South Asia excl. OPEC[c]	−921	−380	+91	+1,240
Near East	+808	+752	−487	+2,120
Near East excl. OPEC[d]	+202	−759	+485	+1,170
Latin America	+275	+327	−2,608	+1,038
Latin America excl. OPEC[e]	+641	+1,093	+450	+2,469
Oceania	−6	−27	−26	−5

[a]Prior to 1975, Egypt and Guinea-Bissau are not included in Fourth World data; in 1975, Egypt alone accounts for $655 million (31 per cent) of the U.S. trade surplus with the Fourth World.
[b]Africa OPEC: Algeria, Libya, Nigeria, Gabon.
[c]East and South Asia OPEC: Indonesia.
[d]Near East OPEC: Iran, Iraq, Kuwait, Saudi Arabia, Qatar, United Arab Emirates.
[e]Latin America OPEC: Venezuela, Ecuador.

NOTE: Exports are f.a.s.; imports, customs value.

SOURCES: Based on U.S. Department of Commerce, *U.S. Foreign Trade: Highlights of Exports and Imports,* December 1972 and December 1973, and U.S. Department of Commerce, *Highlights of U.S. Export and Import Trade,* December 1974; 1975 figures are preliminary ones from U.S. Department of Commerce, Trade Reference Center.

World Military
Transactions

D-1. U.S. Arms Sales and Military Aid to Major Purchasers and Recipients, by Region, FYs 1971-1975 ($ millions)

	U.S. Arms Sales[a]					U.S. Military Aid[b]				
	1971	1972	1973	1974	1975	1971	1972	1973	1974	1975
DEVELOPED COUNTRIES										
NATO	361.7	1,453.0	826.8	1,025.5	2,996.3	282.3	215.4	215.0	117.3	24.4
Other	193.3	209.4	151.2	267.0	302.2	25.9	26.1	12.6	2.9	2.6
Total, Developed	**555.0**	**1,662.4**	**978.0**	**1,292.5**	**3,298.5**	**308.2**	**241.5**	**227.6**	**120.2**	**27.0**
DEVELOPING COUNTRIES										
Sub-Saharan Africa	**16.1**	**2.7**	**2.8**	**13.9**	**34.6**	**14.5**	**13.0**	**12.8**	**13.7**	**13.1**
Ethiopia	–	–	–	7.4	28.0	13.2	12.2	12.2	13.2	12.6
Nigeria	–	2.4	0.7	4.4	4.5	0.2	0.1	–	–	–
Zaire	16.1	0.3	0.8	1.5	1.3	0.4	0.3	0.3	0.4	0.3
Other	–	–	1.3	0.6	0.8	0.7	0.4	0.3	0.1	0.2
Latin America	**49.4**	**109.6**	**111.1**	**211.9**	**154.3**	**23.1**	**23.8**	**18.7**	**21.1**	**18.0**
Argentina	12.8	15.9	16.5	8.6	14.1	0.4	0.8	0.6	0.5	0.1
Brazil	17.8	33.8	16.8	69.1	27.0	0.7	0.7	0.7	0.9	0.9
Chile	2.9	6.3	15.0	75.1	29.0	0.7	0.9	0.9	1.0	0.7
Peru	1.5	0.9	24.8	47.0	23.6	0.5	0.9	0.8	1.0	0.9
Venezuela	1.6	43.5	24.1	4.9	33.5	0.9	0.7	0.9	0.9	0.7
Other	12.8	9.2	13.9	7.2	27.1	19.9	19.8	14.8	16.8	14.7
Middle East and N. Africa	**928.1**	**1,297.4**	**2,948.8**	**7,507.5**	**5,508.3**	**42.8**	**50.2**	**58.4**	**1,548.7**	**177.7**
Iran	398.0	524.0	2,114.5	3,917.1	2,567.9	2.1	0.9	0.3	–	–
Israel	414.7	406.1	192.2	937.3	868.7	–	–	–	1,500.0[c]	100.0[c]
Jordan	16.3	19.5	6.1	61.6	29.6	29.5	45.9	54.9	45.9	74.6
Kuwait	–	–	0.1	30.4	370.5	–	–	–	–	–

Morocco	2.3	7.6	2.5	8.6	294.9	0.7	0.8	0.1	0.6	0.8
Saudi Arabia	96.0	337.3	625.9	2,539.4	1,373.9	0.6	0.4	0.2	0.2	—
Other	0.8	2.9	7.5	13.1	2.8	9.9	2.2	2.9	2.0	2.3
Asia	**90.7**	**149.4**	**238.8**	**264.4**	**484.2**	**3,162.2**	**3,572.5**	**4,320.4**	**1,491.2**	**1,072.7**
China (Taiwan)	63.5	76.7	201.9	95.6	123.1	83.0	91.1	99.4	32.8	2.7
India	0.9	—	—	2.6	7.9	0.2	—	—	0.2	0.1
Indonesia	—	—	0.1	0.1	48.5	18.7	28.1	20.4	16.2	16.0
Khmer Rep. (Cambodia)	—	—	—	—	—	200.4	189.5	174.6	421.7	256.0
Korea, Rep. of	0.5	8.8	1.6	113.1	218.8	633.9	512.2	328.6	111.7	85.7
Laos	—	—	—	—	—	204.2	283.9	288.8	68.0	20.9
Philippines	1.1	0.5	0.7	5.6	31.4	17.8	17.2	33.2	18.1	22.3
Thailand	—	17.0	1.9	20.5	11.4	99.1	110.5	63.7	37.2	34.5
Vietnam, Rep. of	—	—	1.2	—	—	1,901.4	2,339.6	3,310.8	784.7	633.5
Other	24.7	46.4	31.4	26.9	43.1	3.5	0.4	0.9	0.6	1.0
Total, Developing	**1,084.3**	**1,559.1**	**3,301.5**	**7,997.7**	**6,181.4**	**3,242.6**	**3,659.5**	**4,410.3**	**3,074.7**	**1,281.5**
(OPEC Countries)	496.5	909.9	765.4	6,496.2	4,365.3	22.8	30.2	21.8	17.3	17.1
(Countries of special U.S. interest)d	478.7	491.6	396.7	1,146.0	1,210.6	3,022.9	3,416.3	4,202.2	2,918.9	1,098.8
(Non-OPEC, uncommitted countries)e	109.1	157.6	139.4	355.5	605.5	196.9	213.0	186.3	138.5	165.6

aFigures are for foreign military sales *orders* through the U.S. Department of Defense; these are generally delivered in future years.
bU.S. military aid includes Military Assistance Program (MAP) appropriations, arms from the MAP Excess Defense Articles Program (recorded at their acquisition costs), and military assistance service funded (MASF), i.e., military assistance out of the U.S. military budget.
cUnder emergency security assistance legislation waiving payment for U.S. Defense Department export credits to Israel.
dChina (Taiwan), Israel, Khmer Rep. (Cambodia), Rep. of Korea, Laos, and Rep. of Vietnam.
eRefers to all non-OPEC developing countries other than those of special U.S. interest.

SOURCE: U.S. Department of Defense, Security Assistance Agency, Data Management Division, *Foreign Military Sales and Military Assistance Facts,* November 1975, pp. 14, 15, 24, 25, 28, 29, and 32.

D-2. Relative Burden of Military Expenditures, 1972

Per Capita GNP under $100	Per Capita GNP $100-$199	Per Capita GNP $200-$299	Per Capita GNP $300-$499	Per Capita GNP $500-$999	Per Capita GNP $1,000-$1,999	Per Capita GNP $2,000-$2,999	Per Capita GNP $3,000 and Up
Military Expenditures more than 10 per cent of GNP							
Cambodia	Vietnam, S.	Egypt	Iran	Saudi Arabia		Israel	United Arab Emirates
Laos	Yemen, People's Rep.	Jordan	Iraq				
Vietnam, N.			Syria				
Military Expenditures 5-10 per cent of GNP							
Burma	China, Peoples' Rep.	Equatorial Guinea	China (Taiwan)	Albania	Bulgaria	Czechoslovakia	United States
Chad	Nigeria		Korea, Dem. Rep.	Cuba	Hungary	Germany (DRG)	
Somalia	Pakistan		Malaysia	Mongolia	Poland	U.S.S.R.	
	Sudan		Zambia	Portugal	Qatar	United Kingdom	
					Romania		
					Singapore		
Military Expenditures 2-4.9 per cent of GNP							
Ethiopia	Bolivia	Korea, Rep. of	Ecuador	Brazil	Greece	Italy	Australia
India	Central African Rep.	Morocco	Turkey	Lebanon	Spain	Libya	Belgium
Indonesia	Guinea	Thailand		Peru	Yugoslavia		Canada
Mali	Mauritania			South Africa			Denmark
Rwanda	Tanzania			Uruguay			France
Yemen, Arab Rep.	Uganda						Germany (FRG)
	Zaire						Kuwait
							Netherlands
							Norway

Military Expenditures 1-1.9 per cent of GNP

Afghanistan	Dahomey	Cameroon	Algeria	Chile	Argentina	Austria	Switzerland
Burundi	Haiti	Ghana	Colombia	Gabon	Cyprus	Finland	
Upper Volta	Kenya	Honduras	Congo	Rhodesia	Ireland	New Zealand	
	Malagasy Rep.	Liberia	Dominican Rep.		Venezuela		
	Niger	Philippines	El Salvador				
	Sri Lanka	Senegal	Guatemala				
	Togo		Guyana				
			Ivory Coast				
			Nicaragua				
			Paraguay				
			Tunisia				

Military Expenditures less than 1 per cent of GNP

Bangladesh	The Gambia	Botswana	Mauritius	Costa Rica	Trinidad &	Japan	Iceland
Lesotho	Sierra Leone	Swaziland	Oman	Jamaica	Tobago		Luxembourg
Malawi				Malta			
Nepal				Mexico			
				Panama			

NOTE: In 1972, total world arms and military expenditures amounted to $249.6 billion; in 1973, they amounted to $269.6 billion.

SOURCE: U.S. Arms Control and Disarmament Agency, *World Military Expenditures, 1963-1973* (Washington, D.C.: U.S. Government Printing Office, 1975), Publication No. 74, p. 3.

D-3. Sales of Major Weapons to Developing Countries, by Recipient Regions and Supplying Countries, 1968 and 1973 (percentages)

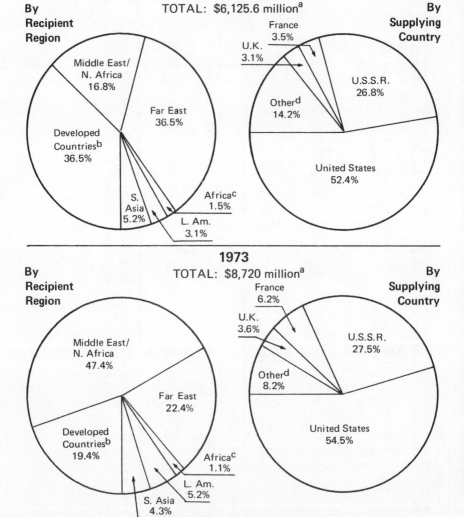

1968

By Recipient Region

TOTAL: $6,125.6 million[a]

By Supplying Country

- Middle East/N. Africa 16.8%
- Far East 36.5%
- Developed Countries[b] 36.5%
- S. Asia 5.2%
- Africa[c] 1.5%
- L. Am. 3.1%

- France 3.5%
- U.K. 3.1%
- U.S.S.R. 26.8%
- Other[d] 14.2%
- United States 52.4%

1973

By Recipient Region

TOTAL: $8,720 million[a]

By Supplying Country

- Middle East/N. Africa 47.4%
- Far East 22.4%
- Developed Countries[b] 19.4%
- Africa[c] 1.1%
- L. Am. 5.2%
- S. Asia 4.3%

- France 6.2%
- U.K. 3.6%
- U.S.S.R. 27.5%
- Other[d] 8.2%
- United States 54.5%

[a] All data in constant 1972 dollars and inflation corrected.
[b] United States, U.S.S.R., and NATO and Warsaw Pact Countries.
[c] Black Africa.
[d] The major "other" suppliers are People's Republic of China, Fed. Rep. of Germany, and Italy.

SOURCE: U.S. Arms Control and Disarmament Agency, *World Military Expenditures and Arms Trade, 1963-1973* (Washington, D.C.: U.S. Government Printing Office, 1975), Publication No. 74, Tables III and IV.

Resource Flows

E-1. Foreign Exchange Receipts and Uses, 1971–1974 ($ billion)

	All Developing Countries				Major Oil-Exporting Developing Countries[a]				Other Developing Countries			
	1971	1972	1973	1974[b]	1971	1972	1973	1974[b]	1971	1972	1973	1974[b]
RECEIPTS												
Exports of goods and services	68.7	79.2	115.0	230.4	23.1	26.4	40.5	127.7	45.6	52.8	74.5	102.7
Exports of goods, f.o.b.	58.0	67.1	99.2	209.3	21.8	24.8	38.2	124.0	36.2	42.3	61.0	85.3
Receipts for non-factor services (gross)[c]	10.7	12.1	15.8	21.1	1.3	1.6	2.3	3.7	9.4	10.5	13.5	17.4
Private transfer receipts (gross)	2.3	2.9	3.8	4.4	0.4	0.4	0.5	0.5	1.9	2.5	3.3	3.9
Official Flows												
From DAC and multilateral agencies (gross)[d]	11.8	13.0	14.6	15.9	1.6	1.5	1.5	1.7	10.2	11.5	13.1	14.2
From OPEC and multilateral agencies (gross)[e]	—	—	1.2	4.2	—	—	0.1	0.2	—	—	1.1	4.0
From socialist countries (net)[f]	0.5	0.5	0.8	1.4	0.2	0.2	0.3	0.7	0.3	0.3	0.5	0.7
Direct investment and other private long-term flows (net)[g]	4.4	5.8	2.8	3.0	0.3	0.5	0.3	0.5	4.1	5.3	2.5	2.5
Private export credits (gross)[h]	5.3	5.2	6.0	7.6	1.7	1.6	2.2	2.4	3.6	3.6	3.8	5.2
Allocation of SDRs	0.7	0.7	—	—	0.1	0.2	—	—	0.6	0.5	—	—
Euro-currency credits	1.0	3.1	8.0	7.1	0.4	1.1	3.1	0.8	0.6	2.0	4.9	6.3
Total Receipts	94.7	110.4	152.2	274.1	27.7	31.7	48.4	134.5	67.0	78.7	103.7	139.6

USES

Debt service on public and publicly guaranteed debt[i]	6.2	7.5	9.8	12.5	1.0	1.5	2.0	2.8	5.2	6.0	7.8	9.7
Amortization	4.3	5.3	6.9	8.7	0.7	1.1	1.5	2.0	3.6	4.2	5.4	6.7
Interest	1.9	2.2	2.9	3.8	0.3	0.4	0.6	0.8	1.6	1.8	2.4	3.0
Other investment income payments (net)[j]	8.8	10.7	12.3[b]	22.2	6.3	7.4	9.3[b]	19.0	2.5	3.3	3.0[b]	3.2
Other uses (net)[j]	0.7	1.4	7.6	30.6	1.2	1.1	6.3	34.1	-0.5	0.3	1.3	-3.5
Changes in reserves[k]	+4.9	+7.9	+11.8	+34.1	+3.5	+2.5	+3.8	+33.1	+1.4	+5.4	+8.0	+1.0
Private transfer payments (gross)	1.3	1.4	1.9	2.1	0.5	0.6	0.9	1.0	0.8	0.8	1.0	1.1
Imports of goods and services	72.8	81.5	108.8	172.5	15.4	18.7	26.1	44.6	57.4	62.9	82.7	128.0
Imports of goods, c.i.f.	61.9	69.3	94.4	150.8	12.7	15.3	21.3	35.3	49.2	54.0	73.1	115.6
Payments for non-factor services (gross)[l]	10.9	12.2	14.4	21.7	2.7	3.3	4.8	9.3	8.2	8.9	9.6	12.4
Total Uses	**94.7**	**110.4**	**152.2**	**274.1**	**27.7**	**31.7**	**48.4**	**134.5**	**67.0**	**78.7**	**103.7**	**139.6**

[a]Algeria, Bahrain, Ecuador, Gabon, Indonesia, Iran, Iraq, Kuwait, Libya, Nigeria, Oman, Qatar, Saudi Arabia, Trinidad and Tobago, United Arab Emirates, Venezuela.

[b]Preliminary.

[c]Covers all services, excluding investment income.

[d]Gross bilateral grants and loans with maturities over one year from DAC countries, and gross flows from those multilateral organizations (other than the IMF) largely financed by the DAC countries.

[e]Gross bilateral grants and loans with maturities over one year from OPEC countries and gross flows from multilateral organizations largely financed by OPEC countries (including the IMF oil facility).

[f]Estimates based on gross commitments.

[g]Includes reinvestment.

[h]Guaranteed private export credits of more than one year's duration, usually including their non-guaranteed portion and, in some cases, other non-guaranteed credits.

[i]For 86 developing countries reporting to the IBRD.

[j]Recorded net short-term capital flows, net long-term capital movements by residents of developing countries, use of Euro-currency credits, and errors and omissions.

[k]Plus sign signifies an increase.

[l]All payments on services, excluding investment income payments to foreigners and freight and merchandise insurance on imports.

SOURCE: Figures obtained from the Research Division, UNCTAD, Geneva.

E-2. External Financial Position of Selected Non-OPEC Developing Countries

	International Reserves		Use of IMF Facility		
	Level of Reserves, Sept. 1975	Change in Level of Reserves, Sept. 1974-Sept. 1975	Fund Holdings of Currency as % of Quota, Nov. 1975	Drawings Out-standing, Sept. 1975	Oil Facility Drawings Out-standing, Nov. 1975
	($ mil.)	($ mil.)		($ mil.)	(million SDRs)
LATIN AMERICA					
Argentina	342.0	–1,177.0	100.0	203.0	76.1
Bolivia	124.3	–56.4	125.1	29.8	–
Brazil	4,496.0[a]	–2,039.0[b]	73.6	–7.0	–
Chile	161.7	–289.8	137.7	341.7	198.3
Colombia	378.0	–52.0	75.0	–	–
Costa Rica	47.5	+21.1	100.0	45.3	30.8
Dominican Republic	153.9	+52.7	75.0	12.5	–
El Salvador	107.0	+27.8	100.0	31.0	17.9
Guatemala	299.3	+97.7	75.0	–	–
Guyana	24.0[g]	–6.9[h]	75.0	0.7	–
Haiti	10.9[c]	–6.5[d]	125.0	18.2	6.4
Honduras	81.1	+50.2	100.0	26.8	16.8
Jamaica	133.3	–74.0	95.6	30.0	–
Mexico	1,399.0[c]	–147.0[d]	73.6	–	–
Nicaragua	128.7	–24.1	100.0	25.9	15.5
Panama	39.4[e]	–3.3[f]	100.0	19.0	17.5
Paraguay	111.4	+34.9	74.9	–	–
Peru	640.1[c]	+119.8[d]	75.0	–	–
Uruguay	189.0	+5.0	111.9	129.0	82.5
MIDDLE EAST					
Egypt	362.0	–241.0	111.4	125.0	–
Jordan	463.8	+130.7	75.0	–	–
Lebanon	1,577.1	+497.6	74.8	–	–
Syria	1,205.0[a]	+638.0[b]	85.8	6.0	–

[a]March 1975 figure.
[b]March 1974-March 1975.
[c]June 1975 figure.
[d]June 1974-June 1975.
[e]December 1974 figure.
[f]December 1973-December 1974.

[g]March 1974 figure.
[h]March 1973-March 1974.
[i]Less than $100,000.

External Debt		Capital Flows			
External Public Debt Outstanding, end-1973	Service Payments On Debt as % of Exports, 1973	Net Change in Guaranteed Priv. Exp. Credits from DAC Countries, 1973-1974	Total Net Flow from DAC Countries and Multilat. Agencies, 1974	Net Bilat. ODA from DAC Countries and Multilat. Concessional Flows, 1974	Bilat. ODA Commitments from OPEC Countries, 1974
($ mil.)		($ mil.)	($ mil.)	($ mil.)	($ mil.)
3,599.1	18.3	−84.0	162.3	15.5	—
770.5	14.8	+8.5	68.3	53.7	—
9,296.7	13.9	+96.7	2,146.8	126.7	—
3,327.0	11.0	−46.3	378.8	14.9	—
2,721.8	13.0	−20.9	146.1	84.0	—
340.9	10.2	+0.5	33.5	15.6	—
430.4	4.5	+2.8	24.7	16.1	—
193.6	5.3	+3.4	39.7	8.0	—
192.3	3.8	+9.8	37.5	21.5	—
228.7	5.4	+2.8	20.7	11.8	15.0
—	—	−0.1	12.3	13.5	—
207.2	3.9	+3.5	31.3	18.8	5.0
458.9	5.0	+17.3	54.8	20.8	—
7,031.1	25.2	+182.5	942.0	26.9	—
487.1	17.8	+3.4	48.6	30.4	—
669.3	16.4	−41.2	160.2	16.4	—
212.3	9.5	−6.5	31.8	21.8	—
2,151.2	32.5	+111.8	637.5	67.9	—
453.3	30.1	−2.3	20.0	5.0	—
2,352.4	34.6	−16.3	168.1	156.6	866.3
323.0	3.7	+4.0	92.8	83.3	128.7
—	—	+12.8	48.2	15.5	84.0
435.5	7.3	+19.4	35.2	15.5	393.9

SOURCE: Figures on international reserves and on use of IMF facilities are from International Monetary Fund, *International Financial Statistics*, Vol. 29, No. 1, January 1976, and from various issues of *IMF Survey* (1975 and 1976); external debt figures are from World Bank, *Annual Report 1975*, pp. 92-95; figures on capital flows are from Report by the Chairman of the Development Assistance Committee, *Development Co-operation, 1975 Review* (Paris: OECD, 1975), p. 183 and Tables 27, 28, and 30.

	International Reserves		Use of IMF Facility		
	Level of Reserves, Sept. 1975	Change in Level of Reserves, Sept. 1974-Sept. 1975	Fund Holdings of Currency as % of Quota, Nov. 1975	Drawings Outstanding, Sept. 1975	Oil Facility Drawings Outstanding, Nov. 1975
	($ mil.)	($ mil.)		($ mil.)	(million SDRs)
Yemen, Arab Republic	n.a.	n.a.	75.0	n.a.	—
Yemen, People's Rep.	62.0[a]	−8.1[b]	125.0	31.9	16.4
ASIA					
Afghanistan	65.2	−2.3	125.0	21.6	—
Bangladesh	n.a.	n.a.	125.5	n.a.	77.3
Burma	143.8	−38.0	137.5	66.4	—
China (Taiwan)	1,258.0	+165.0	100.0	70.0	—
Fiji	n.a.	n.a.	100.0	n.a.	0.3
India	1,449.0	+111.0	125.0	902.0	401.3
Korea	1,271.0	+255.8	125.0	230.9	197.3
Laos	n.a.	n.a.	100.0	n.a.	—
Malaysia	1,362.0	−158.0	71.1	−8.0	—
Nepal	113.3[c]	−17.2[d]	74.9	—	—
Pakistan	540.0	−30.0	173.6	450.0	201.4
Philippines	1,493.0	−42.0	125.0	237.0	96.9
Singapore	3,153.3[c]	+741.7[d]	74.8	—	—
Sri Lanka	69.0	−35.0	114.0	118.0	75.3
Thailand	1,895.0	+124.0	75.0	—	—
Western Samoa	3.6	−1.4	125.0	0.4	0.3
AFRICA					
Botswana	n.a.	n.a.	87.6	n.a.	—
Burundi	33.6	+18.8	100.0	3.9	1.2
Cameroon	55.0[c]	−30.1[d]	100.0	13.4	12.1
Central African Rep.	2.3[c]	+0.5[d]	100.0	8.0	5.0
Chad	3.5[c]	+0.6[d]	105.9	5.8	2.2
Congo	15.0[c]	−4.1[d]	85.1	—	—
Dahomey	24.0[c]	−5.5[d]	83.6	—	—
Equatorial Guinea	n.a.	n.a.	99.9	n.a.	—
Ethiopia	282.9	+39.5	74.7	—	—
Gambia	37.3	+5.6	91.4	—	—
Ghana	191.5	+86.7	100.0	60.4	38.6
Guinea	n.a.	n.a.	100.0	n.a.	3.5

External Public Debt Outstanding, end-1973 ($ mil.)	Service Payments On Debt as % of Exports, 1973	Net Change in Guaranteed Priv. Exp. Credits from DAC Countries, 1973-1974 ($ mil.)	Total Net Flow from DAC Countries and Multilat. Agencies, 1974 ($ mil.)	Net Bilat. ODA from DAC Countries and Multilat. Concessional Flows, 1974 ($ mil.)	Bilat. ODA Commitments from OPEC Countries, 1974 ($ mil.)
—	—	+4.1	36.6	37.3	79.0
—	—	+2.4	12.2	9.8	31.3
973.5	19.9	−2.1	30.8	29.9	85.2
835.5	—	+10.1	485.9	481.9	150.7
417.4	18.6	−0.7	62.0	65.6	—
1,813.2	3.5	+114.5	353.1	−17.7	—
64.7	0.8	+3.3	34.6	13.6	—
12,365.8	20.1	−31.4	1,009.0	1,112.6	276.9
4,413.1	13.9	+78.9	563.4	253.1	—
—	—	+1.8	62.3	58.4	—
1,119.6	2.3	+25.3	216.6	66.6	—
—	—	+0.2	31.4	26.8	—
5,151.2	16.1	+11.4	412.3	356.3	747.1
1,376.2	6.3	+49.0	289.4	147.8	—
525.7	0.4	−8.9	132.8	21.5	—
636.1	12.6	+7.3	88.5	77.9	20.0
750.0	2.6	−6.2	139.4	68.1	40.0
—	—	i	2.1	1.9	—
162.4	2.5	+0.1	7.8	35.4	—
8.6	3.0	−0.2	32.6	32.8	1.0
418.0	5.4	+28.5	111.0	62.0	—
71.9	4.0	−0.9	34.8	35.5	—
55.3	—	−1.3	62.5	63.8	9.5
355.5	10.7	−7.2	48.1	36.5	—
137.5	—	+0.1	30.6	32.5	—
—	—	—	1.0	1.0	1.0
437.6	6.4	−0.5	96.9	109.3	1.0
12.7	0.1	i	9.1	7.4	1.4
666.8	2.3	−3.8	32.2	35.1	—
—	—	−3.5	−1.0	7.5	25.1

External Financial Position (continued)

	International Reserves		Use of IMF Facility		
	Level of Reserves, Sept. 1975	Change in Level of Reserves, Sept. 1974- Sept. 1975	Fund Holdings of Currency as % of Quota, Nov. 1975	Drawings Out- standing, Sept. 1975	Oil Facility Drawings Out- standing, Nov. 1975
	($ mil.)	($ mil.)		($ mil.)	(million SDRs)
Ivory Coast	34.2^c	−53.7^d	100.0	25.5	11.1
Kenya	165.6	−17.9	100.0	78.8	60.8
Lesotho	n.a.	n.a.	75.0	n.a.	—
Liberia	16.6	+4.3	95.3	3.2	—
Malagasy Republic	34.6	−25.2	100.0	22.5	14.3
Malawi	75.8	−6.8	100.1	—	2.3
Mali	4.8	0.0	126.6	11.0	5.0
Mauritania	94.7^c	+25.3^d	95.2	1.8	—
Mauritius	95.8	+80.4	75.0	6.4	—
Morocco	483.0	+85.0	75.0	—	—
Niger	48.4^c	+1.9	83.7	—	—
Rwanda	16.4	+2.3	100.0	2.4	—
Senegal	5.6^c	−27.8^d	100.0	35.2	25.4
Sierra Leone	28.6	−9.1	100.2	13.0	4.9
Somalia	70.3	+43.6	77.7	—	—
Sudan	34.2	−47.2	168.0	133.0	57.0
Swaziland	n.a.	n.a.	87.9	n.a.	—
Tanzania	42.4	+5.0	125.0	85.1	52.1
Togo	64.6^c	+11.0^d	86.2	—	—
Tunisia	428.0	−11.1	75.0	—	—
Uganda	n.a.	n.a.	115.4	37.1	19.2
Upper Volta	76.0^c	+1.8^d	74.9	—	—
Zaire	38.2	−147.4	100.0	118.2	45.0
Zambia	49.9	−234.8	118.4	44.3	18.9

External Debt		Capital Flows			
External Public Debt Outstanding, end-1973	Service Payments On Debt as % of Exports, 1973	Net Change in Guaranteed Priv. Exp. Credits from DAC Countries, 1973-1974	Total Net Flow from DAC Countries and Multilat. Agencies, 1974	Net Bilat. ODA from DAC Countries and Multilat. Conces- sional Flows, 1974	Bilat. ODA Commit- ments from OPEC Countries, 1974
($ mil.)		($ mil.)	($ mil.)	($ mil.)	($ mil.)
882.9	6.3	+41.5	164.3	77.0	–
596.1	5.2	–2.9	153.5	117.5	–
12.8	3.2	–	19.8	19.9	1.5
196.0	6.3	+203.6	348.9	12.5	–
198.9	5.0	–1.9	65.3	60.3	–
267.0	9;0	–1.4	38.6	40.8	–
399.3	1.6	–1.6	104.7	102.3	1.2
92.0	2.1	–4.6	34.4	45.7	52.7
99.5	1.7	+5.7	32.6	25.0	–
1,244.9	9.7	+2.7	111.6	96.9	93.1
116.7	–	–1.1	127.9	130.1	1.4
43.1	1.3	–0.2	45.8	45.7	–
347.2	8.1	+0.3	125.8	97.5	13.5
122.7	8.4	–5.1	6.7	8.5	–
267.7	3.6	–1.1	19.8	31.1	98.0
550.1	11.1	+37.4	110.3	57.2	120.0
34.7	10.5	+2.3	12.8	13.9	–
793.9	6.7	–0.1	161.8	152.5	–
163.2	4.7	+7.9	45.8	36.4	1.2
1,265.8	13.8	–10.0	193.1	142.2	80.4
235.2	5.6	–9.6	0.6	10.9	14.9
119.5	8.3	+2.2	90.6	88.0	–
1,519.1	7.0	+117.7	452.6	180.7	26.0
966.9	28.0	+73.9	162.7	56.5	1.6

E-3. Current Account Deficit of Non-OPEC Developing Countries, 1973-1975 ($ billions)

	1973	1974	1975[a]
Current Account Deficit	-9.4	-30.6	-45.0
Increase (+) in Deficit		+21.2	+14.4
of which:			
Oil price increase		+11.0	+ 1.6
Food and fertilizer price increases		+ 3.5	- 1.0
Manufactures price increases and other trade (primarily with developed countries)		+ 6.7	+13.8

[a]Preliminary estimates.

SOURCE: Report by the Chairman of the Development Assistance Committee, *Development Co-operation, 1975 Review* (Paris: OECD, 1975), p. 37.

E-4. Current Account Balance of the "MSA" Countries,[a] 1973-1975 and 1980 ($ billions)

	1973	1974	1975[b]	1980
Export of goods, f.o.b.	12.2	15.6	15.8	26.3
Import of goods, c.i.f.	14.0	21.9	25.0	44.8
Trade Balance	-1.9	-6.3	-9.1	-18.5
Balance on:				
Non-factor Services	-1.6	-1.9	-2.9	-4.9
Investment Income	-1.0	-1.4	-1.6	-6.7
Private transfers	0.6	0.8	0.9	1.5
Current Account Balance	-3.9	-8.7	-12.7	-28.6

[a]Includes 40 of the 42 countries designated by the United Nations as "most seriously affected" by balance-of-payments difficulties in the current economic situation. These are Afghanistan, Bangladesh, Burma, Burundi, Cambodia, Central African Rep., Chad, Cameroon, Dahomey, Egypt, El Salvador, Ethiopia, Ghana, Guinea, Guinea-Bissau, Guyana, Haiti, Honduras, India, Ivory Coast, Kenya, Laos, Lesotho, Malagasy Rep., Mali, Mauritania, Mozambique, Niger, Pakistan, Rwanda, Senegal, Sierra Leone, Somalia, Sri Lanka, Sudan, Tanzania, Uganda, Upper Volta, Yemen Arab Rep., People's Dem. Rep. of Yemen. Data are not available for Cape Verde and Western Samoa. Also included in the table are Botswana and Malawi which are not classified as "most seriously affected" countries.
[b]Preliminary estimate.

SOURCE: Informal estimates obtained from UNCTAD, New York.

E-5. Foreign and International Bonds Floated by Developing Countries, 1974 and 1975 ($ millions)

	1974	1975[a]
Argentina	—	16
Brazil	25	—
Chile	—	53
China (Taiwan)	20	—
Gabon	—	15
Korea, Republic of	19	—
Lebanon	—	5
Mexico	50	242
Morocco	—	57
Nicaragua	5	—
Panama	9	—
Papua New Guinea	17	25
Philippines	17	—
Singapore	—	12
Sudan	—	9
Total	162	434

[a]Figure is for the first nine months of 1975.

NOTE: The figures in this table include both public and private bonds.

SOURCE: International Bank for Reconstruction and Development, *Borrowing in International Capital Markets,* No. EC-181/753, Third Quarter 1975, pp. 12-13.

E-6. Publicized Euro-Currency Credits to Developing Countries, 1974 and 1975 ($ millions)

	1974	1975[a]
Oil Exporters	795	2,177
Higher Income Developing Countries[b]	4,801	3,814
Middle Income Developing Countries[c]	1,562	756
Lower Income Developing Countries[d]	291	71
Total	7,449	6,818
(Non-Oil-Exporters)	(6,654)	(4,641)

[a]Figure is for the first nine months of 1975.

[b]Argentina, Brazil, China (Taiwan), Colombia, Costa Rica, Dominican Republic, Guyana, Jamaica, Lebanon, Malaysia, Mexico, Nicaragua, Panama, Peru, Uruguay, Zambia.

[c]Bolivia, Cameroon, Egypt, El Salvador, Ivory Coast, Rep. of Korea, Morocco, Philippines, Thailand.

[d]Pakistan, Sudan, Zaire.

NOTE: This table includes only countries that are members of the International Bank for Reconstruction and Development.

SOURCE: International Bank for Reconstruction and Development, *Borrowing in International Capital Markets,* No. EC-181/753, Third Quarter 1975, pp. 24-25.

E-7. Net Flow of Official Development Assistance from DAC Countries as a Percentage of Gross National Product, 1960 and 1970–1977

	1960	1970	1971	1972	1973	1974	1975[a]	1976[a]	1977[a]
Australia	.38	.59	.53	.59	.44	.55	.55	.56	.57
Austria	n.a.	.07	.07	.09	.15	.18	.16	.16	.16
Belgium	.88	.46	.50	.55	.51	.51	.55	.57	.59
Canada	.19	.42	.42	.47	.43	.50	.51	.56	.59
Denmark	.09	.38	.43	.45	.48	.55	.57	.61	.64
Finland	n.a.[b]	.07	.12	.15	.16	.18	.20	.22	.23
France	1.38	.66	.66	.67	.58	.59	.60	.61	.61
Germany	.31	.32	.34	.31	.32	.37	.35	.33	.31
Italy	.22	.16	.18	.09	.14	.15	.14	.14	.13
Japan	.24	.23	.23	.21	.25	.25	.23	.22	.21
Netherlands	.31	.61	.58	.67	.54	.63	.72	.72	.76
New Zealand	n.a.[c]	.23	.23	.25	.27	.31	.36	.41	.47
Norway	.11	.32	.33	.43	.42	.57	.61	.65	.69
Portugal	1.45	.67	1.42	1.79	.59	n.a.[d]	n.a.[d]	n.a.[d]	n.a.[d]
Sweden	.05	.38	.44	.48	.56	.72	.75	.78	.81
Switzerland	.04	.15	.12	.21	.16	.15	.15	.15	.15
United Kingdom	.56	.37	.41	.39	.34	.38	.33	.30	.30
United States[e]	.53	.31	.32	.29	.23	.25	.23	.20	.17
DAC TOTAL									
ODA ($ billions)									
current prices	4.6	6.8	7.7	8.5	9.4	11.3	12.2	13.5	15.0
1975 prices	10.3	12.6	13.2	13.4	11.5	12.7	12.2	12.3	12.6
GNP ($ billions)									
current prices	900	2,020	2,220	2,600	3,100	3,420	3,800	4,400	5,000
ODA as %									
of GNP	.52	.34	.35	.33	.30	.33	.32	.31	.30

[a]Preliminary estimate.
[b]Finland became a member of DAC in January 1975; ODA figures for 1960 are not available.
[c]New Zealand became a member of DAC in 1973; ODA figures for 1960 are not available.
[d]Portugal withdrew from DAC in October 1974; figures later than 1973 are not available.
[e]U.S. ODA amounted to 2.79% of GNP at the beginning of the Marshall Plan (1949).

NOTE: Countries included are members of the OECD Development Assistance Committee, accounting for more than 75 per cent of total Official Development Assistance (ODA). Figures for 1974 and earlier years are actual data. Estimates for 1975, 1976, and 1977 are based on OECD and World Bank estimates of growth of GNP, on information about budget appropriations for aid, and on aid policy statements made by governments. Because of the relatively long period of time required to translate legislative authorizations into commitments and later into disbursements, it is possible to project, with reasonable accuracy, ODA flows (which by definition represent disbursements) through 1977.

SOURCES: Based on Robert S. McNamara, "Address to the Board of Governors," Washington, D.C., September 1, 1975 (Washington, D.C.: World Bank, 1975), p. 39, and on Report by the Chairman of the Development Assistance Committee, *Development Co-operation, 1975 Review* (Paris: OECD, 1975), p. 195.

E-8. Net Flow of Official Development Assistance from DAC Countries, 1960 and 1974
($ millions, $, and percentages)

Countries Listed by 1974 Rank[a]	Total Contribution ($ millions)		Per Capita Contribution ($)		Contribution as Percentage of GNP	
	1960	1974	1960	1974	1960	1974
Sweden	7	402	.09	4.93	.05	.72
Netherlands	35	435	.31	3.22	.31	.63
France	823	1,615	1.81	3.07	1.38	.59
Norway	5	131	.14	3.30	.11	.57
Australia	59	430	.57	3.23	.38	.55
Denmark	5	168	.11	3.33	.09	.55
Canada	75	713	.42	3.17	.19	.50
Belgium	101	271	1.10	2.77	.88	.51
United Kingdom	407	731	.78	1.30	.56	.38
Germany	223	1,430	.42	2.30	.31	.37
New Zealand	n.a.[b]	39	n.a.[b]	1.29	n.a.[b]	.31
Japan	105	1,126	.11	1.03	.24	.25
United States	**2,702**	**3,439**	**1.50**	**1.62**	**.53**	**.25**
Finland	n.a.[c]	38	n.a.[c]	.81	n.a.[c]	.18
Austria	3[d]	60	.04[d]	.79	.04[d]	.18
Switzerland	4	68	.08	1.05	.04	.15
Italy	77	218	.16	.40	.22	.15
Portugal	37	n.a.[e]	.42	n.a.[e]	1.45	n.a.[e]

[a]Rank according to 1974 ODA as a percentage of 1974 GNP.
[b]New Zealand became a member of DAC in 1973; ODA figures for 1960 are not available.
[c]Finland became a member of DAC in January 1975; ODA figures for 1960 are not available.
[d]Figure is for 1961.
[e]Portugal withdrew from DAC in October 1974; figures for 1974 are not available.

SOURCES: Based on Report by the Chairman of the Development Assistance Committee, *Development Co-operation, 1971 Review* (Paris: OECD, 1971), pp. 165 and 175; Report by the Chairman of the Development Assistance Committee, *Development Co-operation, 1975 Review* (Paris: OECD, 1975), pp. 195 and 256-57; and United Nations, Department of Economic and Social Affairs, *Demographic Yearbook, 1961*, Table 4, pp. 126-37.

E-9. Net Flow of Private Voluntary Assistance from DAC Countries, 1970 and 1974 ($ millions, $, and percentages)

Countries Listed by 1974 Rank[a]	Total Contribution ($ millions)		Per Capita Contribution ($)		Contribution as Percentage of GNP	
	1970	1974	1970	1974	1970	1974
Switzerland	11	28	1.74	4.27	.05	.06
Sweden	25	33	3.13	4.03	.08	.06
United States	598	735	2.92	3.47	.06	.05
Norway	4	12	1.01	2.96	.03	.05
Australia	16	37	1.26	2.80	.05	.05
New Zealand	1	6	.50	1.91	.02	.05
Germany	78	177	1.28	2.86	.04	.05
Canada	52	57	2.42	2.51	.06	.04
Belgium	15	18	1.54	1.79	.06	.03
United Kingdom	34	61	.61	1.08	.03	.03
Austria	4	10	.49	1.27	.03	.03
Netherlands	5	20	.40	1.44	.02	.03
Denmark	3	5	.61	1.05	.02	.02
Finland	1	2	.17	.39	.01	.01
France	6	13	.12	.23	.004	.005
Japan	3	9	.03	.08	.002	.002
Italy	5	2	.09	.03	.009	.001
Portugal	1	n.a.[b]	.09	n.a.[b]	.01	n.a.[b]

[a]Rank according to 1974 grants by voluntary agencies as a percentage of 1974 GNP.
[b]Portugal withdrew from DAC in October 1974; figures for 1974 are not available.

NOTE: Private assistance consists of grants by voluntary agencies to developing countries and is net of any government contributions to these agencies. The Development Assistance Committee did not record these flows prior to 1970.

SOURCE: Report by the Chairman of the Development Assistance Committee, *Development Co-operation, 1975 Review* (Paris: OECD, 1975), pp. 206-17.

E-10. Net Flow of Resources from DAC Countries to Developing Countries and Multilateral Institutions, 1964-1966 Average and 1971-1974 ($ millions)

	1964–1966 Average	1971[a]	1972	1973	1974
Official	**6,146.9**	**8,912.3**	**10,084.4**	**11,840.9**	**13,498.7**
Official Development Assistance (ODA)	5,913.0	7,660.5	8,538.2	9,378.0	11,315.6
Bilateral	5,550.0	6,322.5	6,620.9	7,109.6	8,255.4
Grants and grant-like contributions[b]	3,732.6	3,618.2	4,355.5	4,460.4	5,335.9
Development lending and capital[c]	1,817.1	2,704.1	2,265.5	2,649.4	2,919.4
Contributions to multilateral institutions	363.1	1,338.2	1,917.3	2,268.2	3,060.1
Grants	204.2	707.0	997.1	1,055.1	1,464.5
Capital subscription payments	157.3	600.4	869.3	1,126.6	1,535.8
Concessional lending	1.6	30.6	50.8	86.4	59.7
Other official flows[d]	233.9	1,251.8	1,546.2	2,462.9	2,183.1
Private, at market terms	**3,928.1**	**7,965.7**	**8,572.8**	**11,449.5**	**12,832.2**
Private investment and lending[e]	3,016.6	5,134.5	7,125.0	10,253.8	10,350.3
Private export credits	911.4	2,831.3	1,447.8	1,195.7	2,481.9
Grants by voluntary agencies	n.a.[f]	911.1	1,035.7	1,364.5	1,222.0
Total	**10,075.0**	**17,789.0**	**19,693.0**	**24,655.2**	**27,552.9**

[a]Figures prior to 1972 exclude New Zealand and Finland.
[b]Technical assistance, food aid, and other grants.
[c]New development lending, food aid loans, debt reorganization, and equities and other bilateral assets.
[d]Official export credits, debt relief, equities and other bilateral assets, and contributions to multilateral institutions.
[e]Direct investment, bilateral portfolio investment, and multilateral portfolio investment.
[f]Voluntary grants were not recorded by DAC before 1970.

NOTE: Official flows decreased from 61.0% to 48.9% of the total in the 1964–1966 period to 48.9% of the total in 1974; total ODA fell from 58.7% to 41.1%; and bilateral ODA decreased from 55.1% to 29.9%. ODA contributions to multilateral institutions increased from 3.6% to 11.1%; other official flows increased from 2.3% to 7.9%; and private flows at market terms increased from 38.9% to 46.6%.

SOURCE: Report by the Chairman of the Development Assistance Committee, *Development Co-operation, 1975 Review* (Paris: OECD, 1975), p. 217.

E-11. Net Flow of Resources from the United States to Developing Countries and Multilateral Institutions, 1964-1966 Average and 1971-1974 ($ millions)

	1964–1966 Average	1971	1972	1973	1974
Official	**3,427.9**	**3,504.0**	**3,545.0**	**3,445.0**	**4,262.0**
Official Development Assistance (ODA)	3,453.0	3,324.0	3,349.0	2,968.0	3,439.0
Bilateral	3,366.3	2,893.0	2,724.0	2,337.0	2,557.0
Grants and grant-like contributions[a]	2,274.7	1,000.0	1,588.0	1,438.0	1,742.0
Development lending and capital[b]	1,091.6	1,344.0	1,136.0	899.0	815.0
Contributions to multilateral institutions	86.6	431.0	625.0	631.0	882.0
Grants	82.9	185.0	354.0	258.0	344.0
Capital subscription payments	3.7	246.0	271.0	373.0	538.0
Other official flows[c]	−25.1[d]	180.0	196.0	477.0	823.0
Private, at market terms	**1,748.1**	**2,785.0**	**3,360.0**	**3,996.0**	**4,934.0**
Private investment and lending[e]	1,705.3	2,595.0	3,025.7	3,721.4	4,493.4
Private export credits	42.8	190.0	334.3	274.6	440.6
Grants by voluntary agencies	**n.a.[f]**	**599.0**	**669.0**	**905.0**	**735.0**
Total	**5,175.9**	**6,888.0**	**7,574.0**	**8,346.0**	**9,931.0**

[a]Technical assistance, food aid, and other grants.

[b]New development lending, food aid loans, and debt reorganization.

[c]Official export credits, debt relief, and equities and other bilateral assets.

[d]Negative figure results from repayments on old official export credits exceeding new credit extensions during the 1964-1966 period.

[e]Direct investment, bilateral portfolio investment, and multilateral portfolio investment.

[f]Voluntary grants were not recorded by DAC before 1970.

NOTE: Official flows decreased from 66.2% of the total in the 1964-1966 period to 42.9% of the total in 1974; total ODA decreased by almost half, falling from 66.7% to 34.6%; and bilateral ODA dropped from 65.0% to 25.7%. ODA contributions to multilateral institutions increased from 1.7% to 8.9%; private flows at market terms rose from 33.8% to 49.7%; and other official flows increased from 1.1% of the total in 1965 to 8.3% of the total in 1974.

SOURCE: Report by the Chairman of the Development Assistance Committee, *Development Co-operation, 1975 Review* (Paris: OECD, 1975), p. 217.

E-12. Selected U.S. Personal Consumption Expenditures and Net ODA Disbursements, 1974 ($ billions)

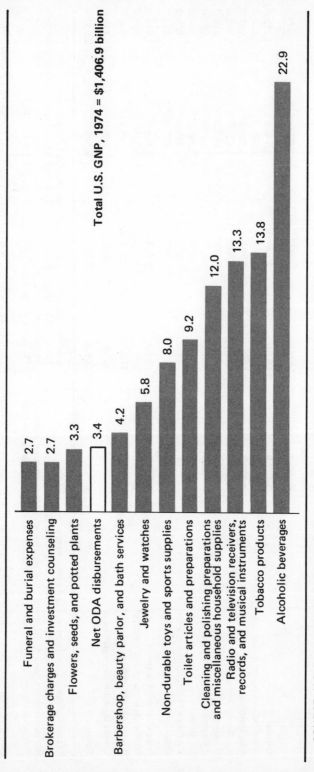

Total U.S. GNP, 1974 = $1,406.9 billion

Funeral and burial expenses	2.7
Brokerage charges and investment counseling	2.7
Flowers, seeds, and potted plants	3.3
Net ODA disbursements	3.4
Barbershop, beauty parlor, and bath services	4.2
Jewelry and watches	5.8
Non-durable toys and sports supplies	8.0
Toilet articles and preparations	9.2
Cleaning and polishing preparations and miscellaneous household supplies	12.0
Radio and television receivers, records, and musical instruments	13.3
Tobacco products	13.8
Alcoholic beverages	22.9

SOURCE: U.S. Department of Commerce, *Survey of Current Business*, Vol. 56, No. 1, January 1976.

E-13. Ten Major Recipients of U.S. Official Development Assistance, Gross Commitments, FYs 1971-1975 ($ millions)

	FY 1971		FY 1972		FY 1973		FY 1974		FY 1975[a]
Rep. of Vietnam	576	Rep. of Vietnam	455	Rep. of Vietnam	502	Rep. of Vietnam	654	Egypt	370
India	455	Bangladesh	286	Indonesia	241	Cambodia	276	Israel	353
Indonesia	177	Rep. of Korea	252	Rep. of Korea	189	India	137	Bangladesh	304
Rep. of Korea	170	Indonesia	240	Pakistan	178	Pakistan	102	India	248
Brazil	118	Pakistan	165	Bangladesh	161	Indonesia	90	Rep. of Vietnam	241
Pakistan[b]	108	Colombia	116	Philippines	124	Bangladesh	80	Pakistan	181
Colombia	98	India	114	Israel	110	Jordan	65	Cambodia	156
Turkey	83	Israel	104	Colombia	97	Philippines	64	Syria	105
Cambodia	77	Philippines	70	Cambodia	93	Colombia	54	Jordan	99
Israel	56	Turkey	67	India	82	Israel	52	Chile	96
Total, 10 Recipients	1,918		1,869		1,777		1,574		2,153
Total, All Recipients	3,429		3,589		4,113		3,906		4,822
10 Major Recipients, as Percentage of Total	55.9%		52.1%		43.2%		40.3%		44.7%

[a]Preliminary.
[b]Includes Bangladesh.

SOURCE: Based on various issues of U.S. Agency for International Development, Office of Financial Management, Statistics and Reports Division, *U.S. Overseas Loans and Grants and Assistance from International Organizations: Obligations and Loan Authorizations.*

E-14. U.S. Economic and Military Assistance, FY 1975[a] ($ millions)

Recipients of U.S. Assistance	Agency for International Development		P.L. 480		Peace Corps	Other[b]	Total Economic Assistance	Military Assistance		Total Economic and Military Assistance
	Loans	Grants	Title I (Sales)	Title II (Donations)				Grants	Foreign Sales Credits	
Latin America	174.5	64.2	66.8	61.0	18.3	263.0	647.8	22.9[c]	134.3	805.0
Near East and South Asia	450.8	561.1	603.8	163.6	6.7	0.2	1,786.2	209.5[d]	391.0	2,386.7
East Asia	98.6	408.0	204.7	36.1	8.7	2.9	759.0	1,072.4	170.7	2,002.1
Africa	70.3	101.0	16.2	118.8	26.7	–	333.0	16.2	54.3	403.5
Oceania	–	–	–	0.3	3.1	63.4	66.8	–	–	66.8
Europe	14.3	13.2	–	0.1	–	–	27.6	3.0	–	30.6
Total, Country Programs	808.5	1,147.5	891.5	379.9	63.5	329.5	3,620.4	1,324.0	750.3	5,694.7
Total, Non-Country Programs[e]	–	384.8	–	80.7	14.4	5.7	485.6	266.6	–	752.2
International Organizations	0.2	177.7	–	–	–	537.8	715.7	–	–	715.7
Total	808.7	1,710.0	891.5	460.6	77.9	873.0	4,821.7	1,590.6	750.3	7,162.6

[a]Preliminary.

[b]Consists of grants to programs such as the Inter-American Foundation and the International Narcotics Control Program, as well as capital subscriptions to international financial institutions and contributions to international organizations.

[c]Includes $4.5 million not included in major programs.

[d]Includes $34.1 million (of which, $10.1 million in materials was not provided under major programs) for Turkey, a NATO member.

[e]General technical services, operating and administrative expenses, freight for voluntary relief agencies, American schools and hospitals abroad, etc.

SOURCE: U.S. Agency for International Development, Office of Financial Management, Statistics and Reports Division, *U.S. Overseas Loans and Grants, Preliminary FY 1975 Data: Obligations and Loan Authorizations, July 1, 1974-June 30, 1975.*

E-15. Economic Aid from U.S.S.R., Eastern Europe, and China to Developing Countries, Gross Commitments, 1970-1974
($ millions)

	1970	1971	1972	1973	1974
Donors					
U.S.S.R.	194	992	610	657	563[a]
Eastern Europe[b]	198	468	832	484	531
People's Republic of China	709	505	553	428	242
Total	1,101	1,965	1,995	1,569	1,336
Recipients					
Africa (excluding South Africa)	589	640	426	443	302[c]
East Asia (excluding Japan)	—	57	—	1	25[d]
Europe	—	—	45[e]	—	—
Latin America (excluding Cuba)	107	259	331	5	429[f]
Near East and South Asia	405	1,009	1,193	1,120	580[g]
Total	1,101	1,965	1,995	1,569	1,336

[a]Over 90% of Soviet commitments were given to Pakistan ($216 million), Argentina ($200 million), and Syria ($100 million).
[b]Bulgaria, Czechoslovakia, Dem. Rep. of Germany, Hungary, Poland, Romania.
[c]Of this, China committed $217 million, mostly to Tanzania, Zambia, Niger, and Mauritania.
[d]All from China to Laos.
[e]All from China to Malta.
[f]Of this amount, $420 million was committed to Argentina, with the U.S.S.R. and Eastern Europe each donating about one half.
[g]Of this amount, Syria received $285 million, Pakistan $216 million, and Bangladesh $54 million, all of which was committed by the U.S.S.R. and Eastern Europe.

NOTE: Short-term commitments are excluded. Grants have, since 1954, made up only 5% of the total. However, grants have accounted for about 15% of China'a aid commitments, compared with less than 2% in other communist countries. All communist economic aid is characterized by concentration on the public sector and close tying of credits to the purchase of donor-country goods. In 1974, net transfers, i.e., gross disbursements less payments of principal and interest on earlier loans, reached a record high due to Soviet grain shipments to India. Excluding these shipments, however, total net transfers were less than in 1973. Chinese credits are the softest: interest-free loans repayable in developing-country products over 10 to 30 years with a 10-year grace period. Eastern Europe's are generally 8 to 10 year loans at 3 to 3.5% interest; the U.S.S.R.'s are normally 12 year loans at 2.5 to 3% interest, with grace periods limited to one year after completion of a project or delivery of goods and repayable in goods.

SOURCE: U.S. Department of State, Bureau of Intelligence and Research, "Communist States and Developing Countries: Aid and Trade in 1974," Report No. 298, January 27, 1976, pp. 1, 3, 21, and 22.

E-16. Concessional and Non-Concessional Aid Disbursements from OPEC Members, 1974 ($ millions and percentages)

	Concessional Aid[a]					Non-Concessional Aid[a]				
	Bilateral	Multi-lateral	Total	As Percentage of: Oil Revenues	As Percentage of: GNP	Bilateral	Multi-lateral	Total	As Percentage of: Oil Revenues	As Percentage of: GNP
	($ millions)					($ millions)				
Algeria	3	32	35	1.0	0.4	—	5	5	0.1	0.1
Iran	378	23	401	2.3	1.1	20	289	309	1.8	0.9
Iraq	210	27	237	3.5	2.3	—	—	—	—	—
Kuwait	328	56	384	5.5	3.6	180	66	246	3.5	2.3
Libya	73	24	97	1.3	1.3	25	7	32	0.4	0.4
Nigeria	2	9	11	0.2	0.1	—	240	240	3.4	1.4
Qatar	42	9	51	3.2	4.6	2	25	27	1.7	2.4
Saudi Arabia	710	100	810	4.1	4.9	30	963	993	5.0	6.0
United Arab Emirates	107	30	137	3.3[b]	3.0	40	129	169	4.1	3.7
Venezuela	20	41	61	0.6	0.3	—	445	445	4.2	2.2
Total	1,873	315	2,224	2.6	1.7	297	2,169	2,466	2.9	1.8

[a]Estimate.
[b]Based on the oil revenues of Abu Dhabi, one member of the United Arab Emirates.

SOURCE: Concessional and non-concessional aid figures are from Report by the Chairman of the Development Assistance Committee, *Development Co-operation, 1975 Review* (Paris: OECD, 1975), pp. 182 and 185. Concessional and non-concessional aid figures as a percentage of oil revenues are based on Report by the Chairman of the Development Assistance Committee, *Development Co-operation, 1974 Review* (Paris: OECD, 1974), p. 44, and as a percentage of GNP are based on *World Bank Atlas, 1975: Population, Per Capita Product, and Growth Rates* (Washington, D.C.: World Bank Group, 1975).

E-17. Recipients of Bilateral Concessional Assistance Commitments from OPEC Members, 1974 ($ millions and percentages)

	$ millions	as percentage of total
Middle East		
Bahrain	69.2	1.8
Egypt[a][b]	866.3	22.6
Jordan[a][b]	128.7	3.4
Lebanon[a][b]	84.0	2.2
Syria[a][b]	393.9	10.3
Yemen Arab Republic[a][b]	79.0	2.1
Egypt/Syria[c]	268.0	7.0
Other	34.7	0.9
Africa		
Guinea	25.1	0.7
Mauritania[a][b]	52.7	1.4
Morocco[a][b]	93.1	2.4
Sahel[a]	6.3	0.2
Somalia[a][b]	98.0	2.6
Sudan[a][b]	120.0	3.1
Tunisia[a][b]	80.4	2.1
Uganda	14.9	0.4
Zaire	26.0	0.7
Other	44.3	1.2
Asia		
Afghanistan[a]	85.2	2.2
Bangladesh[a]	150.7	3.9
India	276.9	7.2
Pakistan[a]	747.1	19.5
Other	60.0	1.6
Latin America		
Guyana	15.0	0.4
Honduras	5.0	0.1
Europe		
Malta	5.0	0.1
Total	3,829.5	100.0
(Islamic countries)	(3,403.0)	(88.9)
(Arab countries)	(2,365.1)	(61.8)

[a]Islamic country as defined (except for Afghanistan, Syria, and the People's Republic of Yemen) by membership in the Islamic Development Bank.
[b]Arab country as defined by membership in the Arab League.
[c]Figure for "Egypt/Syria" is additional to separate figures for Egypt and Syria.

SOURCE: Report by the Chairman of the Development Assistance Committee, *Development Co-operation, 1975 Review* (Paris: OECD, 1975), p. 183.

E-18. Use of the Current Account Surplus by OPEC Members, 1974
($ billions and percentages)

	$ billions	as percentage of surplus
Euro-Currency Deposits	22.8	33.4
(Sterling assets)	(13.8)	(20.2)
United States	11.1	16.3
(Government securities)	(5.5)	(8.1)
(Bank deposits)	(4.2)	(6.2)
(Stock and other securities)	(1.4)	(2.1)
United Kingdom	7.2	10.6
(Government securities)	(3.6)	(5.3)
(Bank deposits)	(1.7)	(2.5)
(Stock and other securities)	(1.9)	(2.8)
Long-term Loans to Other Developed Countries	4.5	6.6
Identified Equity and Portfolio Investment in Other Countries	2.5	3.7
Identified Real Estate	0.5	0.7
Resource Flows to Developing Countries	4.5	6.6
(Concessional bilateral aid)	(2.3)	(3.4)
(Concessional multilateral aid)	(0.4)	(0.6)
(Non-concessional loans and investments)	(0.4)	(0.6)
(IBRD bonds)	(1.4)	(2.1)
Oil Facility	2.6	3.8
Other, Errors and Omissions, and Adjustment for Lag between Oil Exports and Payments (about $10 billion)	12.5	18.3
Total Surplus on Current Account	**68.2[a]**	**100.0**

[a]On a transaction basis. On a settlement (payments) basis, the surplus is estimated to amount to about $58 billion.

SOURCE: Figures obtained from the OECD Secretariat, Paris, 1976.

E-19. Per Capita GNP and Aid Commitments and Disbursements of Selected OPEC and Developed Countries, 1974

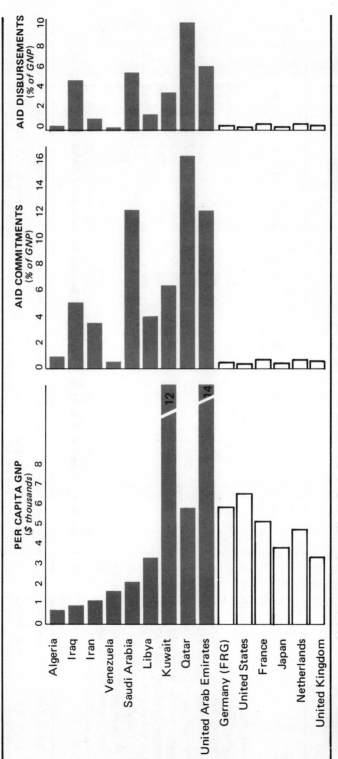

SOURCE: Per capita GNP figures are from *World Bank Atlas, 1975: Population, Per Capita Product, and Growth Rates* (Washington, D.C.: World Bank Group, 1975); OPEC-country aid figures are OECD Secretariat estimates; developed-country aid figures are from Report by the Chairman of the Development Assistance Committee, *Development Co-operation, 1975 Review* (Paris: OECD, 1975), p. 195.

E-20. Aid Commitments from International Organizations to Developing Countries, FYs 1964 and 1968-1974 ($ millions)

	1964	1968	1969	1970	1971	1972	1973	1974	1948-1974
International Bank for Reconstruction and Development	486.4	685.6	1,252.7	1,404.2	1,599.8	1,672.8	1,604.6	3,167.9	17,853.5
International Finance Corporation	18.1	45.3	83.6	90.4	91.9	83.1	136.8	174.9	898.4
International Development Association	207.3	105.4	369.3	569.4	559.0	671.0	1,706.5	1,138.2	6,733.7
Inter-American Development Bank	118.2	385.4	489.2	688.1	614.5	536.3	864.7	1,064.4	6,155.3
Asian Development Bank	—	5.0	65.6	91.5	223.2	265.9	350.6	446.7	1,448.4
African Development Bank	—	5.3	0.1	14.6	18.9	22.1	27.8	50.0	138.7
U.N. Development Programme	122.5	183.8	194.6	174.0	246.7	197.3	179.9	169.3	2,525.5
U.N. Children's Fund and U.N. Regular Programme of Technical Assistance and Specialized Agencies	73.9	56.1	51.3	53.3	84.3	62.8	76.5	137.9	986.2
European Community	63.8	189.9	141.1	98.5	173.3	188.9	251.9	247.2	2,451.0
Total	1,090.2	1,661.8	2,647.5	3,184.0	3,611.6	3,700.2	5,199.3	6,596.5	39,190.7

NOTE: Data for U.N. programs are calendar-year figures, shown in the fiscal year in which the calendar year ends. All other data are for U.S. fiscal years.

SOURCES: U.S. Agency for International Development, Office of Financial Management, Statistics and Reports Division, *U.S. Overseas Loans and Grants and Assistance from International Organizations: Obligations and Loan Authorizations, July 1, 1945-June 30, 1973*, pp. 177-97, and *U.S. Overseas Loans and Grants and Assistance from International Organizations: Obligations and Loan Authorizations, July 1, 1945-June 30, 1974*, pp. 169-94.

About the Overseas Development Council and the Authors

The Overseas Development Council is an independent, nonprofit organization established in 1969 to increase American understanding of the economic and social problems confronting the developing countries, and of the importance of these countries to the United States in an increasingly interdependent world. The ODC seeks to promote consideration of development issues by the American public, policy makers, specialists, educators, and the media through its research, conferences, publications, and liaison with U.S. mass membership organizations interested in U.S. relations with the developing world. The ODC's program is funded by foundations, corporations, and private individuals; its policies are determined by its Board of Directors under the Chairmanship of Theodore M. Hesburgh, C.S.C. The Council's President is James P. Grant.

The authors of *The U.S. and World Development: Agenda for Action, 1976* are listed here in the sequence of the chapters they contributed.

Theodore M. Hesburgh, C.S.C., ODC's Chairman of the Board of Directors, is President of the University of Notre Dame. He was formerly Chairman of the U.S. Commission on Civil Rights and is on the boards of a number of organizations devoted to meeting America's social needs. Father Hesburgh is a trustee of the Rockefeller Foundation, a member of the Council of the International Association of Universities, on the Board of Directors of the Chase Manhattan Bank, and a member of the Presidential Clemency Board.

James P. Grant has been President of the Overseas Development Council since its establishment in 1969. He was formerly Assistant Administrator of the U.S. Agency for International Development, and a Deputy Assistant Secretary of State. Mr. Grant's recent analyses have centered on the world food situation, major structural changes taking place in the international order, and the effectiveness of various development strategies.

Roger D. Hansen, who directed the preparation of this study, is a Senior Fellow at the Council. He is also presently serving as a Senior Research Fellow at the Council on Foreign Relations while working on the Council's 1980s Project. He previously served as U.S. Deputy Assistant Special Trade Representative in the Office of the Special Representative for Trade Negotiations. He is the author of *The Politics of Mexican*

Development (1971); *Mexican Economic Development: The Roots of Rapid Growth* (1971); *Central America: Regional Integration and Economic Development* (1967). His recent articles have examined the global distribution of income and economic opportunity, the "political economy" of North-South relations, the official U.S. response to the "new international economic order" issues, and the need for a new policy framework for U.S.-Latin American relations.

Martin M. McLaughlin, a Senior Fellow at the Council, was concurrently Executive Secretary of the World Hunger Action Coalition during 1974. Mr. McLaughlin was formerly Deputy Director of the Office of International Training in the U.S. Agency for International Development. His recent articles have dealt with food and development issues.

James W. Howe, a Senior Fellow at the Council, was previously a member of the Policy Planning Council of the Department of State and Director of the U.S. aid program to the East African Community. His recent articles have focused on the special problems of the "Fourth World," population, and the international economic order. He is currently engaged in the preparation of a book-length study examining the possibilities of a cooperative international approach to the global energy situation.

Florizelle B. Liser, a Staff Associate at the Council, received her B.A. Degree in political science from Dickinson College in 1973 and her Master's Degree in international affairs from the Johns Hopkins School of Advanced International Studies (SAIS) in 1975. While at SAIS and before joining the Council Staff, she was a Research Assistant at the Brookings Institution.

Overseas Development Council
1717 Massachusetts Avenue, N.W.
Washington, D.C. 20036
(202-234-8701)

ODC Board of Directors

219

ODC Staff

220

Praeger Special Studies

RELATED TITLES

Published in cooperation with the
Overseas Development Council:

BEYOND DEPENDENCY:
The Developing World Speaks Out
      edited by Guy F. Erb and
      Valeriana Kallab

ASSISTING DEVELOPING COUNTRIES:
Problems of Debts, Burden-Sharing, Jobs, and Trade
(Overseas Development Council Studies—I)
      Charles R. Frank, Jr.
      Jagdish N. Bhagwati
      Robert d'A. Shaw
      Harald B. Malmgren

NEW DIRECTIONS IN DEVELOPMENT:
Latin America, Export Credit, Population Growth,
and U.S. Attitudes
(Overseas Development Council Studies—II)
      Colin I. Bradford, Jr.
      Nathaniel McKitterick
      B. Jenkins Middleton
      William Rich
      Paul A. Laudicina

Forthcoming:
WOMEN AND WORLD DEVELOPMENT:
With an Annotated Bibliography
(Overseas Development Council Studies—III)
      edited by Irene Tinker
      Michèle Bo Bramsen
      Mayra Buvinić

**AID PERFORMANCE AND DEVELOPMENT POLICIES OF
WESTERN COUNTRIES:**
Studies in U.S., UK, EEC, and Dutch Programs
      Overseas Development Institute,
      edited by Bruce Dinwiddy

THE APPRAISAL OF DEVELOPMENT PROJECTS:
A Practical Guide to Project Analysis
with Case Studies and Solutions
>   Michael Roemer and
>   Joseph J. Stern

DEVELOPMENT IN RICH AND POOR COUNTRIES:
A General Theory with Statistical Analyses
>   Thorkil Kristensen

DEVELOPMENT WITHOUT DEPENDENCE*
>   Pierre Uri

**ECONOMIC GROWTH IN DEVELOPING COUNTRIES—
MATERIAL AND HUMAN RESOURCES:**
Proceedings of the Seventh Rehovot Conference
>   edited by Yohanan Ramati

**THE WORLD FOOD CONFERENCE AND GLOBAL PROBLEM
SOLVING**
>   Thomas G. Weiss and
>   Robert S. Jordan

PATTERNS OF POVERTY IN THE THIRD WORLD:
A Study of Social and Economic Stratification*
>   Charles Elliott, assisted by
>   Françoise de Morsier

**POPULATION, PUBLIC POLICY, AND ECONOMIC DEVELOP-
MENT**
>   edited by Michael C. Keeley

Also available in paperback as a PSS Student Edition.

Praeger Special Studies
111 Fourth Avenue
New York, NY 10003

222